Stan Henslee

An
Introduction
to the
L A W

Charles Gordon Post received his A.B. and Ph.D. from the Johns Hopkins University. Part of his graduate work was done at the London School of Economics and Political Science. In 1933, he joined the Department of Political Science at Vassar College, where he is now Chairman of the Department. He is the author of *The Supreme Court and Political Questions, Basic Constitutional Cases* (with the late Frances DeLancy and Fredryc Darby), and *Significant Cases in British Constitutional Law*.

An
Introduction
to the
LAW

by

C. Gordon Post

A SPECTRUM BOOK

Prentice-Hall, Inc.

Englewood Cliffs, N.J.

To
the students
past and present
of
Polit 242a

Current printing (last digit):
12 11 10 9 8 7

Library of Congress Catalog Card No.: 63-20413

Printed in the United States of America—C

Preface

The enthusiasm of the writer for his subject stems from a conviction that despite its imperfections, and though its work is never done, the law stands as one of the greatest achievements of mankind. Contrary to popular opinion, the law is not only an absorbing, but an exciting, subject. Most important, it intimately entwines the lives of all of us. Whether the wisdom of legislators and judges be great or small or nonexistent, Samuel Johnson put the matter tersely when he said, "The law is the result of human wisdom acting upon human experience for the benefit of the public."

To introduce so vast a topic is not a simple task. Where to begin and where to end? Happily, the idea of suggesting the answers to certain broad, general questions frequently asked, in the classroom and elsewhere, recommended itself to me. What is justice? How did our courts develop? What did people do before there were any courts? What is the difference between equity and the common law? What is a precedent? What is *stare decisis?* What is a quasi-judicial body? How do judges decide cases? Partial answers to such questions should give the student at least an initial understanding of law and the courts and prepare him for a better comprehension of both in America.

Thus, *An Introduction to the Law* does not pretend to comprehensiveness; it is not intended for lawyers and law students; and it is definitely not a "self-help" legal manual. It is a beginner's book of the law, written primarily for college students whose interests center in the social sciences, and for the general reader.

To Professor Wallace Mendelson of the University of Texas I owe a debt of gratitude. He not only read the entire manuscript but made many valuable suggestions for its improvement. To my colleagues, Dr. Cecil V. Crabb and Dr. Wilfred E. Rumble, Jr., I extend thanks for their patience in discussing with me various matters dealt with herein. For her skill and cooperation in typing the manuscript, I am grateful to Mrs. Lester F. Tubby, Secretary in the Department of Political Science. Finally, for their thoughtfulness, their helpfulness, and their kindness, I wish to acknowledge my indebtedness to three members of the Prentice-Hall staff, Mr. Peter C. Grenquist, Mr. James J. Murray, III, and Mr. Walter E. Langsam.

C. G. P.

Contents

I
Approach to Law, 1

II
Development of Law and the Courts, 18

III
Equity, 40

IV
Trial by Jury and *Habeas Corpus,* 50

V
The Common Law in America, 62

VI
Stare Decisis: The Use of Precedent, 80

VII
Procedure, 105

VIII
The Pre-Trial Conference and Administrative Adjudication, 136

IX
The Judge and His Decision, 153

Notes, 163

Glossary, 176

Charts, 180

Index, 182

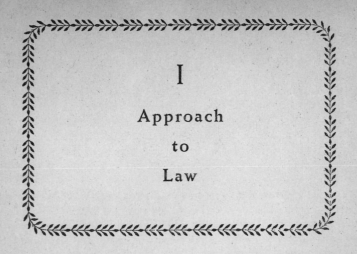

I

Approach
to
Law

The Law Is Everywhere

The law surrounds, guides, restricts, and, if necessary, punishes all of us without exception, from birth to death, and sometimes has its effects upon us before birth and after death.

The law tells you what you must do if you wish to marry and establishes the basic obligations you assume toward husband or wife and children; it requires you to send your children to school for so many weeks in the year and for so many years; it forbids the seduction of your daughter or the sale of narcotics to your son; it tells you how rapidly you may travel on the highway and what you must do in case of accident; it protects you from the dishonest butcher who might sell you horsemeat for top of the round, or the pharmaceutical concern whose claims for its products are extravagant and misleading, or the processor of foods who attempts to cheat you by misrepresenting the quality of his product. If you are a doctor, a lawyer, a dentist, a veterinary surgeon, a certified public accountant, a plumber, or a chauffeur, you must meet certain standards of competence set by law; if you build a loft, a factory, or a theater, structural regulations must be obeyed; if you employ men in a factory, healthful conditions of employment must exist; if you are an employee, your employer cannot prevent you from joining a union; if you wish to borrow money, the law protects you from the unscrupulous moneylender; if you operate a restaurant, standards of cleanliness are demanded by law; the law tells you how to make a valid will and disposes of your estate according to law if you fail to do so. One could go on and on indicating the points of a man's life touched by law.

If you go into a bookshop, pick up a book you wish to buy and say to the owner of the shop, "Put this on my bill," and walk out, you have entered into a contract. If you defame a neighbor, or if you lend your car to a hopelessly drunken friend and he runs into and kills a pedestrian, or if your dog, which is known to be ferocious and has already bitten one person, escapes your premises and bites a passer-by, you have committed a tort or civil wrong and will be liable in damages. If you leave your watch at the jeweler's to be repaired, you are a bailor and the jeweler a bailee, and the latter has the right to hold the property until the charge is paid; the transaction is called a bailment. If you are a customer in a department store or a patron of an amusement park or theater, you are an invitee. If you make a social call for a bridge game, or join a guided tour through a manufacturing establishment, you are a licensee. If your airplane makes a forced landing in a farmer's cornfield or if the artificial lake you have built on your property overflows and runs onto your neighbor's land, you are a trespasser. If you borrow money from a bank to build a house, you are a mortgagor. If you make out a check in payment of a bill or sign a promissory note, your check and the note are negotiable instruments. If your wife does the marketing for the family and charges the food taken, she is acting as your agent and you are the principal.

Thus, it is evident that law is an integral part of our lives. If men lived in a state of complete isolation one from another, one man's path never crossing another's, there would be no need for law. *Custom* might rule that no man's path *should* cross another's, but beyond this a need for any system regulating or guiding the relations of men would be absent. That such a state of affairs never existed is known to all; the truth is that men have always lived in a more or less close connection with other men, that is, in society. Philosophers may quibble that a hermit dwelling in perpetual silence in a hillside cave or a raven-fed Simeon Stylites dwelling for thirty years on top of a pillar sixty feet high disproves the validity of so bald a statement; the exceptions, however, are so rare as to prove the rule. Living in society, no matter how primitive, men have always been subject to law.

Law: Subject to Change

As social organization developed from a predominantly agricultural to a predominantly technological and urban system, and as the relations of men became more and more intimate, the greater was the need of law. A basic force at work here is change, which necessarily has its effect upon the law. Habits, manners, modes of thought, the production of goods, the distribution of goods, the very size of the population, are far different today than they were a century and a half ago. The United States in 1800 had a population estimated at 5,308,483. Today, the population is close to 180,000,000. In 1800, though there were cities like Boston, Charleston, Philadelphia, Baltimore, and New York, relatively few people lived in them; most people engaged in agricultural pursuits and some 90 per cent of the Representatives in Congress came from agricultural constituencies. Today, more than half of the population, city-oriented, live in over one hundred and fifty great, sprawling metropolitan areas. In 1800, the majority of people satisfied their own needs (except for iron, salt and firearms), making their own shoes, clothing, and shelter, and producing their own food. Today, the overwhelming majority of us depend upon others, often great corporate bodies, for the very necessities of life and for the opportunity to earn a living that will secure those necessities. In 1800, most people lived in relative isolation. Roads were poor, transportation was slow, and there are records of men and women who were born, grew up, married and had children, and died, within the confines of a single county. Today such isolation is gone. The railroad, the automobile and good roads, the modern press services, the airplane, radio and television, have brought to us an intimacy with more and more people and conditions, not only in the adjoining county and the state capitol, but in Berlin, Moscow, Nairobi, Amritsar, Accra, and Peiping.

This is a far cry from the relative simplicity of the 1800's. And, since the Civil War, the Congress, the state legislatures, and the courts have tried to keep abreast of the changes in the underlying conditions of our lives. Sometimes they were successful, sometimes not. Steam locomotives were fast and dangerous, and measures had to be taken to protect the lives of passengers as well as the lives and property of those who lived along the railroad's right of way. With the advent of an even more lethal instrument, the automobile, there came speed limits, licensing, compulsory liability insurance, and problems relating to congestion and parking in the cities. Strict rules and regulations followed the development of the airplane and the creation of the great passenger- and freight-carrying airlines. As men became less able to provide their own food, they became more dependent upon what they found in cans in the markets, thereby creating numerous opportunities for fraud on the part of the processors. Often, in fact usually, the consumer did not know, and could not know, what he was buying. Horsemeat in beef stew, turnips in strawberry jam, and reconstituted eggs (old eggs deodorized with formaldehyde) in cakes found their way to the dinner table. Furthermore, the use of chemical preservatives became standard practice. Coal tar dyes and borax in sausages, alum in bread, salicylic acid in canned cherries, saltpetre in corned beef, sodium sulphite in pickles, whether harmful or not, were adulterants, of which the consumer was unaware. Various proprietary remedies, purchasable in any drugstore, contained habit-forming and dangerous drugs such as opium and laudanum. The consumer sought protection through law; and today the canner must specify on the can just what the can contains. Today, also, the use of dangerous drugs is strictly supervised and regulated.

Sometimes the courts recognized the underlying changes, sometimes they did not. In 1897 New York passed a law which limited the number of hours a man might work in a bakery to not more than ten hours a day nor more than sixty hours a week. There were good reasons for this law. The workers had to work at night in a warm, moist, flour-saturated atmosphere and the incidence of respiratory diseases among bakers was high. The 1897 law was adopted as a health measure to protect both worker and consumer. The New York courts found it to be a valid use of the State's police power. The United States Supreme Court, however, held the law to be unconstitutional on the ground that it violated the "liberty" of the due process clause of the Fourteenth Amendment.[1] Earlier, the Supreme Court had held that "liberty of contract" was part of the "liberty" of that clause. The Court, speaking through Mr. Justice Peckham, conceived of the employer-employee relationship as one of equality. The idea was that the employer could offer such hours of labor and wages as he chose; freedom of contract meant that the man looking for work could accept the offer or not, and any law which interfered with this supposed freedom was unconstitutional. Even in 1905, when this case was decided, there was no such equality, and it meant that men could starve if they did not want to accept the employer's offer.

There is such a thing as "judicial lag": it was not until Mr. Roosevelt's attack upon the Supreme Court in 1937 that the justices began to revise and bring up to date constitutional doctrines relating, among other things, to labor, manufacturing, and agriculture.

In another area, however, the courts were keeping abreast of social developments; this was in the swiftly expanding realm of the automobile.

In 1910, the New York legislature enacted that "Any person operating a motor vehicle who, knowing that injury has been caused to a person or property, due to the culpability of the said operator, or to accident, without stopping and giving his name, residence, including street and street number, and operator's license number to the injured party, or to a police officer" or "reporting the same to the nearest police station, or judicial officer, shall be guilty of a felony punishable by a fine of not more than five hundred dollars or by imprisonment for a term not exceeding two years" [2] or both.

One Edward Rosenheimer was indicted for violation of this statute. In the Court of General Sessions, the defendant *demurred* to the indictment. In effect, he said "Yes, it is true that I did not do what was required of me by the law at the time of the accident, but the law is unconstitutional in that it compels me 'to be a witness against myself,' contrary to Art. I, §6, of the state constitution."

The Court of General Sessions sustained the demurrer and discharged the defendant from custody; and this judgment was affirmed by the Appellate Division of the Supreme Court.

The law only required that he give his name and address. But if he did, in fact, cause the accident one thing would lead to another and he would be on hand to be sued by the injured party or even arrested and charged with crime. The lower courts viewed this as unconstitutional self-incrimination. However, to uphold in this way a man's right to run away from an accident for which he was responsible is to ignore the rights of the injured party and to make a mockery of a constitutional clause. The New York Court of Appeals, recognizing the competing claims of both constitutional clause and statute, and the need of some control of the automobile in behalf of all citizens, reversed the lower courts. "When we bear in mind," said the court,

> not only the great danger occasioned by the use of motor vehicles, but also the fact that the great speed at which they can be run enables the person causing injury to readily escape undetected, leaving parties injured in person or property unable to tell from whom they shall seek redress, I think it involves no violation of public policy or of the principles of personal liberty to enact that as a condition of operating such a machine the operator must waive his constitutional privilege and tell who he is to the party who has been injured or to the police authorities. . . .[3]

And so the state has intervened to reduce, resolve, or remedy the numberless conflicts of a changing society. Anti-trust acts, pure food and drug acts, labor legislation, unemployment insurance acts, social security acts, factory acts, and acts prohibiting certain types of racial discrimination have been enacted by the Congress and the state legislatures. The courts, too, have played an important role in adopting new views to new situations.

But change is not everything. Men want a degree, at least, of certainty and stability in their daily lives. They like to know where they stand today and some idea of where they shall stand tomorrow. They know, too, that out of the past there have come good and reasonable rules for the governance of society. "There are two principles inherent in the nature of things," says Alfred North Whitehead, "recurring in some particular embodiments whatever field we explore—the spirit of change, and the spirit of conservation. There can be nothing real without both. Mere change without conservation is a passage from nothing to nothing. Its final integration yields mere transient non-entity. Mere conservation without change cannot conserve." [4]

Conflict: The Basis of Law

One of the most wonderful developments in the history of mankind, more important than the wheel, the lever, or the steam engine, has been the willingness of men to submit their disputes to third parties. When or how this willingness first manifested itself is known to no one; it is enough that in the early accounts of man of which we have reliable knowledge, this tendency has been revealed. True, history abounds with instances where men, individually or collectively, have taken the law in their own hands and sought restitution or revenge; but these are exceptions, frowned upon by society, and bringing in their wake severe penalties. These exceptions, however, serve a purpose in that they point up the nature of men without law and indicate the *raison d'être* of law.

The fundamental basis of law may be summed up in two words: human conflict. The hypothetical state of nature, so forcefully described by Hobbes, finds each man a law unto himself. Each man is his own legislator, his own judge, his own executive. "[D]uring the time men live without a common Power to keep them all in awe," wrote Thomas Hobbes, "they are in that condition which is called Warre; and such a warre, as is of every man, against every man." [5] Under such circumstances, he declared in the *Leviathan*,

> there is no place for Industry; because the fruit thereof is uncertain: and consequently no Culture of the Earth, no Navigation, nor use of the commodities that may be imported by Sea; no commodious Building; no Instruments of moving, and removing such things as require much force; no Knowledge of the face of the Earth; no account of Time; no Arts; no Letters; no Society; and which is worst of all, continuall feare, and danger of violent death; And the Life of man, solitary, poore, nasty, brutish, and short.[6]

This state of total conflict is anarchy, from which man, according to Hobbes, sought escape through a compact creating a society, and later a compact creating a government. Each man contracted to give up certain of his natural rights—the right to be his own legislator, his own judge, and his own executive—in return for which his person and property were to be protected by a government acting as the agent of society. Although society did not originate in a social compact, the condition of conflict (in a somewhat less extreme form than that described by Hobbes) is still beneath the surface of society;[7] this is why we have government and law. "But what is government itself," asked Madison, "but the greatest of all reflections on human nature?"; and he continued, "If men were angels, no government would be necessary." [8] Men do commit fraud, embezzlement, theft, murder, mayhem, arson, manslaughter, assault and battery, seduction, and rape; men exploit their fellow men; they cheat and lie; they kill thousands of other men every year on the highways; they play on the confidence of the trusting and mislead the unwary. This is not a pretty picture, nor is it the whole picture; for man *is* a social animal, he cannot live apart from his fellows, and he does aspire to fair play and decency in his relations with others. While he is dominated by self-interest, he has feelings for justice and equity and the welfare of humanity.[9]

What Is Law?

The term "law" is by no means easy to define. Legal scholars disagree as to its definition. Unlike the chemists who do not continually ask "What is chemistry?" or the medical men who are not plagued by the question "What is medicine?" legal scholars and philosophers have produced over the decades a great literature in answer to the question, "What is law?" [10] Charles Evans Hughes, later Chief Justice of the United States Supreme Court, declared that "We are under a Constitution, but the Constitution is what the judges say it is. . . ." [11] Mr. Justice Holmes believed that "The prophecies of what the courts will do in fact, and nothing more pretentious, are what I mean by the law." [12] And Karl Llewellyn held that "What these officials [judges, sheriffs, clerks, jailors, or lawyers] do about disputes is, to my mind, the law itself." [13] There is truth but not the whole truth in any of these definitions; if true, then what do we call the constitutional clause, or the statute, which creates the judge, the court, and the official?

Let us look at law—constitutional, statute, judge-made, administrative, even international law—in terms of its objectives. Broadly speaking, a definition of the term will include objectives such as internal and external security, the general welfare and prosperity. In a more limited sense, the object of law is to enforce standards of social behavior; and to provide the rules whereby the relations of individual to individual, of group to group, of government to citizen, may be such that a certain fairness is realized between them and conflict is avoided. And where conflict cannot be avoided, the law provides a means of adjudication or peaceful settlement through the instrumentality of a third party, namely, the courts.[14]

We may state the matter in another way. The basic subject matter of the law (and the reason for so profound an interest) is human experience. Over the centuries, the law has been wrought of many ingredients, among them, human passion, human frailty, and human greed; taken together, they add up to human conflict from which, in the hands of judges and legislators, there have emerged rules of conduct for individuals and groups, in countless relationships, as entities in a society. It has been wrought, too, out of centuries of struggle on the part of man to free himself from the restrictions of absolutist kings and arbitrary governments.

A study of courts and their personnel as such is a study of the institutional setting in which judges, attorneys, and sometimes juries play important roles; here the facts of a dispute are determined through evidence given by witnesses, according to certain procedural rules; here legal concepts are invoked by the attorneys in behalf of their clients; here the law is explained by the judge for the guidance of the jury in reaching a verdict. This whole framework of people and ideas, this unique setting, has been built with two principal characters in mind: the plaintiff and the defendant.

The Law Is Human

In approaching a study of law and the courts it is well to remember what seems to be a universal truth: that only men, individually or collectively, have interests. My automobile has not the slightest interest in getting me from New York to Kansas City; my lawn mower does not languish during the winter months and yearn to be out cutting the grass. It may be a convenient mode of expression, but the United States or the State of Illinois can have no "interests" or "policies." Only men, acting properly in the name of the United States, can have a foreign policy; only men, duly elected to the Congress of the United States, can declare war; only men, acting under authority of State law, can execute the murderer. An institution like a court is without life; it has no power to weigh evidence and make a decision, unless men are an integral part of the institution—as they are. This seems self-evident, as indeed it is; but often enough, a court is spoken of as though it were a disembodied spirit far removed from the affairs of men. A court is not, as Mr. Justice Holmes said in another connection, "a brooding omnipresence in the sky." [15] The judges, the attorneys, and the juries are men and women, all of them human and therefore fallible. Fallible men reach verdicts, fallible men plead for their clients, fallible men prosecute, and fallible men pronounce judgment. It may also be said, sadly enough, that some judges and prosecutors have been, not only fallible, but dishonest, grossly prejudiced, and venal; but these are the exceptions.

That grand old slogan, much admired by Americans, "a government of laws, not of men," [16] is meaningless as it stands because government cannot exist without men, good or bad; government and men are inseparable.

Law: An Inexact Science

It is important to remember that the law is not an exact science. It is unfortunate but true that many people, unfamiliar with law and the courts, tend to see the issues in a lawsuit from a one-sided, prejudiced, standpoint. People oftentimes, unaware of their own ignorance or naïveté, complain when the outcome of cases does not accord with their own views. They blame the personnel of the courts. With competent judges and jurors who can see through the arguments of the other side, a lawyer ought to be able to advise a client with certainty as to the conclusion of his case.

The truth is that lawyers deal in probabilities, not in certainties.

Before we condemn the lawyers, let us consider another profession—medicine. Medical men will tell you that there is a great deal that they do not know about the human body and its pathology; like the lawyers, they cannot guarantee results. People are different in their physical, mental, and emotional make-ups, and a cure in one case is no guarantee that it will be effective in a similar case. It is probable that, in medicine, no two cases are exactly alike.

In fact, there is implicit in the law's view of the doctor a realization that he cannot with absolute certainty predict the outcome of an operation or a course of treatment. The law recognizes varieties, too, of medical skill and competence. The court in the New York case of *MacKenzie v. Carman* said,

> The law thus requires a surgeon to possess skill and learning which is possessed by the average member of the medical profession in good standing, and to apply that skill and learning with ordinary reasonable care. *He is not liable for a mere error of judgment, provided he does what he thinks best after a careful examination.* He does not guarantee a good result, but he promises by implication to use the skill and learning of the average physician to exercise reasonable care, and to exert his best judgment in the effort to bring about a good result." [17] As Judge Holloway said in a Montana case, "The object of the law on the one hand is to guard the patient against the wrongful practice of ignorant or negligent men who hold themselves out as physicians or surgeons, and on the other to protect the faithful practitioner of ordinary learning, skill, and ability from loss in reputation or purse on account of matters for which it would be unreasonable to hold him responsible.[18]

No doctor can say for certain what the outcome of a case will be. He faces the nature of the patient, and his own competence: he represents the human element as much as the patient.

Here is a rough parallel with the law. As each patient is an individual case presenting his own peculiar mental, emotional, and physical characteristics (about all of which there may be inadequate knowledge), so with the law. Each case is individual, each case is particular, and two cases are rarely, if ever, alike, if only because two similar cases may be litigated in different courts by different judges, different attorneys, and different jurors. The human element of a case centers not only in the litigants themselves but in the court.

An extreme case of this unpredictability is that of two men who stole a few chickens. One of them was captured and tried. The jury brought in a verdict of guilty and the judge, who thought the offense a trivial one, sentenced him to a brief imprisonment. The other thief, learning of the light sentence given his erstwhile partner in crime, gave himself up to take his trial at the next sitting of the court. Unfortunately for the prisoner, another judge presided at his trial, a judge who thought that men who started out by stealing chickens ended by committing more atrocious crimes. This judge sentenced the poor fellow to "transportation," that is, to a penal colony in Australia.[19]

What Is Justice?

The symbol of justice which adorns many a court house has descended to us from the classical goddess of justice, Astraea, a virgin with stern but majestic countenance, holding a pair of scales in one hand, a sword in the other. The scales represent judgment, the sword, enforcement. In later representations the goddess is blindfolded, betokening impartiality.

To describe the symbol of justice is a simple matter; to define justice is another matter. Like Pilate, who asked "What is truth?" and turned away not waiting for an answer,[20] many a lawyer would ask "What is justice?" knowing full well that no definitive answer was forthcoming. A judge may say, "My business is not justice; it is the law." A lawyer might say to a client, "The justice of your claim is clear—now let us see what the law has to say about it." The Archbishop of Canterbury began an address before a group of British barristers with the words, "I cannot say that I know much about the law, having been far more interested in justice." [21]

Justice, or the lack of it, is inherent in two factors instrumental in the legal resolution of disputes: one is the system itself; the other is the men who administer the system.

A system of law which would permit a man to be arrested, to be kept uninformed of the charge against him, and to be held incommunicado for thirty days; a system which would allow the "third degree" or the coerced confession; a system which would deny a defendant *habeas corpus,* counsel, and bail; a system which would see a man condemned before he was heard in his own defense or which denied him the right to call witnesses in his own behalf; all these actions, or any one of them, would, in the United States today, be deemed the essence of injustice. And the history of Anglo-American law as a system is replete, from a present-day point of view, with such iniquity. This is not to say that such practices were illegal; they were unjust.

"I think it is a hard case," said Lord Chief Justice Jeffreys in 1684 in the trial of Thomas Rosewell for high treason, "that a man should have counsel to defend himself for a two-penny-trespass, and his witnesses examined on oath; but if he steal, commit murder or felony, nay, high-treason, where life, estate, honour, and all are concerned, he shall neither have counsel, nor his witnesses examined upon oath. . . ." [22] Interestingly enough, in 1695, by Act of Parliament,[23] a person accused of high treason was allowed counsel, but one hundred and forty-two years had to elapse before this right was extended to other felonies.

Torture was once an accepted mode of eliciting evidence, and occasionally, although more and more rarely, one learns that the "third degree" is still with us. Until 1772,[24] a prisoner who refused to plead either guilty or not guilty could not be tried at all; he was thereupon subjected to the *peine forte et dure*. The prisoner was stretched out on his back, his arms and legs secured by chains, and weights placed upon his body, the weights being increased each day until he either pleaded or died. Also, in the early part of the nineteenth century the application of the death penalty was indiscriminate, senseless, and vicious. Murder, killing or maiming cattle, treason, picking a pocket, marking the edges of coin of the realm, arson, forgery, cutting hopbinds growing on poles in any plantation of hops, extortion, the wandering about of a soldier or sailor without a pass, wounding tax officers in the execution of their duties, and being found in the company of gypsies—these were a few of the offenses incurring the death penalty. And it made no difference whether the offender was a man, a woman, or a child.

To consider what appears to be a modern injustice in the English system, let us note that the Court of Criminal Appeal has no power upon appeal to order a new trial of a convicted person.[25] If there has been significant irregularity or serious misdirection during the trial, the appellate court can only upset the conviction and substitute a verdict of acquittal. In 1952, a committee was appointed by the Lord Chancellor and the Home Secretary to study the question of whether the Court of Criminal Appeal should be so empowered. By a vote of five to three, the committee recommended no change on the following grounds: (1) that a second trial would only slow down the administration of justice which should be swift and final; (2) that to place a man twice in jeopardy would be offensive to public opinion; (3) that the second trial could hardly be a fair one; (4) that the second trial might become the "normal" practice and thus destroy public confidence in the administration of justice; and (5) that the practice of a second trial might make judge and jury of the trial court less careful.[26]

Professor Goodhart tells the story of a young wife who was brutally raped. The defendant maintained that it was not rape since the woman had consented to his advances; he was, however, found guilty by a jury on evidence so clear and so overwhelming as to leave no room for doubt that he had shockingly attacked her. On appeal to the Court of Criminal Appeal his conviction was quashed "owing to an error concerning the admission of certain evidence." He returned to his village a free man; his story that the wife had consented was seemingly vindicated, with the result that gossip drove the husband and wife to another part of the country.[27]

On the noncriminal side of the English system in the first half of the nineteenth century, certain of its characteristics, amounting to injustice in themselves, were its slowness, its recognition of an excessive number of technicalities, and its reliance upon old and outworn modes of procedure. Those of you who have read Charles Dickens' *Bleak House* will comprehend a little the workings of the Court of Chancery. "My feeling . . . is the feeling common, I suppose," wrote Dickens, "to three-fourths of the reflecting part of the community in our happiest of all possible countries; and that is, that it is better to suffer a great wrong than to have recourse to the much greater wrong of the law." [28] Dickens had been in Chancery several times in order to protect *A Christmas Carol* from unscrupulous and piratical publishers; he won his cases but he could never recover costs from the defendants. "I shall not easily forget the expense, and anxiety," he wrote, "and horrible injustice of the *Carol* case, wherein, in asserting the plainest right on earth, I was really treated as if I were the robber instead of the robbed. . . . I know of nothing that *could* come, even of a successful action, which would be worth the mental trouble and disturbance it would cost." [29]

Prior to the reform of Chancery in 1852,[30] the Court was understaffed and the original officials were allowed to employ underpaid deputies to do their work for them. When the parties employed their own solicitors, they still had to pay fees to the Six Clerks in Chancery; and they were required to pay fees for innumerable documents, some of them totally useless. In addition, the wheels of Chancery turned slowly. In the course of a Chancery suit lasting several years there would naturally occur births, marriages, and deaths. Dickens was not exaggerating when he wrote,

Innumerable children have been born into the cause [*Jarndyce v. Jarndyce*]; innumerable young people have married into it; innumerable old people have died out of it. Scores of persons have deliriously found themselves made parties in Jarndyce and Jarndyce without knowing how or why; whole families have inherited legendary hatred with the suit. The little plaintiff or defendant who was promised a new rocking-horse when Jarndyce and Jarndyce should be settled, has grown up, possessed himself of a real horse, and trotted away into the other world. Fair wards of court have faded into mothers and grandmothers; a long procession of Chancellors has come in and gone out; the legion of bills in the suit have been transformed into mere bills of mortality; there are not three Jarndyces left upon the earth perhaps, since old Tom Jarndyce in despair blew his brains out at a coffee-house in Chancery Lane. . . .[31]

In our own country, an understaffed judiciary and the great increase in the number of causes in our courts, particularly personal injury cases, result in delays which tend to undermine the administration of justice. There was a total of 52,973 actions "brought in the Supreme Court [New York] during the court year ending June 30, 1955, an increase of almost 1,200 over the preceding court year." On that date "there were pending, and undisposed-of, almost 47,000 cases in the Supreme Court." The time required "between the date when a case is placed on the trial calendar and the date when it is reached for trial ran to 45 months in one county and ranged from 9 to 40 months in eleven other counties. . . ." [32]

Dissatisfaction with the administration of justice in New York has led to proposals for reform: "What does the citizen expect and what is he entitled to receive from his court?" The answer was "justice." Of what does "justice" consist? Good laws, good judges, and a good court system. Granted that a definition of "good" admits of a variety of meanings, it seems obvious that if the citizen cannot expect a reasonably speedy trial the machinery of justice must be creaky and in need of repair.

Thus, it is obvious that the judicial system itself can retard or further the realization of justice. Great strides have been taken in England since the middle of the last century to eliminate a cumbersome judicial system and to erect in its place a smoothly operating system of courts of advantage to the litigants. We may say that in the United States, too, effective reforms have been made in our court systems.

The judicial system itself, as we have just seen, can be a major aid or hindrance to justice. Even more crucial, however, for justice, are the judges: no matter how excellent a court system may be on paper, no matter how good it may be philosophically, it will never be any better than the men who administer it.

In the United States the quality of judges is certainly high; on the other hand, there has been judicial corruption. The purchase of judgeships, judicial connivance with corrupt policemen and underworld characters, and the acceptance of bribes are not unknown. One has only to read Raymond Moley's *Tribunes of the People*[33] for a hair-raising account of court corruption as revealed by the Seabury investigations of the early 1930's. One judge bought his appointment for $10,000. Another received a fee of $190,000 in connection with the lease of piers belonging to the City of New York. During the investigation a New York Supreme Court Justice disappeared and has not been seen since. "The genius of sardonic comedy," says Moley, "never imagined a more weird gathering than that which attended the dinner in honor of Magistrate Vitale at the Tippecanoe Democratic Club. While judges, politicians, and the underworld made merry, six gunmen entered the hall, lined up the guests, and walked out with thousands of dollars of loot. Soon after, it was disclosed that Magistrate Vitale had effected the return of many of the stolen articles within a few hours after the burglary." [34] This kind of thing composes the dregs of judicial corruption and is by no means a common phenomenon in the United States.

Less sensational and more to the point are the following two cases.

In September, 1919, a number of Negroes, assembled in their church, were attacked by a body of white men and in the melee which followed a white man was killed. Great excitement ensued: Negroes were hunted down and shot, and on October first another white man, Clinton Lee, was killed. Several Negroes were arrested and indicted for the murder of Lee. After the arrest, a mob marched to the jail with the intention of lynching the Negroes but were prevented by the presence of Federal troops. The indictment was returned on October 29th; on November 3rd the defendants were brought into Court, informed that a certain lawyer had been appointed to defend them, and were at once placed on trial before a white jury, from which Negroes had been excluded.

The defense counsel did not dare to ask for time to prepare an adequate defense, nor did he dare to demand a change of venue, nor even to challenge a juryman. He had no preliminary consultation with the accused, called no witnesses, and did not put the defendants on the stand. The trial lasted about three-quarters of an hour, and in less than five minutes the jury brought in a verdict of murder in the first degree and the judge sentenced them to death.

The conviction was sustained by the state's highest court and the Governor set the date for the execution. The prisoners then appealed to a Federal District Court for a writ of *habeas corpus* on the ground that the trial was a violation of the due process clause of the XIVth Amendment to the United States Constitution. The District Judge refused to issue the writ, holding that the alleged facts were insufficient *prima facie* to show nullity of the original judgment. From this ruling, an appeal was made to the United States Supreme Court.

The Supreme Court reversed the order of the District Court, ordering it to hear the case. This time the Negroes received a fair trial that resulted only in prison sentences.

According to Mr. Justice Holmes, there never was a chance for these men to be acquitted. "No juryman could have voted for an acquittal and continued to live in Phillips County, and if any prisoner by any chance had been acquitted by a jury he could not have escaped the mob." [35]

Speaking for the majority of the Supreme Court, Mr. Holmes said, ". . . if the case is that the whole proceeding is a mask—that counsel, jury and judge were swept to the fatal end by an irresistible wave of public passion, and that the State Courts failed to correct the wrong, neither perfection in the machinery for correction nor the possibility that the trial court and counsel saw no other way of avoiding an immediate outbreak of the mob can prevent this Court from securing to the petitioners [the Negro prisoners] their constitutional rights." [36]

In this situation, the trial court was so dominated by the mob that only one verdict and one sentence were possible. The trial itself was a pretence. Had the sentence of the trial court been carried out, a "legal" lynching, figuratively speaking, would have taken place. By any stretch of the imagination, it is difficult to understand the unwillingness of the highest court of the state to order a new trial. This is not to say that the Negroes were necessarily innocent; at best, the determination of guilt or innocence is not a simple matter. But here there was condemnation before trial; there were prejudice, fear of the mob, an inadequate defense, and a timid appellate court.

The essence of justice, I think, is to be found in the case of *People v. Zackowitz*.[37] No mob was involved; no racial prejudice distorted judgment; and the trial was no pretence.

Joseph Zackowitz was indicted for the shooting and killing of Frank Coppola. Shortly after midnight, November 10, 1929, Zackowitz and his wife, "Fluff," were returning to their home from a dance. On the way, Zackowitz dropped into a store to purchase a newspaper, while his wife walked on. When he caught up with her, he found her in tears. She said that she had been insulted by four young men who were repairing an automobile on the other side of the street. Zackowitz immediately crossed the street, upbraided the boys, and told them that "if they did not get out of there in five minutes, he would come back and bump them all off." Returning to their apartment, Zackowitz induced his wife to tell him what had been said. One of the young men "had asked her to lie with him, and had offered her two dollars." Enraged once again, Zackowitz returned to the scene of the encounter where a battle of words took place, followed by blows; Zackowitz kicked Coppola in the stomach; Coppola— at least there was some evidence to this effect—went for Zackowitz with a wrench; whereupon Zackowitz pulled out a gun and shot Coppola. Zackowitz and his wife fled from Brooklyn to Manhattan where, about two months later, the former was apprehended by the police and indicted for murder in the first degree. Zackowitz pleaded self-defense.

"At the trial," said Judge Cardozo speaking for the majority of the Court of Appeals, "the vital question was the defendant's state of mind at the moment of the homicide. Did he shoot with a deliberate and premeditated design to kill? Was he so inflamed by drink or by anger or by both combined that, though he knew the nature of his act, he was the prey to sudden impulse, the fury of the fleeting moment?" [38]

Shortly after the arrest the apartment of Zackowitz was searched and there, in a radio cabinet, were found three pistols and a tear gas gun. These weapons, none of which had fired the fatal shot, were laid out before the jury. "The end," said Judge Cardozo, "was to bring persuasion that here was a man of vicious and dangerous propensities. . . . The District Attorney tells us in his brief that the possession of the weapons characterized the defendant as 'a desperate type of criminal,' a 'person criminally inclined.' " [39] The prosecutor succeeded in creating an atmosphere of professional criminality, an endeavor "the more unfair in that, apart from the suspicion attaching to the possession of these weapons, there is nothing to mark the defendant as a man of evil life. He was not in crime as a business. He did not shoot as a bandit shoots in the hope of wrongful gain. He was engaged in a decent calling, an optician regularly employed, without criminal record, or criminal associates. If his own testimony be true, he had gathered these weapons together as curios, a collection that interested and amused him." [40]

Now Judge Cardozo was not suggesting that Zackowitz was innocent of premeditation and deliberation, but if the defendant approached the four young men the second time with intent to kill, why did he not shoot at once? "How reconcile such a design with the drawing of the pistol later in the heat and rage of an affray?" [41] These were questions the jurors had to ask themselves in order to draw a line between *impulse* and *deliberation*. "The sphygmograph," said Cardozo,

> records with graphic certainty the fluctuations of the pulse. There is no instrument yet invented that records with equal certainty the fluctuations of the mind. . . . With only the rough and ready tests supplied by their experience of life, the jurors were to look into the workings of another's mind, and discover its capacities and disabilities, its urges and inhibitions, in moments of intense excitement. Delicate enough and subtle is the inquiry, even in the most favorable conditions, with every warping influence excluded. *There must be no blurring of the issues by evidence illegally admitted and carrying with it in its admission an appeal to prejudice and passion.*[42]

The "evidence illegally admitted" was the evidence of the pistols and tear gas gun, and the characterization of Zackowitz therefrom as a man of murderous propensities. The rule of evidence is that character is never an issue in a criminal prosecution unless the defendant chooses to make it one. In this case, Zackowitz's character was an issue from the start, and it was made an issue by the prosecution. In a real sense charged with murder, he had also to answer to a second charge, bad character. Zackowitz was thus forced to take the stand to defend his character. Cross-examination revealed that he had no license for the pistols.

> That fact disclosed, the prosecution was at liberty to prove the possession of the weapons in an attempt to impeach his credibility, since possession was a felony. All this may be true, but the evidence was not offered or admitted with such an end in view. It was received at a time when there was nothing to show that the defendant was without a license, and without suggestion that any such evidence would be brought into the case thereafter. The jury were not told that the possession of the weapons had significance only in so far as possession without a license had a tendency to cast a shadow on the defendant's character and so to impair the faith to be given to his word. . . . They were told in effect through the whole course and tenor of the trial that irrespective of any license, the mere possession of the weapons was evidence of a murderous disposition, which, apart from any bearing upon the defendant's credibility as a witness, was evidence of guilt.[43]

The judgment of conviction was reversed and a new trial ordered. In the second trial, Zackowitz was charged with manslaughter and sentenced to twenty years in jail.

These two cases—*Moore v. Dempsey* and *People v. Zackowitz*—are the products of highly organized and sophisticated legal systems in which the defendants were protected in many ways: by rules of procedure, rules governing the admissibility of evidence, and due process. In the first case apparently no one except the defendants wanted more than a token recognition of the rules; in the second, to all intents and purposes the rules were scrupulously observed by an able judge. In the first case, there was *gross injustice,* there to be seen by all; in the second, the injustice was more subtle and, in the minds of three dissenting judges, no injustice at all (see Judge Pound's dissent). In each case, the injustice done at the trial level was corrected by a higher court.

Both cases give ample point to the concluding remarks in a report of the National Commission on Law Observance and Enforcement:

Specific changes in the machinery of criminal prosecutions, such as have been suggested, will help lessen unfairness by defining limits which must not be overstepped and providing the accused with a more efficient legal remedy if there is transgression. But changes in machinery are not sufficient to prevent unfairness. Much more depends upon the men that operate the machinery. And whatever limits are imposed by statute, prosecuting officials and trial judges must necessarily be left with great powers and wide discretion. The most important safeguards of a fair trial are that these officials want it to be fair and are active in making it so. As Mr. Wigmore has said: "All the rules in the world will not get us substantial justice if the judges and the counsel have not the correct living moral attitude toward substantial justice." [44]

The law, not abstract principles of justice, is the concern of judges and lawyers. But Justice *is* important; it is a quality, a sense of fair play, a sense of decency, in judges and counsel. It was evident in a Holmes or a Cardozo; it was evident in the English judge when he questioned counsel's delving, upon cross-examination, into a witness' past to impair her credibility; counsel responded that he had every right to do so. "Yes," replied the judge, "you have every right, but I consider it a most indecent thing to do." It is true that judges and counsel must work within the framework of the law; but within that framework there is scope for justice, and therein lies the distinction between a great judge and a competent one.

II

Development
of
Law and the Courts

Legal traditions and practices in the United States today reflect a great heritage from England—the common law. This chapter will suggest how this law originated and how it developed; and it will discuss our adoption of this law, modified to meet the new circumstances and conditions of America. But first, for purposes of comparison, we should consider just how disputes were settled before the dim beginnings of a modern court system.

Resolution of Conflict: Anglo-Saxon and Norman

The mode of trial in late Anglo-Saxon England, just before the Norman Conquest, was indeed primitive. There were no judges in our sense of the word, no attorneys, no policemen, and from the vantage point of the twentieth century, no rational method by which the allegations of either a plaintiff or a defendant could be proved "beyond a reasonable doubt."

The administration of justice was largely local. England was divided into vills or townships, a number of which comprised the hundred while a number of hundreds formed the shire. The hundred moot and the shire moot were the courts respectively of the hundred and the shire. Besides these public courts, there were courts of private jurisdiction, headed by the Lord of the Manor.

The magistrates, to use a modern term, were the alderman, the reeve, the shire-reeve (sheriff, as he came later to be called), the bishop, and those tenants of the lord whose attendance at court was expected. The jurisdiction of these courts extended to such matters as treason, homicide, cattle-stealing, battery, debt, and to disputes over the possession of land.

The procedure followed in these courts was fairly uniform. Let us suppose that Richard Jones claimed that John Doe owed him a sum of money. Richard would appear before the shire court and make this allegation under oath. John would respond by saying, as Blackstone has it, "hear this, ye justices, that I do not owe unto Richard Jones the sum of ten pounds, nor any penny thereof, in manner and form as the said Richard hath declared against me. So help me God." [1] The oaths having been properly taken, the court then decided which of the parties would go to the proof, usually the defendant. The proof consisted in the appearance of twelve (the number varies) neighbors or oath-helpers or compurgators, each of whom asserted under oath that he believed in his conscience that the defendant "saith the truth." Had John been unable to find the proper number of oath-helpers or if the required form were not followed by each of them, then "the oath bursts" and John's claim that he owed Richard nothing is demolished. There was a saying, "fail in a syllable, fail in your case." Oath-helpers were not witnesses; they did not swear that John did not owe Richard ten pounds; they merely swore that John was to be believed. They were character witnesses.

In criminal cases, twelve freemen served as accusers before either the hundred court or the shire court. They would present, under oath, the names of those whom they believed to have committed a crime. Guilt or innocence would then be determined either by compurgation or by the ordeal. With the latter, God intervened in the administration of justice.

Charged with crime, a man would have to submit to ordeal by fire or water or dry bread. Holding a hot iron in his hand, the accused had to walk about nine feet. According to the Laws of King Athelstan,[2] the hand would then be bound and three days later examined by a priest. If the wound were foul, the accused was guilty; if clean, he was innocent. Or the accused might be required to plunge his arm into a pot of boiling water to retrieve a stone; again, the condition of the burn would conclude the verdict. Tied up and thrown into a stream, a man would be deemed faultless if he sank, since the pure waters had accepted him; if he rose quickly to the surface he was guilty, for the waters had rejected him; obviously, either result could make him the loser. And, in another ordeal, if the unfortunate accused choked on dry bread, he was pronounced guilty.

It will be noted that the oath as well as the opinion of neighbors played important and often decisive roles in the Anglo-Saxon trials. We may raise our eyebrows at so naïve a method of proof, yet it is probably true that a rough justice was accomplished. We must bear in mind that the England of that day consisted chiefly of scores of little hamlets, in which men were born, grew up, and died, living intimately with their neighbors and knowing the reputation of each for integrity, responsibility, and fairdealing.

We must be mindful, too, that the oath meant much more then than it does now. God was closer to men, He was part of their lives and ever watchful for the least transgression. Men believed in miracles and divine intervention: the man who swore falsely might be struck dead on the spot or suffer some worse fate after death.

It is probably true that the family and relatives of a murdered man would take the law in their own hands and begin a blood feud. Society, however, came to frown upon private vengeance. In time a practice prevailed which allowed the feud to be bought off. The Laws of Alfred [3] provide, in part, that "If a man strike out another's eye, let him pay IX. shillings . . . as 'bōt' (reparation). . . . If a man strike out another's tooth in the front of his head, let him make 'bōt' for it with VIII. shillings. . . . If a man's arm, with the hand, be entirely cut off before the elbow, let 'bōt' be made for it with LXXX. shillings." Every man's life had its value. According to the Laws of Athelstan, the king's life was valued at 30,000 "thrymsas," [4] a sheriff's at 4,000, and a thegn's at 2,000. This was called the *wergild,* or the price of homicide. In general, part of the wergild went to the king "for the loss of a subject," part to the lord "for the loss of a vassal," and part "to the next of kin."

The Norman kings made use of the shire moot, the hundred moot, the shire-reeve or sheriff, and the old modes of trial, compurgation, and the ordeal. The Normans, themselves, added a new method of settling disputes, namely, trial by battle. This was another means of proof in which divine intervention played a part, the assumption being that God would strengthen the arm of the innocent or upright contender.

Readers of Scott's *Ivanhoe* will recall that the beautiful prisoner Rebecca was charged by her captor, Bois-Guilbert, with sorcery. This she denied, declaring that the testimony delivered against her was false. Unable to wage combat herself, "She doth offer, by a champion instead thereof, to avouch her case, he [the champion] performing his loyal *devoir* in all knightly sort, with such arms as to gage of battle do fully appertain, and that at her peril and cost. And therewith she proffered her gage." It was Ivanhoe who appeared at the last moment to do battle for her.

"The herald, then seeing each champion in his place, uplifted his voice, repeating thrice—*Faites vos devoirs preux chevaliers!* . . . The Grand Master, who held in his hand the gage of battle, Rebecca's glove, now threw it into the lists, and pronounced the fatal signal words, *Laissez aller."* The two knights—Ivanhoe and Bois-Guilbert—charged each other and each was struck to the ground. Ivanhoe leaped to his feet to fight with his sword, but Bois-Guilbert did not rise, for he was dead, although the spear of his opponent barely touched his shield. "This is indeed," cried the Grand Master, "the judgment of God." Thus did the fair Rebecca establish her innocence and thus did she escape the flames.

Trial by battle was the usual mode of settling a conflict over the possession of land. At first, the parties to the dispute were the actual participants in trial by battle unless barred by youthfulness or sex, but in time the parties began to employ professional "champions" who would do their fighting for them.

Imperfect as was the judicial system in this early period, crude as were the methods of proof, and naïve as were men in their submission to fear and superstition, there was still a forum, however stiff and formal, to which men could go with their grievances and be heard. There was something else, too. The law was on the way to becoming a rule of life. Men were getting away from the feud, they were outgrowing the practice of private vengeance, and they revealed an increasing willingness to submit their disputes to third parties—the courts.

So much for the *modes* of settling disputes before, and for many decades after, the Conquest.

Feudalism

Of the early post-Conquest influences which fostered the development of law and the courts in England, the system of landholding was perhaps the most significant; for upon these landholding arrangements rested both the structure of the central government and the highly important tax system.

William I assumed "ownership" of all English land and proceeded to parcel it out in great tracts to his most important followers. These men who held land directly of the king were his *tenants-in-capite* or tenants-in-chief. In return for the land, they rendered services of various kinds to the king.

The king was the lord of all the lands, but his tenants-in-chief had the power of sub-infeudation which meant that they could grant any part of their domain, or all of it for that matter, to inferior tenants who would, in turn, owe them certain feudal services.

Feudalism was not entirely foreign to the English before the Conquest. The first William extended it and moulded it in such a way as to enhance his own power. In France, for example, the sub-infeudatories, at whatever level, were expected to support their *immediate* lord in war, even against the king. In England, William would have none of this. Tenants of William's tenants-in-chief and so on down the line were bound to the king by an allegiance superior to that owed any sub-infeudatory.[5] A centralized allegiance, based upon a system of landholding, must have contributed psychologically to the strength of the central government and, in turn, to the growth of a central judiciary whose jurisdiction would ultimately cover the whole of England.

Let us look more closely at these landholding arrangements. Holding real property in subordination to some superior was a dominant feature of the feudal system and was called *tenure*.

Tenures were divided into the free and the unfree, the latter represented by the villein who was bound to his land and required to perform certain agricultural services for his lord. If he fled his place he could be recovered by a command to the sheriff to apprehend the fugitive and to return him to his lord.

There were four free tenures: *frankalmoign, chivalry, serjeanty,* and *socage*. The tenant in frankalmoign was obliged to pray for the grantor while he lived and to offer masses for his soul when he died. This was a spiritual tenure, the tenants being in the main religious corporations. A tenant in chivalry (knight service) was required to serve his lord in war and to provide a number of armed retainers for the same purpose; he could, however, escape this service by a money payment known as a *scutage*. Grand serjeanty involved the tenant in duties of a personal nature to the king, such as carrying his sword or serving as an officer in the king's household. A tenant holding land by petty serjeanty was expected to present to the king each year some small instrument of war: a lance, a bow, or a sword, for example. The tenant in socage was under obligation for certain agricultural services to his lord, but by the payment of a quit-rent he could escape these.

It might appear that the feudal relationship of the king to his tenants-in-chief, and of the tenants-in-chief to their sub-tenants, and of the sub-tenants to *their* sub-tenants, was a simple matter. Quite the reverse is true. Not only were the relationships complex, they were financially onerous. Knight service included payments to the lord for three purposes: to ransom the lord if a captive of one of his enemies, to make the lord's eldest son a knight, and to bear part of the marriage expenses of the lord's eldest daughter. These *aids,* as they were called, of the tenant were supposed to be reasonable. When a tenant died his *fief* (the lands granted him by his superior) descended to his eldest son preferably, but before coming into possession (not ownership), if he were of age, he had to pay to the lord what was euphemistically called a *relief*. On the other hand, if the heir were not of age, the lord assumed custody of the heir and his lands and all the profits therefrom, no accounting being required. This was spoken of as *wardship*. On reaching the age of twenty-one, the ward could take possession of his heritage upon the payment of a certain sum of money. If the heir were a woman, she could take possession on the same conditions as a man but at the age of fourteen. The lord could also marry off his female wards; and a ward who refused to wed the lord's choice of a husband was mulcted of an amount of money equal to her marriage price, that is, the sum her suitor would have paid the lord for the privilege of marrying her. Double the market value of the marriage was the fine imposed upon the woman who married without the lord's consent.

This merely suggests the complexity of the system. Out of this welter of intricate relationships it is clear that the king was going to have to decide disputes between himself and his tenants and between his tenants as to who owed what and to whom. To these sources of conflict we may add others: the Crown lands, the sheriff's court and other local courts, all of them yielding revenue to the king and over which he kept a watchful eye.

It is little wonder then that the king was in need of a bookkeeping department, an agency to oversee the collection and disbursement of his revenues. The Exchequer, as we shall see, was to fulfill this need.

The Curia Regis

First, let us go back a little. With the coming of the Normans, the old Anglo-Saxon *Witenagemot* was replaced by the *Curia Regis,* a legislative, executive, and administrative organ by means of which the king governed the country and controlled his own officials. It was a court of law as well.

Unlike the Witenagemot which consisted of the wise men of the realm, the Curia was composed of the king's tenants-in-chief. These men advised the king, recommended new laws, and adjudicated disputes arising between the great men of the country, the king, counseled by the Curia, giving judgment.

Remember that the older courts—the shire court and the hundred court —still flourished. The power of the sheriff was enhanced for a time under the Norman kings. He was the king's chief officer in the shire, the chief of police as it were who could raise the "hue and cry" and call out a *posse comitatus* to arrest a thief or murderer. He was the watchdog of the king's fiscal interests in the shire, and the holder of a court. By royal charter and the powers inherent in the feudal relationship, manorial and franchise courts throve, their jurisdiction extending to both civil and criminal matters.

Now in this early Norman period, a new and special institution grew within the Curia Regis which was important for the future of the English judicial system. This was a "thesaurus," a treasury—the Exchequer. This "oldest official offshoot of the *curia regis*" was a royal bookkeeping department, concerned with debits and credits and the royal revenues. It was, in fact, the fiscal committee of the Curia Regis. To this place the sheriff came periodically to settle the accounts of the shire. Great lords came to pay their debts to the king or to dispute the amount of the debt claimed. As a consequence, we find the barons of the Exchequer sitting as a law court. The Exchequer was clearly in operation as a distinct entity in the reign of Henry I (1100-1135).

Henry I had died in 1135 leaving no male heir. He had hoped that his daughter, Matilda, would secure the crown, but the barons in council chose Henry's nephew, Stephen of Blois. Stephen was not a statesman and, according to the *Chronicle,* "he was a mild man, and gentle and good, and did not exact the full penalties of the law." [6] He was unable to control the barons, allowing them to build and fortify castles; he provided no supervision over the sheriffs who assumed illegal powers, forgetting that they were servants of the king. Disputes which rightfully should have gone to the Curia were settled in the shire courts, and feudal lords abused their judicial powers.

Matilda and a group of barons made war upon Stephen. This struggle ended only a year before the king's death with the Treaty of Wallingford. It was agreed that Stephen should be king but that upon his death the crown should go to Matilda's son, Henry of Anjou. Henry II, the first Plantagenet, inherited a confused and disorderly kingdom.

When Henry II came to the throne there was no clear distinction between civil and criminal law. Crime was a wrong against an individual, to be remedied by either blood or money. Trial by battle, compurgation, and the ordeal were still used as methods of deciding cases. Trial by jury was undeveloped.

Henry was a strong-minded, vigorous king who worked unceasingly to strengthen his government and to centralize the judicial system. He recognized the inadequacies of the older modes of trial and encouraged the use of the jury. He insisted that crime was not only a wrong against an individual but a wrong against the State; crime violated the "King's Peace." He claimed for the Curia Regis jurisdiction over all serious crime. Finally, and this is crucial in connection with the development of the common law, he made the royal writ a powerful weapon in a struggle to curb the powers of the local courts and to enhance the powers of his own courts.

Writs

What was the royal writ? It was a formal, written order of the king, issuing out of the Chancery. It was directed to an inferior officer, or to a private individual, commanding him to do whatever was specified in the order. If it were disobeyed, the officer or private person would be in contempt of the royal authority and subject to punishment.

The royal writ did not commence litigation; litigation followed only if the writ were disobeyed or ignored. The royal writ was not an original writ, nor was it a judicial writ. It was simply an *executive* writ.

The writ was of Anglo-Saxon origin. Efforts have been made to trace the writ back to the time of King Alfred in the ninth century with only partial success. The earliest writ which has come down to us was issued during the reign of Aethelred II, sometime between the years 984 and 1001. It runs as follows:

> King Aethelred sends friendly greetings to Earl Aelfric and Wulfmaer and Aethelweard and all the thegns in Hampshire. And I inform thee, and all of you, that Bishop Aelfheah sent to me the charter of the land at Chilcomb, and I had it read before me. Then I was greatly pleased with the ordinance and the pious benefaction which my ancestors, when Christianity first began, established for the benefit of the holy foundation; and the wise king Alfred afterwards renewed in the charter which was read before me. It is now my will that it shall be assessed for all purposes at one hide,[7] just as my ancestors formerly established and freed it, whether there be more land there or whether there be less.[8]

The importance of the old executive writ cannot be underestimated. It was a powerful and all-pervasive instrument of government in the hands of the Norman kings, who used it regally—"do this" or "do not do that"—and in connection with matters great and small, such as an order to stop "people fishing in the Thames to the detriment of the fisheries of the monks of Rochester." The executive writ in the Norman period was usually not as long as Aethelred's writ; ordinarily it was a brief, bare-bones order.

For two reasons, the executive writ was of great significance. First, its use contributed to the decline of the local courts and the rise of the king's courts. Second, from the executive writ there developed the *original* writ upon which the future common law was to be in part based.

Executive Writs and the Local Courts

It is a long and involved story, but we can give a sampling of the means by which the king's court asserted its supremacy over the local courts. One must remember, however, that this supremacy was not asserted at once and that the paucity of early records prevents specific dates from being attributed to some of the following instruments.

By the *writ of right* emanating from the king, the presiding officer of a nonroyal court was commanded to do "full right" to a particular plaintiff in his suit against a particular defendant; and "if you do not," so ran the writ, "the sheriff shall." That is, if the demandant could not find justice in a feudal court or a hearing or if there was untoward delay, then the case was to be removed to the sheriff's court. The sheriff was the king's chief officer in the county.

The writ *Praecipe* at first applied only to the king's tenants—the *tenants-in-capite;* but Henry II extended its use to the tenants of an intermediate or mesne lord. The writ was directed to the sheriff, who was ordered to command the defendant "to render something [a debt or a piece of land] to the plaintiff, and if he does not, bid him appear at Westminster before me to show me why not."

The Grand Assize of Henry II provided that when a plaintiff in the manorial court claimed a piece of land in the possession of another and offered to do battle, the tenant in possession of the land could decline the offer and demand the writ *de pace habenda;* this forestalled further steps in the original process. The plaintiff, having secured the proper writ, would then carry the action to the king's court, where title would be determined by lawful knights of the shire. The tenant-in-possession "put himself on the Grand Assize" and thus escaped trial by battle and the manorial jurisdiction. The Grand Assize ruled out trial by battle in cases of disputed lands. It also ruled out the jurisdiction of the feudal courts over such matters. Dispossession could only follow after the question of possession had been decided in the king's court.

The Assize of *Novel Disseisin,* one of the Petty Assizes, was issued in 1166. This provided that if a man were, without a judgment, disseised (dispossessed) of his free tenement by another man, the first man was to be without further question repossessed of his seisin. The sheriff was required, by writ of novel disseisin, to summon a jury of twelve "legales homines" of the vicinity and its task was to answer the question, Has *A,* without a judgment, been turned out of his freehold by *B* since the king's coronation? If the answer were in the affirmative *A* was put in possession of his property without more ado, and *B* was fined; if the answer were in the negative, then *A* would be fined for his false claim. The point of *novel disseisin* is that, in a conflict over the title to land, a party must not simply turn the other party out, but must bring an action and settle the matter before the king's justices.

In 1176, Henry issued another Petty Assize, the Assize of *Mort d'ancestor.* Let us suppose that a tenant dies and that his former feudal lord refuses to recognize his [the tenant's] son as heir. The Assize of *Mort d'ancestor* required that in such a situation a jury should be summoned and asked the following questions: Did the father of the claimant die seized (in possession) of the land? Did the claimant bring the action within the prescribed time? Is the claimant the legal heir? If the answer to all three questions is "Yes," the claimant was seised of his property.

Note that the *Grand Assize,* the *Assize of Novel Disseisin,* and the *Assize of Mort d'ancestor* required that title to disputed lands should be determined by a number of "lawful men," jurors, in other words, who decided matters of fact.

By a writ of *tolt,* the sheriff could remove a land case from a feudal court where justice was delayed or refused, to his own court. The writ specified that in the particular case the sheriff would be acting as a royal justice.

Finally, by a writ of *pone,* a land plea could be called up from the sheriff's court to the king's court—the Court of Common Pleas; but this, of course, came later in history.[9]

It must not be supposed that the Norman and Plantagenet kings were interested in abstract justice; above all, they were interested in enhancing their power and in enlarging their revenues through centralization of the judicial system. Rather than see fees for court actions and writs go into the coffers of the feudal lords, the king preferred to see them go into his Treasury. It must be stressed, however, that the development of the king's courts was popular with the people. The great majority of people disliked the feudal courts or even the sheriff's courts, for feudal lords and sheriffs were often partisan and high-handed, and not seldom guilty of extortion and misconduct. In fact, Magna Carta provided that the sheriff's courts could not hear pleas of the crown and thus limited severely the criminal jurisdiction of that court. And the Statute of Gloucester,[10] 1278, prohibited suits for goods in the king's courts unless the goods taken had a value of over forty shillings; this was interpreted to mean that the county courts could only entertain suits for goods whose value was under forty shillings.

At this point, we may leave the subject of writs and consider the courts. This is quite proper, for the use of the executive writ and the king's courts grew side by side. It was largely after the courts began to take on a distinct form that another kind of writ appeared. This was the original writ. We shall come to this matter in a moment.

The Common Law Courts

By the end of the thirteenth century there were three common law courts: the Court of Common Pleas, the Court of King's Bench, and the Exchequer. The first of these was concerned with disputes between subjects (mainly civil offenses); the second, with disputes to which the king was a party (mainly criminal offenses); the third was concerned primarily with matters of revenue. The jurisdiction of each of these courts, however, was ill-defined, with much overlapping.

We have already mentioned the earliest offshoot of the Curia Regis: the Treasury, or, as it later came to be called, the Exchequer. One of the chief concerns of the Norman and Angevin kings was revenue and a "Thesaurus" or treasury was early established at Winchester where both the Domesday Book and the Great Seal were kept. It was staffed by barons and headed by a Justiciar. To this place, twice a year, came the sheriffs and others to give a financial accounting of their stewardship or to pay their debts to the Crown. Royal rents, county dues, taxes on every hide of land for purposes of defense, fines collected in the local courts, and feudal exactions such as aids and reliefs—all had to be paid over to the king. It was inevitable that disputes would arise and that the

Justiciar and the barons would be deciding cases involving financial issues.

But the Exchequer began to widen its scope and to assume jurisdiction over disputes between subjects; in fact, the Exchequer assumed the role of court of last resort in such cases. Shortly, however, Henry II ended this practice and reserved to himself and his Council those causes in which the Curia or the Exchequer failed to do "justice." This was the germ of the court which was later called the Court of Common Pleas; it sat wherever the king happened to be.

These early kings made frequent "progresses" through the country, supervising local administration, protecting their interests, impressing the people with their power and dignity, and dispensing justice. These "progresses" occasionally carried the king to France. To bring a suit in the Curia was often an arduous and an expensive undertaking: the records show that a plaintiff was required to take himself and his witnesses from one part of England to another, or even across the Channel. The inconvenience of such a system, as well as the impossibility of the king and his court being in all places at all times, led to two innovations.

The first was the system of the itinerant justices or *justices in eyre.* During the reign of Henry I, the practice began of sending out into the counties a number of judges of the Curia. These men, it is true, heard pleas both civil and criminal, but a larger part of their work consisted in the collection of revenue and the detection of fraud on the part of sheriffs and other revenue officials. During the reign of Stephen, the justices in eyre simply did not function and it was Henry II who renewed the practice. These itinerant justices were not popular. They squeezed the people for all they were worth.

However, there is one thing to remember. On circuit these justices sat with the full county court and became a "link between the Curia Regis and the shire moot, between royal and popular justice, between the old system and the new." [11] The periodic presence of the king's justices throughout the realm gave to the law a uniformity and a certain commonness.

During the reign of Henry II, judges were dispatched to the counties to take assizes of *Mort d'Ancestor, Novel Disseisin,* and *Darrein Presentment.* [12] Ordinarily, in civil cases, litigants from whatever part of England had to travel to Westminster, or wherever the king happened to be, to get their disputes before a court. A change came in 1285. By the Statute of Westminster II, [13] Edward I sent his regular judges on circuit, each one sitting with two "discreet" knights in each county and trying matters of fact at what were called courts of assize and *nisi prius.* The purpose of the statute was to lessen the congestion in the Common Pleas and King's Bench. The assize judges were given jurisdiction over civil cases commenced in either of the two courts. The sheriff would receive a direction to summon a jury to Westminster *"unless first"* (nisi prius) the justices of assize held court in the county. It was thus possible for a civil suit to be settled locally. This system is still in operation in England. The practice of sending out justices in eyre was abandoned toward the end of the fourteenth century.

The second innovation was the establishment in Westminster of a permanent court of two clerks and three laymen who "were not to depart from the King's Court" and who were to hear all the complaints of the people and "do justice." This represents a further development of the Common Bench or Court of Common Pleas.

This central court apparently had no clearly defined jurisdiction. It heard both Pleas of the Crown and Common Pleas, that is, criminal and civil cases, but it was an institution distinct from the Exchequer for it had its own seal. In the course of his "progresses," John heard many cases with his judges; such hearings were heard "coram rege," before the king. The pleas entertained by the new court at Westminster were "coram justitiariis de Banco," before a bench of justices. Upon the return of the king to Westminster these two courts did not merge.

The third court was the Curia Regis itself. Here the king heard the crown pleas. As this court developed, it was to be called the Court of King's Bench. This was the last great court to be established as a judicial body. This court followed the king, as did the early Court of Common Pleas. Its writs were returnable, however, not to Westminster as was the case of the Court of Common Pleas, but to wherever the king happened to be within the realm. There was a chief justice and three puisne (associate) judges. Its jurisdiction extended to breaches of the King's Peace —to crimes and misdemeanors. This court also served, most importantly, as an appellate tribunal correcting errors and hearing appeals from the Court of Common Pleas.

No one knows just when this court ceased to follow in the footsteps of the king. At least, by the time of Richard II, the King's Bench became fixed at Westminster.

In this account of the creation of a judge-made law common to all England we have so far discussed two closely allied foundational developments: the use of the executive writ and the consequent decline of the local courts, shire, feudal and franchise; and the corresponding growth of the royal courts. It now remains to consider another element in the underpinning of the common law and that is the *original writ*.

Original Writs

"The most common three stages in the history of the early common law writs were indeed the following:" says R. C. Van Caenegem, "an executive writ of redress for a certain wrong as a royal favour; the same writ but judicialized, still given in way of a favour; finally, the same writ, but given out by chancery as a matter of course to all plaintiffs who complained about the wrong for which the writ had been drafted and were willing to pay a moderate, current fee. . . ." [14]

An original writ was an order *issuing from the Chancery,* "as a matter of course." It was issued upon payment of a fee, in the king's name, and affixed to it was the Chancellor's Great Seal. Back of the writ lay the authority of the king.

The writ accomplished three things: first, it gave the plaintiff access to the king's court; second, it authorized a designated court to assume jurisdiction and to try the case; third, it directed the sheriff to summon the defendant to court. The writ specified the alleged wrong and ordered the defendant either to right the wrong or to show cause before the king's judges why he should not.

Here is an example of an original writ:

The King to the Sheriff greeting. If *A* shall make you secure for the prosecution of his claim, then put *X* through gages and safe pledges that he be before our justices, etc., *on such day* to show

wherefore by force and arms he made assault on said *A* at Trumpington and beat and wounded and maltreated him so that his life was despaired of.

wherefore by force and arms he made assault on said *A* at Trumpington and wounded and maltreated and imprisoned him.

wherefore by force and arms he broke the close of said *A* at Trumpington.

wherefore by force and arms he broke the millstone of said *A* of the value of forty pounds at Trumpington, and took and carried off his goods and chattels of great value.

wherefore with force and arms he entered into one messuage in Trumpington which *M* demised to the said *A* for a term which is not yet passed and ejected him, the said *A,* from his farm aforesaid

and other enormous things did, to the great damage of him the said *A* and against our peace; and have there the names of the pledges and this writ.[15]

At first, all manner of wrong was the subject matter of the writs. A writ often had no special name; any alleged wrong might make up the complaint. In time, however, fairly common wrongs began to be described in fairly common terms by the chancery clerks who drew up the writs. In time, too, after many writs had been issued for a similar complaint, a hardening process set in and a particular type of writ came to be associated with a particular type of action.

If, for example, *A* claimed that *B* owed him, and had unjustly detained, one hundred pounds, and *A* goes to court to collect the money, the process is called an *action for debt;* the necessary writ in such a case would be a *writ of debt.* If *A* claimed that *B* had come upon his land by force and arms and had cut down and carried off his wheat, the suit against *B* would be an *action of trespass,* and the necessary writ, a *writ of trespass.* There was a *writ of detinue* and an *action of detinue* for the recovery of specific chattels wrongfully detained or their value in money. For breach of a simple contract, that is, a contract not under seal, the plaintiff secured a *writ of assumpsit* and the action was an *action of assumpsit.* For breach of contract under seal, damages could be recovered by means of an *action of covenant,* the enabling writ being called a *writ of covenant.*

The Common Law

We have now reached a point at which it is possible to answer the question: what is the common law? This law was the fabric woven, with the slow, hesitant persistence of a tortoise, by the judges of King's Bench, Common Pleas, Exchequer, and Assizes. These courts were parts of a centralized judicial system of general jurisdiction. They had almost completely supplanted the old manorial and shire courts. Their interpretations and pronouncements would, with some exceptions, establish a uniform, and so-called "unwritten" law. It was a fabric woven out of custom, precedent, and the wisdom of judges.

According to Blackstone, the common law consists of *general customs* "which are the universal rule of the whole kingdom, and form the common law, in its stricter and more usual signification"; *particular customs* "which for the most part affect only the inhabitants of particular districts"; and *certain particular laws* "which by custom are adopted and used by some particular courts, of pretty general and extensive jurisdiction." [16]

General Customs

General customs, "or the common law, properly so-called," is "that law, by which proceedings and determinations in the king's ordinary courts of justice are guided and directed." Under this heading would come such matters as the inheritance of land, the transfer or acquisition of property, remedies for civil injuries, various temporal offenses and the manner and degree of punishment, and "an infinite number of minuter particulars, which diffuse themselves as extensively as the ordinary distribution of common justice requires." [17] More particularly, Blackstone gives several examples of common law doctrines:

> that there shall be four superior courts of record: the chancery, the king's bench, the common pleas, and the exchequer;—that the eldest son alone is heir to his ancestor—that property may be acquired and transferred by writing;—that a deed is of no validity unless sealed and delivered;—that

wills shall be construed more favourably, and deeds more strictly;—that
money lent upon bond is recoverable by action of debt;—that breaking the
publick peace is an offence, and punishable by fine and imprisonment;—
all these are doctrines that are not set down in any written statute or ordinance, but depend merely upon immemorial usage, that is, upon common law,
for their support.[18]

Blackstone, quite rightly, at once anticipates a question from the
student. Just how and by whom are these customs to be known and
their validity determined? His answer is "by the judges in the several
courts of justice." The judges, Blackstone says, "are the depositories of
the laws; the living oracles, who must decide in all cases of doubt, and
who are bound by an oath to decide according to the law of the land." [19]
One may ask, however, by what criterion or criteria are judges to determine the validity of a general custom?

To make a particular custom a valid part of the common law the
following standards, according to Blackstone, must be met:

(1) "That it have been used so long, that the memory of man runneth
not to the contrary." This means that if anyone can remember the in-
ception of a custom, "it is no good custom."

(2) "It must have been *continued*." No interruption in a custom is allowed and a revival, though it gives the custom a new beginning, "will be
within time of memory" and therefore void.

(3) The custom must have been *"peaceable* and acquiesced in." In
other words, the alleged custom must not have been subject to dispute
for such dispute would indicate a lack of general consent.

(4) A custom must be *reasonable*. Here Blackstone is speaking of
"artificial and legal reason," by virtue of which "a custom may be good,
though the particular reason of it cannot be assigned; for it sufficeth, if
no good legal reason can be assigned against it." A custom of a parish
whereby a man is forbidden "to put his beasts into the common till the
third of October" would be a good and reasonable custom though "it
would be hard to shew the reason why that day in particular is fixed
upon, rather than the day before or after." On the other hand, a custom
which allows no man to put his cattle in the common until the lord of
the manor has first put his cattle in is a bad and unreasonable custom
since the lord may "never put in his; and then the tenants will lose all
their profits."

(5) Customs should be *certain*. A custom that requires land to descend
"to the most worthy of the owner's blood" is a bad custom and void,
"for how shall this worth be determined?" However, a custom that lands
shall descend to the oldest living male "of the blood" is certain and
therefore good.

(6) Though established by consent, a custom when established must
be *compulsory*. A custom that all inhabitants of an area shall be taxed
for the upkeep of a bridge is a good custom; a custom "that every man

is to contribute thereto at his own pleasure, is idle and absurd, and indeed no custom at all."

(7) Customs must be *consistent* with each other. Customs cannot be set up one in opposition to the other; "contradictory customs cannot both be good nor both stand together." [20]

Particular Customs

The second component of the common law—*particular customs* —may be explained by a brief consideration of the customs of *Gavelkind* and *Borough-English*.[21] The system of Gavelkind, of Saxon origin, was retained in Kent after the Normans had introduced the law of primogeniture. This system, quite contrary to primogeniture, was a mode of descent whereby land descended to all sons equally, and if there were no sons, then to the daughters. In fact, it is thought that the law of Gavelkind was general in England before the Conquest.

Borough-English, again directly contrary to the law of primogeniture, was a custom whereby the youngest son inherited the estate in preference to his older brothers. Two chief explanations for the custom of *Borough-English* have been propounded. One is that, as Blackstone delicately puts it, "the lord of the see had antiently a right to break the seventh commandment with his tenant's wife on her wedding-night; and that therefore the tenement descended not to the eldest, but the youngest, son; who was more certainly the offspring of the tenant." [22] Blackstone does not hold this theory to be valid, for he cannot learn that "this custom prevailed in England" though it did in Scotland until abolished by Malcolm III. A more valid reason for the custom has been put forth, not only by Blackstone, but by other authorities, including Littleton: "That the youngest Son, after the Death of his Parents, is least able to help himself, and most likely to be left destitute of any other Support; and therefore the Custom provided for his Maintenance by casting the Inheritance upon him." Blackstone, himself, hazards a guess that the practice descended from British and German ancestors to whom it came from the Tartars. The Tartars were shepherds and herdsmen and as soon as the eldest sons were capable of leading a pastoral life they were given an allotment of cattle by their father and migrated to a new habitation. The youngest son is naturally, says Blackstone, "the heir of his house, the rest being already provided for." [23]

Certain Particular Laws

The third component of the common law in Blackstone's view "are those peculiar laws, which by custom are adopted and used only in certain peculiar courts and jurisdictions." [24] Blackstone has reference here to civil and canon law. A word may be said of each of these.

By civil law—or Roman law, or Roman civil law—is meant that system of law in operation in the Roman Empire and set forth particularly in the compilations of Roman jurists (Justinian and his successors) and comprising the Institutes, the Codex, the Digest and the Novels collectively called the *Corpus Juris Civilis*. The Institutes (A.D. 533) comprise an elementary account of Roman law; the Codex, a collection of imperial constitutions and rules of law; the Digest (or Pandects), an authoritative compilation of the Roman law; the Novels, or, more properly, Novellae Constitutiones, a collection of those constitutions which were issued after the publication of the Codex.

After several centuries of neglect and oblivion, the Roman law was rediscovered and a new vogue and authority was given to this system. Americans are too apt to think of Roman law as a phenomenon of antiquity no longer of importance. The influence of Roman law has been immense. The jurisprudence of more than half of the civilized world is based upon Roman law: all Europe except England and Russia, Turkey, Egypt, South Africa, the Philippines, Japan, all of Central and South America, Mexico, Quebec, and our own State of Louisiana, though in Quebec and Louisiana the criminal law is based upon the common law.

In civil law countries, the law is codified. It is not based upon the decisions of the courts but upon the principles and propositions of the law which have been sanctioned by the legislature. In France, a lawyer does not rest his case upon judicial decisions and precedents but upon the codes. In French law, there is no doctrine of *stare decisis* although there are volumes of reported cases. The theory is that each and every case is to be decided on its merits, provided always that the decision is based upon the code.

The oldest of the modern civil law codes is the French Civil Code, adopted in 1804. Before this time, France had no general law for the country as a whole. The laws of the different parts of France were spoken of as "customs"; the custom of Orleans, the custom of Normandy, the custom of Paris. Voltaire quipped that in traveling through France one changed laws more often than one did horses. At any rate, due to the prominence of Paris, its laws or the customs of Paris became in time the law for the greater part of the French people. It is true, too, that after the revival of legal learning in Italy around the middle of the eleventh century, the renewed study of Roman law extended to Paris, which became one of the great centers of Roman law education. The custom of Paris became, therefore, more and more patterned upon Roman law.

It was not until the promulgation of the Code Napoleon that a uniform law was established for the whole of France. In all, there are eight codes in France: the Civil Code which is divided into three parts—the law of persons, the law of property and ownership, and the law for acquiring property; the Code of Criminal Procedure; the Commercial Code; the Penal Code; the Code of Civil Procedure; the Code of the Forest; and two Codes of Military Justice.

The Roman law, upon which these French codes are based, also touched England, but failed to take root there. With the withdrawal of the Romans from England, their civilization, including their law, departed with them; but after the conversion to Christianity, there must have been some Roman law influence upon Anglo-Saxon jurisprudence through the medium of the learned ecclesiastics who had much to do with making the laws and the administration of justice. In 1149, Vacarius, a jurist who had studied at Bologna, a great civil law center, was invited to England, where he taught civil law at Oxford. The legal treatises of both Glanvill and Bracton are marked by a variety of Roman principles and even terminology. But, as a system, the Roman law never reached deep into English life, and finally was rejected. Roman law was "frustrated by the obstinacy of the national character, concentrated and enshrined in the very tissue of the common law itself. Centuries of litigation had hardened its texture, practice and precept at the Bar and on the Bench and in the busy chambers of the Inns of Court had clothed it with a resilience that defied destruction and, by anticipating new necessities, rendered complaint less specious." [25]

This does not mean, however, that English law "knows nothing" of Roman law, for this would not be true. As an example, one may quote the words of Tindal, C. J., in giving judgment in *Acton v. Blundell,* decided in 1843, a case concerning rights in a subterranean watercourse and in which counsel cited the Digest:

The Roman Law forms no rule binding in itself upon the subjects of these realms; but in deciding a case upon principle, where no direct authority can be cited from our books, it affords no small evidence of the soundness of the conclusion to which we have come, if it proves to be supported by that law, the fruit of the researches of the most learned men, the collective wisdom of ages, and the groundwork of the municipal law of most of the countries in Europe. The authority of one at least of the learned Roman lawyers appears decisive upon the point in favour of the defendants.[26]

Besides such individual cases, in which the Roman law reveals its presence, certain courts in England were to a large extent influenced by the Roman law: the Court of Chancery, the Court of Admiralty, and the ecclesiastical court. Scrutton says that "every Chancellor from 1380 to 1488 was a clerk [clergyman]; until the end of Wolsey's Chancellorship in 1530 only a few lay holders of the office are found, and up to that year 160 Ecclesiastics had held the office. In this clerical preponderance, the advantages of the Civil Law, familiar to the Chancellors by their early training, and as the system in use in the ecclesiastical Courts, are obvious." [27] Courts of Admiralty, with jurisdiction over maritime matters, originally developed outside the common law. Their proceedings indicate a strong "resemblance to those of the civil law" but as Blackstone says, the law of England "doth not acknowledge or pay any deference to the civil law considered as such; but merely permits it's [sic] use in such cases where it judged it's determinations equitable, and therefore blends it, in the present instance, with other marine laws: the whole being corrected, altered, and amended by acts of parliament and common usage." [28]

"Canon law" is the term applied to ecclesiastical jurisprudence and comprises the Papal decrees known as the *Decretals* (1234), the *Sept* (1298), the *Clementines* (1317), and the *Extravagantes* (1500), besides rules from Scripture, the writings of the early Church fathers, and ordinances of Church councils. It is obvious that Canon law would be in its origins and development exclusively, or almost exclusively, Roman. With the clerical separation in England after the Conquest, a whole hierarchy of ecclesiastical courts was formed whose business was extensive. Offenses against divine law, claims of Church dues, the distribution of property for Church use, all questions affecting marriage, and all controversies as to the validity and interpretation of wills, and other matters, were claimed by the Church as coming within the jurisdiction of its courts, not always with success. But the amount of business was so great and the problems so infinite that a *Corpus Juris Canonici* had been produced rivaling the *Corpus Juris Civilis*.

Blackstone declares that it may seem odd that he includes these laws in the category of *leges non scriptae,* or unwritten laws, since "they are set forth by authority in their pandects, their codes, and their institutions; their councils, decrees, and decretals; and enforced by an immense number of expositions, decisions, and treatises of the learned in both branches of the law." [29] In other words, they appear to be properly placed under the head of *leges scriptae,* or written law. But, Blackstone follows the view of Matthew Hale that the civil and the canon law have force and effect in England not because they are written but rather because "they have been admitted and received by immemorial usage and custom in some particular cases, and some particular courts; and then they form a branch of the *leges non scriptae,* or customary law." [30]

It seems appropriate at this point to explain the meaning of the term "unwritten law." The term might suggest that it related to laws which are handed down orally from generation to generation, never being committed to stone or papyrus or paper. And it is true that in prehistoric ages the laws were traditional for the very good reason that no one could write. True, also, is the fact that men have claimed the right to commit a crime by virtue of the "unwritten law," as, for example, where a husband finds his wife *in flagrante delicto* and immediately shoots her paramour. A grand jury may fail to indict under the circumstances, or a jury might acquit, but there is no unwritten law which itself condones such an act. No, the term "unwritten law" refers to that part of the law which is observed and applied in the court and which has not been enacted or promulgated in the form of statute or ordinance. Thus, the common law is part of the "unwritten" law because it has not been enacted by Parliament or a state legislature, and consists of the rules or principles or maxims, supposedly originating in custom, accepted by the courts, applied by successive generations of judges, and as binding as a rule of law or a rule of conduct. But, this law is "written" in that it is contained in literally thousands of reported cases.

There is another point to consider. In the last paragraph I spoke of the common law as "supposedly originating in custom." Blackstone makes common law and custom almost, if not entirely, synonymous. The picture that is created in our minds is that of a practice which is followed from time immemorial by the great mass of the people; that this practice or custom is finally recognized and applied by the courts, by which I mean that the courts evolve a legal rule from the custom and that henceforth violation of the rule will result in punishment—imprisonment, damages, fine, as the case may be. For example: let us say that over the centuries the inheritance of realty by the oldest living son became the general practice. Let us say that no act of a legislative body, no edict of a king, said that the oldest son had to inherit the realty; it was just the custom; this was the way property had descended and should descend. Let us suppose that the second son contests this practice when his father dies, claims half the real estate, and goes to court to make good his claim if he can. He is unfortunate, however, in that the judges do not look with favor upon his claim. Their procedure is to ask "What is the common practice?" "Is the practice so widespread and universal in the kingdom that it amounts to a general custom?" The judges listen to the arguments, consider the precedents, and in our hypothetical situation the plaintiff has no direct precedents because the courts have never before been faced with a conflict such as this, and the only precedent, if it be a precedent, which the defendant has to offer is that from time immemorial the eldest son has always inherited. The judges, finding that the practice is universal in the kingdom, make a rule, secure the eldest son in his property, and deny the claim of the second. Such is the image in our minds; the judge is merely finding or discovering the law; he is impelled, as it were, to the rule of primogeniture by general custom. Blackstone would like to believe this; he suggests in uncertain certainty when he says, "And indeed it is one of the characteristic marks of English liberty, that our common law depends upon custom; which carries this internal evidence of freedom along with it, that it probably was introduced by the voluntary consent of the people."

This view of law as legally recognized custom is too simple and suggests too passive a role for the judges. C. K. Allen, in *Law in the Making*, has this to say:

The cardinal fact in the settlement of our medieval law is the gradual domination of a permanent central tribunal over the jurisdiction of local courts. This process, beginning under Henry I, may be said to have become irresistible under Henry III; royal justice establishes approximate uniformity in essentials as against the bewildering diversity of local custom, and the supreme custom becomes the custom of the King's Court. . . . Beyond doubt, the greater part of this process of consolidation was the conscious task of the King's expert advisors. Its effect has not been fully realized until modern times. Our old books, in the desire to generalize about the principles of the Common Law, are often naively unconscious of its artificial ingredients. For example . . . St. Germain gives the following examples of customs "that properly be called the common law"—the system of courts and judicature; freedom from arbitrary imprisonment (as confirmed by Magna Carta); freedom and equality of justice; primogeniture and other customs of inheritance; certain feudal customs, such as wardship and marriage; feoffment with livery of seisin; the principle that a term of years is a chattel-real; distress for rent; trial by jury.[31]

But as Mr. Allen declares, "Excepting perhaps the general principles of 'freedom,' there is scarcely an item in this catalogue which cannot be traced to the direct influence of judicial practice, or—e.g. trial by jury— to a direct borrowing or importation." [32]

To return for a moment to our example of the descent of real property, Mr. Allen says that though primogeniture might be thought of as a purely native custom, "it seems to have been established as a general custom of the realm by the deliberate encouragement of the judges." [33] Certainly, primogeniture "did not occupy the position of a general custom at the end of the twelfth century, but seems to have been regarded as peculiarly appropriate to military tenures. Yet after the lapse of another century, it had become the general rule of descent. The persuasive learning of the judge is not difficult to detect behind this development." [34]

Mr. Allen's view, and it seems a reasonable one, is that "there *is* a native law of the community," [35] sociological, real, and human. This was the view of Savigny; but Mr. Allen holds that "in the development of this fundamental law, interpretation by constituted authority plays an indispensable part, and this in an increasing degree as the system of law develops into more complex but more settled forms." [36]

There is still another matter to consider and that is the relationship of common law to statute law. Sometimes, a statute is merely declaratory of the common law. Where this is the case, the statute is to be "construed together with, and in the light of, the common law, the "Legislature being presumed to know the common law on the subject and to enact the statute as merely declaratory thereof, and to be so interpreted in the light of its origin and common law definition"; but this is true only where the statute does not depart from the governing common law principles. As a general rule, where the rule of the common law and the rule of the statute as to a given subject differ, the statute will prevail. There was a time when almost all crimes were common law crimes; today, in New York, all crimes are statutory but many of the sections of the Penal Code are merely declaratory of the old common law crimes.

By the end of the fourteenth century, the basic forms of the common law had emerged. The three courts—King's Bench, Common Pleas, and Exchequer—were in operation at Westminster and their judges were appointed to administer "the law and Custom" of the realm. This was a broad mandate and meant that the judges were free to evolve principles and rules of law in the thousands of cases that came before them. True, some law, for example, the Assize of Clarendon and the Statute of Westminster II, was enacted by king and Council, but the incidence of such legislation though significant, was sporadic. The rules, announced and applied in concrete cases by the judges in the central courts, and based theoretically upon the general customs and the juridical notions of the times, were carried through the country by the circuit or Assize judges. The common law was the result.

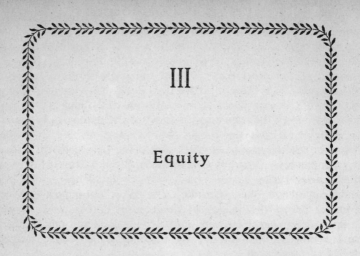

III

Equity

The common law was a hard law, a limited law. The time came when the common law judges yielded to a static conservatism, gloried in procedural technicalities, and hewed to a line so straight as to render their courts much outdated in its laws. The Chancery did have the power to create new writs and this power was regularized by a clause in the second Statute of Westminster (1285): "And whenever in future it shall happen in the chancery that a writ is found in one case, but none is found in a similar case falling under the same law and requiring a similar remedy, let the clerks of the chancery agree in making a writ; or let them adjourn the plaintiffs into the next parliament, and write down the cases in which they could not agree and refer them to the next parliament, and let a writ be made by those learned in the law so that for the future it shall not befall that the court shall delay over-long in doing justice to complaints." [1] Yet we must remember that the Chancery in the thirteenth century was still not a court. The Chancellor or his clerks heard only the plaintiff's case and issued a writ, possibly a new writ; the Chancellor did not conduct a trial and reach a decision; this was done by a common law court. But, sometimes, in spite of second Westminster, that court would "quash" the new writs. As a result, the plaintiff was without a remedy.

Suppose that an ancient, massive, and shapely oak tree stands on John Doe's property. Richard Roe, a neighbor, claims that this tree in fact stands on his property and that he intends to cut it down for what appears to him to be a good and sufficient reason. John Doe's protests are unavailing. When Richard threatens to begin operations, John goes to court, and explains the whole matter to the judge; but the judge is not helpful. In effect, John would be told, "Just wait. Let Richard cut the tree down and then sue him for damages." John would plead, "But, I

40

don't want damages, I want the tree." Perhaps the response would be a murmured "Sorry."

This hypothetical case suggests the origin of equity. It was to meet such a situation as this that equity developed. In fact, it is not too much to say that equity developed out of the inadequacies of the common law.

Briefly, by equity is meant a body of rules formerly enforced in a Court of Chancery and quite distinct from the rules enforced in a common law court. In its broadest sense equity means fair-dealing.

The common law courts had one chief remedy for all injuries of one sort or another and that was damages or money payments. For breach of contract, the common law would award damages; it would not force a party to a contract to carry out its terms, but, within limits, equity would. A common law court might tell John Doe to wait and let Richard Roe cut down a prized oak on his property and then sue for damages; but equity would issue an injunction which would restrain the threatening party until the question of the ownership of the particular piece of land could be resolved in court.

The king was the fountainhead of justice, the dispenser of mercy, and those who could find no relief in the common law courts would humbly petition the king for a remedy. These petitions were referred to the Chancellor; in dealing with them he began to exercise and develop judicial power, and to play a more important role in the administration of justice. In the fourteenth century, complainants began to submit their petitions directly to the Chancellor, instead of to the king, praying him "to do what is right for the love of God and in the way of charity." The Chancellor, if agreeable to the appeal, would summon the plaintiff's adversary and examine him in connection with the alleged wrong done by him. In time, a formal procedure developed. Having considered the petition or "bill" as it was called, the Chancellor ordered the defendant before him to answer the complaint. The order was contained in a writ called a *subpoena* and failure to appear incurred a fine. The defendant appeared; he was interrogated by the Chancellor and he had to answer on oath the charges alleged in the plaintiff's bill. There was a certain flexibility in the procedure; the Chancellor decided questions of law; he determined the facts of the case without the aid of a jury; and he resolved the conflict.

There were thus four essentials to a Chancery or equity proceeding: (a) a petition addressed to the Chancellor by a plaintiff complaining of (b) an alleged wrong to be done by some specified person or persons, and asking (c) that the wrongdoer be sent for to answer the complaint, and (d) that a remedy be provided.

For purposes of illustrating the role of equity we may well consider three equitable devices: the injunction, specific performance, and the trust. All three were in use in the fourteenth century.

Injunction

An injunction is a court order. It is directed to a person, enjoining him from doing certain acts. For one to ignore or to violate an injunction is to invite penalties.

Here is an example of an early fifteenth-century application for an injunction. John Craven and Simon Irby captured a number of the enemy at the battle of Agincourt (1415). William Buckton, Esquire, wrongly deprived Craven and Irby of their prisoners and "against their will and assent hath ransomed them," delivering them up "without any satisfaction made thereof to the King of that which belongeth to him . . . and to the utter undoing of the poor estates of the said suppliants . . ." [2] Craven and Irby discovered that the sum of 200 marks, part of the ransom money, was in the hands of one Maude Salvayn, the wife of the Treasurer of Calais, and they petitioned the Lord Chancellor "to grant to the said suppliants a writ directed to the . . . Treasurer of Calais him firmly charging and *enjoining* that the said sum . . . may be kept, and delivered to no one, until it be tried by right and law to whom it belongeth . . ." [3]

In the hypothetical case of the oak tree, the complainant would go to equity and commence an action for an injunction. A writ of summons would be served upon the troublesome neighbor and at the same time, if the court granted the application, an interlocutory or temporary injunction would be issued to him which he would violate at his peril. This temporary injunction would be operative until the trial of the action. If, at that time, John Doe makes good his claim that the tree is, in fact, on his property, then the court would make the injunction permanent.

The common law courts would not issue injunctions and why they would not is a question that must remain unanswered. In most situations, to wait until the damage has been done and then to sue for a money payment is the height of absurdity. If a company falsely brands its product, or makes claims for it which are not true or which are definitely misleading, it would not do merely to wait until someone were injured and sue the company for damages. If a neighbor dumps refuse in his backyard from which offensive gases drift over an adjoining property to the discomfort of the owner, it is not enough that the latter sue the former for the tort of nuisance; anyone would want the nearby dumping of such noxious refuse prohibited.

Two cases very nicely illustrate the role of equity in the English system before the great reforms of 1873-1875. Both relate to Johanna Wagner, a singer of considerable repute and sister of the composer, Richard Wagner. Miss Wagner had entered into a contract with Lumley, the manager of Her Majesty's Theatre in London, whereby she agreed to sing at his theater for a period of three months, during which time she was not to sing elsewhere except with the written permission of the manager. Gye, the manager of a rival theater, the Royal Italian Opera, knowing the nature of the agreement between Lumley and Miss Wagner, induced the singer to break her contract and to sing for him at his theater.

Lumley brought suit against Gye[4] in the Court of Queen's Bench (a common law court) alleging special damage. Gye demurred to the complaint; in effect, he appeared in court and said, "The facts stated in the declaration are correct; but what of it, there is no cause of action." The question he raised was this: are the facts as alleged by the plaintiff— namely, that the defendant had maliciously induced Miss Wagner to break her contract with Lumley, thus causing great damage to him— sufficient, as a matter of law, to entitle him to recover damages?

Gye argued that to sustain such an action against him it would be necessary for Lumley and Miss Wagner, the parties to the contract, to stand in the relationship of master and servant. The authorities are clear, Gye argued, and an action will lie by a master against a person who induces a servant to leave his employ unlawfully; but, these authorities apply only to employment contracts in trade, manufacturing, and household service and not to the employment of a theatrical performer. The defendant's attorney urged that Lumley's only remedy was against the party breaking the contract, Miss Wagner.

The court overruled the demurrer, holding that the nature of the service contracted for was immaterial.

The question of law having been settled, Lumley sued Gye before a jury whose business it was to determine the amount of damages.

Specific Performance

Now, Lumley could have sued Miss Wagner for damages, too; but Lumley did not want damages from Miss Wagner, he wanted her to live up to the terms of her agreement with him and to sing in his theater. He wanted, in other words, specific performance. At the time of which we are writing, a common law court could not help him; he had to go to an equity court called the Court of Chancery.[5]

Here, Lumley was not altogether successful. The court refused to enforce Miss Wagner's positive agreement to sing at Her Majesty's Theatre, but it did *compel performance* of another clause of the contract, namely, her promise not to sing elsewhere, by an injunction. There were thus three avenues open to Miss Wagner: (1) not to sing at all; (2) to sing for Lumley; or (3) to sing for Gye or someone else during the period of the contract. If she followed the last course, she would be in contempt of court for violating the terms of the injunction and suffer a period of time in jail.

There were thus certain things that equity would not do, such as compel a man to fulfill a promise of marriage or compel the performance of a promise of personal services, as we have just seen.

"The remedy by specific performance was invented," said the court in *Ryan v. Mutual Tontine Association*, "and has been cautiously applied, in order to meet cases where the ordinary remedy by an action for damages is not an adequate compensation for breach of contract." [6] Where the ordinary remedy of damages was sufficient, equity would not demand specific performance. An extremely valuable consideration, of great importance to the plaintiff, was required before equity would act.

Specific performance would give relief in a case such as the following. Determined to found a new college, Cambridge University, through its Chancellor, entered into a contract with the defendant for the acquisition of certain lands adjoining the land already held by the institution. In return for this land, the university agreed to turn over to the defendant a piece of property "lyeing in the sayd toun." [7] This property given in exchange was, according to the complainant, of greater value than the property to be received. The defendant, after agreement had been reached and the contract signed and sealed, "of self wille and wythoute any cause," [8] refused to turn the land over to the university. The complainant, in equity, sought to compel the defendant to meet his contractual obligation as "trowth, good feith and consiens requiren in this caas." [9]

Here, the land "was especially desired by the university because of its location; no other piece of land nor any amount of damages would be an indemnity for the loss of the bargain. Furthermore, what damage could be assessed? . . . Specific performance alone would give relief." [10] In fact, many cases involving specific performance relate to contracts for the transfer of real property.

Uses or Trusts

When one person turns over to another person certain properties such as real estate or securities, to be used for the benefit of a third person, the arrangement is called a trust. The person conveying the property is the donor; the person receiving it is the trustee; and the person for whose benefit the agreement is created is the beneficiary.

The story of the trust is an interesting one. Its origin goes back to the English Middle Ages when such an arrangemnt was called a *use*.

The practice of the use developed, in part at least, in arriving at some mode of providing Franciscan friars with food and shelter. The followers of St. Francis, dedicated to good works, preaching, and poverty, could hold no property, and yet these friars had to have some place to lay their heads at night and needed food to sustain themselves. The problem was solved by the transfer of lands and buildings by willing donors to a

local community for the benefit or use of the friars. In the t
century,

> Alexander, the master of the Priest's House at Canterbury . . . gave   m
> [the friars] a piece of ground and built them a temporary chapel, but when
> he was for presenting them with the building, he was told that they might
> not possess houses and lands, and the property was thereupon made over
> to the corporation of Canterbury to hold in honourable trust for their
> use. . . .[11]

The use became very popular. In the fourteenth century, the exactions of
knight service began to be evaded by the simple process of conveying one's
land to a number of friends for one's own benefit. One escaped the burdens
of wardship and marriage, for a party of six or eight or ten persons who
possessed the land as joint tenants could have no heir and no daughter.
In the same way, the forfeiture of a person's lands to the king upon conviction of either treason or felony was prevented. The Statutes of Mort-
main, which severely restricted the amount of property a religious organization could hold, were evaded by the use, for the religious house could
not "possess" the land; it could only enjoy its use and benefits. If a person
transferred his property to a number of persons for his own benefit, a
creditor could not seize the estate in satisfaction of a debt because the
debtor had no estate to seize. The medieval common law prohibited the
willing of land except, for example, in Kent, where the custom of
Gavelkind [12] prevailed. But even this rule of the common law was evaded
by means of the use. *A* would convey his property to *B, C, D, E,* and *F,*
the joint tenants, with directions as to the disposition of the estate after
his death.

The penny-pinching Henry VII did nothing about the use despite the
fact that through this device he was shorn of his feudal dues. His high-
living and extravagant son, however, had other ideas. Henry VIII pushed
through Parliament in 1536 a bill which is called the Statute of Uses.[13]
The purpose of the act is indicated in the popular title given it: An Act for
the Transmutation of Uses into Possession, that is, the conversion of the
equitable estate into a legal estate subject to the rules of the common law.
The act did secure the estates of the religious houses for the Crown but
it failed to abolish the use. There were loopholes in the act and in no
time at all uses of land, as distinguished from legal estates, reappeared in
full flower. The device began to be called a trust.

Now, the important point is that the common law courts would not enforce the use, for its eyes were solely upon the possessor of the property
and the beneficiary was not the possessor. A beneficiary could not go to
law and demand his rights in the premises, for legally he had none. And,
true it was, there were corrupt trustees who got hold of a man's property
and turned it to their own benefit, forgetting the beneficiary. The Chancel-

or, however, in the name of equity and good conscience did not hesitate to step in and enforce the use. Let us suppose that Richard Roe conveys his lands to John Doe for his (Richard's) use and benefit. Richard no longer "owns" the property for title is now in John, but the former is supposed to have all the advantages of "ownership." Suppose that John is a rascal and a knave and that once title is in his hands he fails to carry out the honorable agreement. Richard is not only without his estate, he is without any benefits from that estate. Richard would go into Chancery, and if his allegations were correct, the Chancellor would compel John Doe to administer the estate strictly in accordance with the terms of the use.

The impression has, no doubt, been given that the use or trust was a bad thing. It has been called a "dodge" and in some respects it was. Yet it had its good side.

Consider the rights of women, or the lack of them, before their emancipation. It was said of an earlier time, that husband and wife are one, that one being the husband. When a woman married, all of her property, according to the common law, became the property of the husband. The wife could inherit a dozen fortunes; the husband could fritter them away and, in the end, desert his wife and leave her penniless. Here the trust was (and is) of great importance in the financial protection of the wife. A considerate father would enter into a trust agreement with a friend (now a bank or trust company) by which the latter would receive certain specified properties, the income from which would go to the daughter. A husband might benefit from the income but he could not touch the principal. A wife was thus protected against the unscrupulous fortune hunter or irresponsible ne'er-do-well. And equity would enforce the agreement in behalf of the beneficiary.

Common Law and Equity

Shakespeare did not study law but he knew much about it. It is probably true that the people of the sixteenth century, undiverted by radio, television, many periodicals and newspapers, found the sitting of a court a matter of real interest and perhaps entertainment; at least, a trial was something different in the ordinary run of their lives. Shakespeare, like others, probably picked up a fair knowledge of law simply by attending the sessions. At any rate, his plays are filled with references to such matters as common law and equity, crime and punishment, bastardy, bankruptcy, contract, treaties, felony, and trials.

One of Shakespeare's trials is of interest here and that is the trial of Antonio in *The Merchant of Venice*. It is of interest because, although abbreviated and arranged for the purposes of the play, it nicely distinguishes common law and equity.

You will remember that Bassanio is deeply in love with Portia but has not the means, he believes, to compete with his rivals for her hand. His friend, Antonio, would gladly lend him the money but at the moment his fortunes are at sea; however, Antonio declares that he will borrow the money for Bassanio and goes to Shylock, who agrees to lend him 3,000 ducats to be repaid in three months. If Shylock is not repaid by the prescribed date then

> let the forfeit
> Be nominated for an equal pound
> Of your fair flesh, to be cut off and taken
> In what part of your body pleaseth me.

Antonio confidently expects his cargoes to arrive long within the three months period and that Shylock will be repaid; but unfortunately, such is not the case. Storms and pirates, apparently, have beset Antonio's fleet and it is suggested that Antonio's fortune lies at the bottom of the sea.

At any rate, Shylock is not repaid on the appointed date and he moves for judgment in the Duke's court in Venice. The Duke attempts to persuade Shylock to "qualify his rigorous course" but Shylock is obdurate and insists upon the letter of the bond, namely, a pound of flesh. Shylock is even offered 6,000 ducats but no, he will have his bond.

Now, Portia appears disguised as an attorney to defend Antonio. She examines the bond, or the contract, attempts to dissuade Shylock from his course without success, and then:

Portia: A pound of that same merchant's flesh is thine: The court awards it, and the law doth give it.
Shylock: Most rightful judge!
Portia: And you must cut this flesh from off his breast: The law allows it, and the court awards it.
Shylock: Most learned judge! A sentence! Come, prepare!

This was the common law at work. It was a hard law and fully enforceable. "If a person borrowed £500 from a money-lender," says George W. Keeton, "and agreed to pay a penalty of £1000 if the money were not repaid on January 1, if the debt was not satisfied—even if the debtor tendered £500 on the morning of January 2—the creditor could insist on the letter of his bond, refuse the £500, and imprison his debtor until he paid the £1000 in full. Similarly, in the sphere of property law, if a person mortgaged an estate worth £10,000 to secure an advance of £1000, repayable in six months, if he were unable to repay in full at the expiration of the six months, his estates became the absolute property of his creditor at common law." [14]

As Shylock stands over Antonio, the knife raised, the learned Portia, who practices on the chancery or equity side as well as at the common law, says:

> Tarry a little; there is something else.
> This bond doth give thee here no jot of blood;
> The words expressly are "a pound of flesh":
> Then take thy bond, take thou thy pound of flesh;
> But, in the cutting it, if thou dost shed
> One drop of Christian blood, thy lands and goods
> Are, by the laws of Venice, confiscate
> Unto the state of Venice.

This sounds like equity. If the Elizabethan playgoer substituted in his mind an "estate" for a "pound of flesh," he might have cheered when equity stepped in to soften the rigors of the common law. For, by Shakespeare's time "Chancery was granting relief against forfeitures in special cases of hardship, as where the delay was due to accident, or the fraud, fault, or sharp practice of the mortgagee . . ." [15] Had property, not flesh, been the bond, Shylock would have received only his principal, with interest from the date due. Shakespeare, of course, did not allow Shylock even that.

The Fusion of Equity and Law

Nineteenth-century England was dominated by a spirit of reform. Parliament abolished the slave trade, passed factory acts, revised the poor laws, regulated, to a degree, the labor of children, reorganized local government, prohibited public executions, improved the prison system, and perhaps most important of all, wiped out the rotten-boroughs, extended the suffrage, and made the House of Commons a more truly representative body. [16]

The courts and the law were not immune to this reforming spirit. The courts and their procedures, whether appellate courts or courts of first instance, all of them troubled by overlapping jurisdictions, a lack of coordination, and highly technical processes, were subject to parliamentary scrutiny and reorganization. A new system of County Courts was created by statute in 1846. [17] The jurisdiction of the ecclesiastical courts over wills and matrimonial matters was abolished in 1857 and two courts established to assume these jurisdictions: the Court of Probate [18] and the Court of Divorce and Matrimonial Causes. [19] The last vestige of benefit of clergy was abolished in 1827. [20] The number of capital offenses by 1856 had been reduced to three: treason, murder, and the burning of army and navy storehouses. [21] The forfeiture of a convicted felon's property to the state, thus leaving his dependents virtually penniless, was remedied in 1870. A criminal defendant was given the right to testify in his own behalf and to call his own witnesses. In 1836, the accused was no longer denied the right to counsel.[22] The common law forms of action, so complicated, so exacting, were abolished and cases henceforth were to be commenced with a simple writ of summons.[23]

Even equity, starting out as a court in which flexibility was a prime characteristic, had become, like the common law courts earlier, a rule-ridden, technical, complex maze of outworn, cumbersome, and expensive precedents and practices.

The apex of the reform movement, as far as the courts were concerned, was the passage of the Judicature Acts, beginning in 1873.[24] The whole court system was thoroughly reorganized, simplified, and made more efficient. These acts brought to an end the separation of law and equity. The jurisdiction of the old common law courts and Chancery was assumed by the High Court. The rules of the common law and equity were not amalgamated; they remained pretty much the same. But the rules of both systems were henceforth to be applied by all the courts. If there were conflict, equity was to prevail.

The end result was that if a person sought damages, the court assuming jurisdiction would act like a common law court; if, in the same court, another person seeks an injunction, the court would act like an equity court and apply the rules of equity.

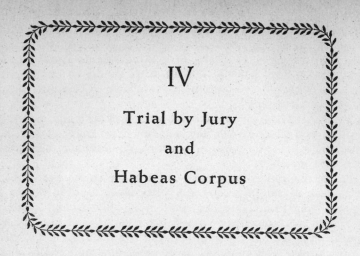

IV

Trial by Jury

and

Habeas Corpus

Trial by jury and the writ of *habeas corpus* were vitally significant instruments in a fair administration of justice as understood by Englishmen and later by Americans. In the foregoing chapters, mention has been made of each of these developments; it is now appropriate to consider them more fully.

The Jury

There are two kinds of juries: the grand jury and the petit or petty jury. Since we shall deal at greater length with each of these in the chapter on Procedure, it is enough to say here that the grand jury is a body of local persons, chosen by law, whose duty it is to examine evidence against a person suspected of crime. The evidence is presented in an *ex parte* proceeding by a prosecuting attorney and his witnesses, and the grand jury must then determine whether the evidence is strong enough to hold the suspect for trial. If the grand jury is convinced that the evidence is sufficient, it will return a "true bill," or bill of indictment, charging the suspect with a specific crime. The indictment is an accusation and the grand jury is an accusatory body.

The petty jury is likewise a body of local citizens, usually twelve in number, who are chosen by law to hear and to decide a case in a civil or criminal court. Was the defendant negligent as alleged by the plaintiff? Is the defendant guilty as charged in the indictment? These are questions the trial jury must answer after hearing the evidence from both sides.

Henry II fostered the idea of the King's Peace, by which crime was no longer considered a wrong against an individual, but rather a wrong against the state. He extended the jurisdiction of the Curia Regis to all major crimes. He made use of experts in the law and sent out itinerant justices.

Finally, aside from his use of the writ, Henry took steps to lessen the use of compurgation (the clearing of an accused person by the oaths of others) and the ordeal by fire or water in favor of a more rational method of determining guilt or innocence.

The grand and petty juries did not develop from the practice of compurgation; the best opinion, at least, holds that in all likelihood these juries had their origin in the *Inquest*.[1] This device came to life in the later Roman Empire when the Imperial Treasury found itself embroiled in tax disputes over the ownership of a particular farm or piece of land. Treasury officials would select a number of the most responsible individuals in the neighborhood in which the disputed land was located and expect them to determine the issue from their own knowledge. This practice was adopted by the Frankish emperors and later by the Normans, who carried it to England. The compilation known as the Domesday Book was based upon the Inquest.

In time, the inquest was made available to ordinary litigants in civil, that is, noncriminal, cases. It was an advantageous instrument to both king and people. For the former, it meant a step in the direction of a more closely knit nation; it meant, too, a more precise knowledge of revenue sources. For the latter, it meant ultimately the decline of trial by battle, which was hardly a satisfactory method of getting at the truth of an issue.

This significant advance in England's administration of justice came as a result of the Grand Assize, to which we have already referred.[2] Instead of submitting to trial by battle in a land dispute, the defendant could apply to the king to issue a writ to the appropriate sheriff ordering him to summon sixteen knights of the county to determine on oath the party to whom the disputed land belonged. According to Glanvill, four knights were chosen by the parties to the dispute, and they in turn selected twelve other knights, all of whom appeared before the king's justices to testify on the question of possession. These jurors or "recognitors" were not determiners of fact on the basis of evidence presented by witnesses; they themselves were witnesses.

The petty or possessory assizes were applicable when a person had been ejected from his freehold—he had been disseised—and went to law to get his land back. A writ would be issued which directed the sheriff to summon twelve men to appear before the king's judges to answer under oath the question, "Has there been a disseisin?" This is a question of fact, and we find that the recognitors are still witnesses who are likely to know the facts.

It was Henry II who was responsible for extending the practice of the fiscal inquest to criminal procedure. The itinerant judges were primarily interested in the revenues and rights of the Crown; jurors (freeholders, and representatives of every hundred, borough, and township in the shire) called for that purpose would swear to the amount of profit that had fallen to the Crown in the way of feudal dues and benefits. The king's justices were also quite interested in the doings or misdoings of the sheriffs. But these preoccupations did not preclude examination of the misdoings of the people themselves. The role of the inquest in criminal procedure emerged when the jurors were required on oath to name those persons in the county or hundred whom they seriously suspected of crime. This practice was recognized and made standard procedure by the Assize of Clarendon, the first section of which provides:

> In the first place, the aforesaid King Henry, with the consent of all his barons, for the preservation of the peace and the keeping of justice, has enacted that inquiry should be made through the several counties and through the several hundreds, by twelve of the most legal men of the hundred and by four of the most legal men of each manor, upon their oath that they will tell the truth, whether there is in their hundred or in their manor, any man who has been accused or publicly suspected of himself being a robber, or murderer, or thief, or of being a receiver of robbers, or murderers, or thieves, since the lord king has been king. And let the justices make this inquiry before themselves, and the sheriffs before themselves.[3]

These twelve men were the ancestors of the present-day grand jury. They constituted a jury of presentment: they made the initial accusation. The accused one then went to the ordeal, for, as the second section of the Assize provides, when a person has been accused, he shall "be arrested and go to the ordeal of water." [4]

Henceforth, for several centuries, there were to be but two modes of accusation: (1) the "appeal," where one individual charged another with committing a crime; and (2) presentment by the jurors.

There was, however, a later development. This was the petty jury, which replaced the ordeal as the determiner of guilt or innocence. It will be remembered that the ordeal was, in effect, a religious ceremony; in the application of the test the priest was the directing officer. In a sense, he was a judge. It was the priest, for example, who examined the burnt hand and, depending upon the condition of the wound, adjudged the accused guilty or innocent. But when, in 1215, the Fourth Lateran Council forbade the participation of priests in such ceremonies, the ordeal was doomed.

There was, thus, a jury of accusation, but there was now no method of testing the accusation. "Apparently," says Edward Jenks, "the judges who found themselves called upon for a practical solution of the difficulty got into the habit of asking the accused whether he would submit to a trial by the 'country,' i.e. by a second jury, chosen from the neighbours present. The purely voluntary character of this submission is shown by the (to us) amazing fact that, until the year 1772, a prisoner who refused to plead before such a tribunal could not be tried at all; he could merely be subjected to the *peine forte et dure*—to judicial torture—to compel him to plead." Jenks continues,

> Apparently the pressure literally applied to the accused to "put himself upon his country" was successful in establishing the . . . jury of trial in criminal cases, as an ordinary institution, soon after the close of the thirteenth century. At any rate, a statute of the year 1352 makes a clear distinction between the jury of indictment ("grand jury") and the "jury of deliverance," by enacting that no member of the former should be put upon the latter, if the accused objected.[5]

But, as yet, we are nowhere near our modern jury. The petty jury, like the grand jury, consisted of witnesses who decided cases largely from their own knowledge of the events. Petty jurors were not yet listening to the evidence presented by each side; there appears to be little weighing of evidence, and there was no requirement that a verdict must be reached on the basis of evidence presented in court. "As to such evidence as the jury may have in their own consciences," says Blackstone, "by their private knowledge of facts, it was an antient (sic) doctrine, that this had as much right to sway their judgment as the written or parol evidence which is delivered in court. And therefore it hath been often held, that though no proofs be produced on either side, yet the jury might bring in a verdict." [6]

In general, accusation by the grand jury was tantamount to conviction, despite the presence of a petty jury. Furthermore, judges and crown prosecutors were not loathe to intimidate a jury and even to punish the jurymen if they returned a verdict deemed improper by the judge. The petty jury was not independent. And it was not until the last quarter of the seventeenth century that in reaching a verdict the jury attained a real independence; at the same time, the jury was required to make use only of information elicited in court.

The juryman's lot in the sixteenth century was a hazardous one. Even doing his sworn duty might mean a fine and imprisonment: consider the case of Sir Nicholas Throckmorton.

In 1554, this gentleman was tried for high treason.[7] Throckmorton was implicated in Sir Thomas Wyatt's rebellion against Queen Mary, in that he allegedly contemplated the death of the Queen, waged war against her within the realm, and adhered to the Queen's enemies. Throckmorton pleaded "not guilty." When the jury returned to deliver its verdict, one Sendall, a clerk of the Crown, asked the panel: "How say you, is master Throckmorton knight, there prisoner at the bar, guilty of the Treasons whereof he hath been indicted and arraigned in manner and form, yea or no?" Whetston, foreman of the jury, answered, "No."—Thomas Bromley, the Lord Chief Justice, then asked, "How say the rest of ye, is Whetston's Verdict all your Verdicts?" And the jury answered, "Yea." [8] The Lord Chief Justice warned the jury: "Remember yourselves better, have you considered substantially the whole Evidence in sort as it was declared and recited? the matter doth touch the queen's highness, and yourselves also, take good heed what you do." [9] To this threat, Whetston responded bravely: "My Lord, we have thoroughly considered the Evidence laid against the prisoner, and his Answers to all these matters, and accordingly we have found him not guilty, agreeable to all our consciences." [10] Throckmorton was discharged for the alleged treason contained in the indictment, but the Lord Chief Justice instructed the lieutenant of the Tower to take him prisoner again "for there are other matters to charge him with." [11]

One of the attorneys for the Crown then appealed to the court: "And it please you my lords, forasmuch as it seemeth these men of the Jury, which have strangely acquitted the prisoner of his Treasons whereof he was indicted, will forthwith depart the court; I pray you for the queen, that they, and every of them, may be bound in a recognizance of £500 a piece, to answer to such matters as they shall be charged with in the queen's behalf, whensoever they shall be charged or called." [12] Whetston pleaded with the Court: "I pray you, my lords, be good unto us, and let us not be molested for discharging our consciences truly? we be poor merchant-men, and have great charge upon our hands, and our livings do depend upon our travails; therefore it may please you to appoint us a certain day for our appearance, because perhaps else some of us may be in foreign parts about our business." [13] The report of the Throckmorton trial ends with the words: "The Court being dissatisfied with the Verdict, committed the Jury to prison." [14]

Four of the jurors delivered themselves out of prison by admitting that they had offended in acquitting Throckmorton; the remaining eight were called before the Council in the Star Chamber where they affirmed "that they had done all things in that matter according to their knowledge, and with good consciences, even as they should answer before God at the day of judgment." [15] The Lords were unimpressed and the luckless jurors were fined a thousand marks apiece and imprisoned "till further order were taken for their punishment." [16] Finally, five of the eight jurors were freed upon payment of £220 apiece; the other three were delivered out of the Fleet upon payment of a fine of £60. Such were the hazards of jury duty in sixteenth-century England.

It was not until 1670 that a change came in the law regarding the verdict of juries.

William Penn, Quaker and founder of Pennsylvania, and William Mead, were tried before the Recorder at the Old Bailey Sessions[17] for certain alleged "trespasses, contempts, unlawful assemblies, and tumults." The jury acquitted both Penn and Mead. The Recorder, dissatisfied with the verdict, fined each juror 40 marks to stand committed until paid. One of the jurors, Edward Bushell, refused to pay the fine and sought his freedom by means of a writ of *habeas corpus* in the Court of Common Pleas.[18] The court discharged the prisoner. Speaking for the court, Chief Justice Vaughn declared that "if the judge, from the evidence, shall by his own judgment first resolve . . . what the fact is, and so knowing the fact, shall then resolve what the law is, and order the jury penally to find accordingly, what either necessary or convenient use can be fancied of juries, or to continue trials by them at all?"[19] Henceforth, juries were free to reach their own verdicts without fear of punishment by the judges. A judge might berate a jury for a verdict which was contrary to the weight of evidence but he could do no more, unless the jury was actually corrupt.

Blackstone believed trial by jury to be supremely important in criminal cases. "In times of difficulty and danger," he said, harking back to a time when judges served only during the pleasure of the king, "more is to be apprehended from the violence and partiality of judges appointed by the crown, in suits between the king and the subject, than in disputes between one individual and another, to settle the metes and boundaries of private property."[20] In eighteenth-century England, hostile critics of the government were usually charged with sedition. So vague a charge was a danger to the liberty of the subject if judges were inclined to favor the government. But as Edward Jenks says, "Happily, in the days when this danger was greatest, the sturdy independence of juries was a real safeguard against oppression, and a strong justification of the jury system."[21] Juries also tended to reduce somewhat the severity of the English law. "It is a melancholy truth," wrote Blackstone, "that among the variety of actions which men are daily liable to commit, no less than an hundred and sixty have been declared by act of parliament to be felonies without benefit of clergy; or, in other words to be worthy of instant death."[22] Among these offenses (the number was increased to well over 200 by the year 1800) were picking pockets to the amount of twelve pence or over, maiming cattle, consorting with pixies, stealing in shops to the value of five shillings or over, and stealing to the value of forty shillings or over in dwelling houses. Blackstone deplored the frequency of capital punishment, "so dreadful a list," he said, "instead of diminishing, increases the number of offenders. The injured, through compassion, will often forbear to prosecute; juries, through compassion, will sometimes forget their oaths, and either acquit the guilty or mitigate the nature of the offence."[23] Sir Samuel Romilly, a leader in the reform of the English criminal law, relates the case of Elizabeth Hobbs. She was tried in 1732 for stealing in a dwelling house, two guineas, two half-guineas, and forty-four shillings in money. She confessed the fact and the jury found her guilty, but found that the money she had stolen was worth only thirty-nine shillings.[24] In the same year, William Sherrington was tried for stealing privately in a shop goods which he had sold for one pound, five shillings; the jury found that the goods were worth only four shillings tenpence.[25]

In a word, between the liberties of the people and the powers of the Crown, and to the advantage of the former, there were two barriers: presentment (the grand jury or jury of accusation) and the trial jury.

Trial by jury has been deemed one of the monumental achievements of Western man. Sir William Blackstone spoke of the trial jury as a *Palladium* (a safeguard) which must remain sacred and inviolate if the Englishman is to enjoy his liberty; he considered the jury as "the glory of the English law," and declared that the most transcendent privilege any subject can enjoy or wish for is "that he cannot be affected either in his property, his liberty, or his person, but by the unanimous consent of twelve of his neighbours and equals." [26] By 1765, when the first volume of the *Commentaries* appeared, Blackstone had good reason to speak highly of the jury, for its development by this time was impressive.

But trial by jury was not destined to remain forever the glory of either English or American justice. In recent decades, this ancient institution has been subjected to a searching examination and re-evaluation and has been found wanting. Later in this volume we shall discuss the inadequacies of the jury and its decline as a useful device in the administration of justice.

Habeas Corpus

When, in 1938, the old *writs* of *certiorari, mandamus,* and *prohibition* (which were directives that a higher court might issue to a lower court) were abolished by Act of Parliament, and the simpler and more practical *Orders* of *certiorari, mandamus,* and *prohibition*[27] substituted for them, there was no compelling reason why the writ of *habeas corpus* should not have been made an *Order,* too; but, according to Mr. R. M. Jackson, "It is understood that the framers of the statute did not care to run the risk of being thought subversive; they feared that any interference with *habeas corpus* would offend people, and that a sound bill might founder on this point." [28] Thus, in England, *habeas corpus* remains a writ, unsullied by a legislative desire for simplicity or convenience, untouched by the twentieth century, sacrosanct in its long and honored career, a basic safeguard for the rights and dignity of the subject. For of what avail are the rights of man if he has no means of escaping arbitrary, improper, or wrongful imprisonment? *Habeas corpus* is the means whereby the validity of imprisonment is tested.

Originally, the writ of *habeas corpus* was an order directed to the sheriff, bidding him to "have the body" of the accused person brought before the court for trial. Later, in the fifteenth century, the writ issuing from the Court of King's Bench was used to control, and thus to weaken, commitments made by the feudal courts. In the sixteenth century the writ was recognized as a means of protecting the liberty of the person.

Before the fifteenth century, however, the writ was defective in three particular respects. The jailor was not required to make an immediate return to the writ. He might delay for a second writ of *habeas corpus* called an *alias* writ: "We command you, as we have before [*sicut alias*] commanded you." The jailor might even wait for a third writ called a *pluries* writ which was similar to the first and second except for the words, "as we have *often* commanded you" [*sicut pluries praecepimus*].

Secondly, a man might be moved from prison to prison. In this way the jailor often circumvented the demand to produce the "body" in court, since his prisoner's "body" was, conveniently, no longer in his jail. Such a practice was the reason for the provision in the Habeas Corpus Act of 1679: "That if any person or persons, subjects of this realm, shall be committed to any prison, or in custody, of any officer or officers whatever for any criminal or supposed criminal matter, that the said person shall not be removed from the said prison and custody into the custody of any other officer or officers . . . or where the prisoner is removed from one prison or place to another within the same county . . . shall suffer and incur the pains and forfeitures" provided by the Act.[29] The Act also prohibited the sending of a prisoner to a jail in Scotland, Ireland, Jersey, Guernsey, Tangier, or other ports beyond the seas.

In the third place, the Crown attempted to circumvent the writ by ordering a person imprisoned by "special command of the king," and holding that such command, in and of itself was sufficient to justify commitment and detention. Just what this meant is indicated in *Darnel's Case* or the *Case of the Five Knights*.[30]

Charles I, intent upon continuing the war against France, and unable to secure any financial aid from Parliament, resorted to a forced loan. The war was not a popular war and the prospect of a forced loan was even less popular, and various people refused to subscribe at the rate proposed. The nonsubscribers of high rank were bound over by recognizances to tender their appearance at the Council-board, and some of them were committed to prison. Among those in prison, only five, including Darnel, sought their freedom by *habeas corpus*. In response to the writ, the Warden of the Fleet Prison answered that Darnel "was and is committed by the special command of his majesty." [31] No reason for the detention was given.

Despite long and able argument in the Court of King's Bench, the five knights were remanded to the custody of the Warden; the Warden's *return* (reply) to the writ of *habeas corpus* was deemed sufficient. In the text of this decision Lord Chief Justice Hyde declared that "the king hath done it [ordered the original commitment], and we trust him in great matters, and he is bound by law, and he bids us to proceed by law, as we are sworn to do, and so is the king. . . . If in justice we ought to deliver you, we would do it; but upon these grounds, and these Records, and the Precedents and Resolutions, we cannot deliver you, . . . you must be remanded [recommitted to prison]." [32] A review of the records, that is, of precedents, had led the Court to aver that "where the cause of the commitment hath been expressed, there the party hath been delivered by the court, if the case so required; but where there hath been no cause expressed, they have ever been remanded; or if they have been delivered, they have been delivered by the king's direction, or by the lords of the council . . ." [33] This was in reply to counsel for the prisoners, who during the trial had argued that the warrant of imprisonment "by the special command of his majesty" was too general, no offense being specified. If the Warden's reply were upheld by the court, they argued, the king could order an indefinite imprisonment of the subject, without accusation, without trial, and release might come only with death. As we have seen, it was upheld. But reaction against this kind of arbitrary action was soon to come.

The decision of the court in the *Case of the Five Knights* was one of a series of events which moved Parliament to draw up the *Petition of Right* and to compel the king to agree to it. Obviously, private property was endangered if the king continued to exact forced loans; and the defenses of the common law would be rendered nullities if he could order commitment and detention, with no opportunity to get one's case in court, for those who refused to accept what they deemed to be illegal taxation. The Petition of Right was not a law; it was, as its title indicates, a petition; but it was a vital constitutional document. Charles I reluctantly accepted it. The Petition declared in part:

By the statute called the Great Charter of the Liberties of England, it is declared and enacted that no freeman may be taken or imprisoned, or be disseised of his freehold or liberties or his free customs, or be outlawed or exiled or in any manner destroyed, but by the lawful judgment of his peers or by the law of the land; and in the eight and twentieth year of the reign of King Edward III it was declared and enacted by authority of Parliament that no man, of what estate or condition that he be, should be put out of his land or tenements, nor taken, nor imprisoned, nor disinherited, nor put to death, without being brought to answer by due process of law:

Nevertheless, against the tenor of the said statutes and other the good laws and statutes of your Realm to that end provided, divers of your subjects have of late been imprisoned without any cause showed; and when for their deliverance they were brought before your Justices by your Majesty's writs of *habeas corpus,* there to undergo and receive as the court should order, and their keepers commanded to certify the causes of their detainer, no cause was certified, but that they were detained by your Majesty's special command . . . and yet were returned back to several prisons, without being charged with anything to which they might make answer according to the law. [34]

The Petition prayed that the king would not do this kind of thing; and the king said that he would not.

After the Restoration, Charles II attempted to undermine *habeas corpus* by the arbitrary imprisonment of political offenders. Mr. Francis Jenkes, a businessman of London, alarmed because of the decline of trade occasioned by the French, who laid ruinous duties on English woolens and whose silks and "other unnecessary commodities imported hither" were beggaring "many thousands of our honest and industrious weavers," and believing that only Parliament could afford any kind of remedy, moved that the king be petitioned to call a new Parliament. Mr. Jenkes made this proposal in the Guildhall before the Common Council. His speech was reported to the king and the Lord Chancellor, and shortly thereafter he was summoned to appear at the Council-board. A member of the council asked Jenkes: "How came you to meddle with matters of state?" to which Jenkes replied: "I thought any of his majesty's subjects, in an humble manner, might petition his majesty for a remedy of any grievance whatsoever." "Do you think," he was asked, "anyone may petition for a parliament?" and Jenkes replied, "I believe they may." Here the king said, "I will take care that none such as you shall have to do with the government." [35]

Jenkes was committed to prison by the Privy Council for sedition. Through counsel he sought release by *habeas corpus,* but the Lord Chief Justice would not issue the writ for "no other reason but that it was vacation." [36] For the same reason, the Lord Chancellor would not grant the writ. Jenkes then sought release on bail in the Quarter Sessions. Here, the justices refused to do anything on the grounds that Jenkes was committed by a superior court, "and we, who are an inferior one, cannot bail him." [37] It was many weeks before Jenkes was released on bail.

It was this case, added to Lord Clarendon's practice of imprisoning political offenders in distant or unspecified prisons, that led to the Habeas Corpus Act of 1679. This act was limited to persons not yet convicted but imprisoned for an alleged crime, except treason or felony "plainly or specially expressed in the warrant of commitment." The writ might issue in term or out of term, and if any judge, the Lord Chancellor included, "shall deny any writ of *Habeas Corpus,* by this act required to be granted, being moved for as aforesaid, they shall severally forfeit to the prisoner or party grieved, the sum of five hundred pounds. . . ." [38] If any officer of government—sheriff, minister or deputy—"shall neglect or refuse to make the returns aforesaid, or to bring the body of the prisoner or prisoners according to the command of the said writ, within the respective times aforesaid," he shall "for the first offense forfeit to the prisoner or party grieved, the sum of one hundred pounds," and for the second offense, two hundred pounds, and "shall and is hereby made incapable to hold or execute his said office." [39] A person delivered or set at large by *habeas corpus* shall not "at any time hereafter be again imprisoned or committed for the same offense by any person or persons whatsoever, other than by the legal order and process of such court wherein he or they shall be bound by recognizances to appear, or other court having jurisdiction of the cause";[40] violation of this provision would incur a penalty of five hundred pounds to be paid to the prisoner or party grieved. As has been mentioned, the act forbade the removal of a prisoner from one prison to another to escape obedience to the writ, and made illegal the sending of a British subject as prisoner to "Scotland, Ireland, Jersey, Guernsey, Tangier, or into other parts, garrisons, islands, or places beyond the seas. . . ."[41]

This act represented a decisive advance in behalf of the liberty of the person. Blackstone says that "to bereave a man of life, or by violence to confiscate his estate, without accusation or trial, would be so gross and notorious as an act of despotism; as must at once convey the alarm of tyranny throughout the whole kingdom. *But confinement of the person, by secretly hurrying him to gaol, where his sufferings are unknown or forgotten, is a less public, a less striking, and therefore a more dangerous engine of arbitrary government."* [42] Blackstone calls the Habeas Corpus Act "that great bulwark of our constitution." [43] These words of Blackstone are to be found, quoted with approval, by Hamilton in the *Federalist Papers,* No. 84.

It is fair to say that though the writ of *habeas corpus* was issuable at common law its present form in England has had its origin in the Act of 1679. The rights thereunder were thought by the American colonists to be the privileges of British subjects, although the Lords of Trade and Plantations had no such notion. The statute was reenacted in some of the colonies, while in Virginia the rights contained therein were conceded under the royal prerogative. In all the new state constitutions provision was made for the writ of *habeas corpus.* It is the only writ specified in the Constitution of the United States. Debate on the writ at the Convention centered, not on the writ itself, but whether provision should be made for its suspension. As finally worded, the writ was not to be suspended "unless when in Cases of Rebellion or Invasion the public Safety may require it." And as new states came into the Union, specific provision for the writ was incorporated into their constitutions.

We have already examined one case—*Moore v. Dempsey*—in which *habeas corpus* played a major role. Let us discuss one other: *United States v. Wong Kim Ark,*[44] decided by the Supreme Court of the United States in 1898.

Wong Kim Ark, born in San Francisco, was the son of Chinese parents domiciled in the United States. At the age of seventeen he traveled to China for a short visit, returned to the United States, and was permitted to enter by the collector of customs on the ground that he was a native born citizen. In 1894, he made another visit to China, but upon his return to the United States he was denied admittance on the ground that he was *not* a citizen of the United States. This meant that Wong Kim Ark was not permitted, by Federal authority, to land on United States soil. Through counsel, Wong Kim Ark sought release by means of *habeas corpus*. In the *habeas corpus* proceeding which followed, a federal district court ordered Wong Kim Ark's discharge on the ground that he was a citizen of the United States. The United States appealed to the Supreme Court and the order of the district court was affirmed.

The words *habeas corpus* mean "that you may have the body." The words, however, have acquired a significance that far transcends their literal translation. In the long struggle to build a governmental edifice dedicated to a decent relationship between governors and governed, *habeas corpus* became, and still is, an important keystone. From England the colonists brought the writ to America. Today, guaranteed as it is in every state constitution and in the Constitution of the United States, *habeas corpus* remains a stalwart device for the protection of our liberties.

V

The Common Law

in

America

In theory, the colonists in Massachusetts Bay or Virginia or other English settlements in North America brought the law of England with them. "Our ancestors," said Mr. Justice Story, speaking of the common law, "brought with them its general principles, and claimed it as a birthright; but they brought with them and adopted only that portion which was applicable to their situation." [1]

This is the theory and in a broad, general way, it is true; but it certainly was not our *earliest* ancestors in this country who brought with them the common law. In the earliest years, the struggle to survive and the taming of an unfriendly environment necessitated the presence of no lawyers as lawyers. For several decades, anyway, there would not have been sufficient business to attract the craftsmen of Westminster. Furthermore, as a class, lawyers were not highly regarded. In fact, in Massachusetts, the citizen was required to plead his own cause in the courts. The 1641 Body of Liberties, taken from the legal books of the Old Testament, provided that "Every man that findeth himselfe unfit to plead his owne cause in any Court, shall have Libertie to imploy any man against whom the Court doth not except, to helpe him, Provided he give him noe fee, or reward for his paines." [2] A Virginia act of 1645 (repealed in 1656) expelled "mercenary attorneys." One trained lawyer, Letchford, "was not permitted to practise his profession." [3] Farmers, merchants, seamen, served as judges, and in New Hampshire, it was not until 1754 that a lawyer became chief justice.[4] The administration of justice was, in those early years, as Reinsch says, "rude, popular, summary . . . in which refined distinctions . . ." [5] had no place.

But as the population in the colonies increased, as the arrangements of society became more complex, as business and farming and shipping began to assume larger proportions in the lives of the people, as more

62

men entered into agreements with other men, as they sold and bought property and willed land and personal effects, in short, as more opportunities for illegal and dishonest dealings arose, the need for lawyers became apparent. The 1648 revision of the Massachusetts Body of Liberties omitted the above-quoted Article 26. This does not mean that henceforth in Massachusetts a group of trained lawyers, already at hand, began to practice. The truth is that there were few trained lawyers; the attorneys of the day were mostly laymen.

The period of the rough and ready, popular law, however, did not last long. Within fifty or sixty years of the original settlement, lawyers and judges were busy with contracts, debts, trusts, frauds, matters of inheritance, with writs and actions. The times were beginning to demand more than the judicial attitude that "every tub must sit on its own bottom." And in the several colonies, although there was no strict duplication of the English system of courts, judges were presiding at the Assizes, the Common Pleas, Chancery, the Exchequer, courts of Oyer and Terminer which were empowered to *hear and determine* all treasons, felonies, and misdemeanors, admiralty and appeal courts. The English judicial system was gradually being adapted; and English law was being invoked in the settlement of disputes. As law and the courts became more sophisticated, there was need for men trained in the law.[6]

Colonial Legal Training

Let us consider for a moment the training of most eighteenth-century American lawyers. John Adams, after graduating from Harvard, taught school in Worcester, Mass. Here, in 1756, he decided to become a lawyer. Continuing to teach to pay his expenses, he was turned loose, without much direction, in the library of James Putnam, a practising attorney. Adams read Coke's *Institutes of the Laws of England,* Hawkins' *Pleas of the Crown,* and Matthew Hale's *History of the Common Law of England.* In addition, and this was an important part of the lawyer's training, "he followed the court sessions closely, wrote simple writs for his master, searched precedents, and in this manner absorbed the rudiments of practical law in a country town."[7] Adams' apprenticeship expired in 1758. He returned to the neighborhood of Boston and sought a patron who would present him to the Superior Court and recommend his admission to the bar. He approached Jeremiah Gridley, the leader of the Boston bar. Gridley examined Adams briefly, suggested certain readings, emphasizing particularly the common law, and agreed to present him to the court. Adams sought the support of other leaders of the bar. "Of Mr. Adams," said Gridley to the court, "as he is unknown to your honors, it is necessary to say that he has lived between two and three years with Mr. Putnam of Worcester, has a good character from him and all others who know him, and that he was with me the other day several hours, and I take it he is qualified to study the law by his scholarship, and that he has made a very considerable, a very great proficiency in the principles of law, and therefore, that the client's interest may be safely intrusted in his hands. I therefore recommend him, with the consent of the bar, to your honors for the oath." [8] This is a far cry from the legal aptitude tests, the law school, and the bar examinations, of the present day. The experience of Adams was the experience of all American lawyers of the time and for many decades thereafter. There were no textbooks as we know them, no readily available collections of cases or extensive law libraries.

Had Adams been born a few years later, he might conceivably have attended Tapping Reeve's law school in Litchfield, Connecticut. Reeve graduated from Princeton in 1763, remained there to teach for a time, and then moved on to Hartford to read law in the office of Judge Jesse Root. Admitted to the bar in 1772, Reeve settled in Litchfield and began a practice. Soon, young men applied to him for permission to study law under his tutelage. One of the first was Aaron Burr, Reeve's brother-in-law. Thus, in 1774, was the first law school established in America. The school prospered and attracted students from many parts of the country; and as the number of students increased, Reeve began to deliver lectures and to organize moot courts. When Reeve was made a judge of the Superior Court, a former student and graduate of Yale, James Gould, joined him in the conduct of the school. The school continued until 1833 by which time, it is estimated, more than a thousand lawyers had received part of their training there. [9]

Blackstone's Commentaries

Shortly before the Revolution, however, there was published in England a legal work which was destined to have a profound and lasting effect upon American law and American legal education. This was William Blackstone's *Commentaries on the Laws of England*. [10] The first volume appeared in 1765 and by 1769 all four volumes had been published. This English edition was more in demand in the colonies than it was in England. In 1771-1772, the *Commentaries* were published in America.

To understand the nature of Blackstone's achievement, one must remember that, prior to the appearance of the *Commentaries,* the common law consisted of a confused mass of precedents contained in a variety of sources and hard to find. After all, there were few *Reports* in England and even fewer in America. What Blackstone did was to systematize the precedents and to present them in a comprehensive and orderly fashion within the covers of four volumes. The common law was all there—organized, detailed, well-indexed—and the well-turned sentences of the new legal god fell into the laps of judges and attorneys like manna from heaven.

True, prior to, during, and after the Revolution, there was considerable antagonism to anything English, including the common law. There were judges, says Reed who "tried to decide . . . cases [not covered by legislation] by the light of reason and abstract justice, but soon felt the necessity of leaning upon precedent as a more concrete and safer guide. . . . The judges were thus driven back upon English precedents." [11] And, continues Reed, had it not been for Blackstone's *Commentaries,* "it is possible that, in our early patriotic reaction against everything English, the codifying spirit, already expressed in state constitutions, would have produced also statutory codes, behind which judges would not have gone. Had this taken place, our law would have been organized upon the Continental principle. . . . The general content of the English common law would have been incorporated into these codes in the same way as the European civil law had absorbed local customs. Blackstone, however, provided an admirably comprehensive, lucid and up-to-date systematization of the English common law, suitable alike as a reference authority for the courts and as a textbook for students." [12] Blackstone was the backbone of the curriculum at the little school in Litchfield.

But the patriot lawyers did not reject Blackstone *in toto.* Certainly, they would have rejected his views of the powers of Parliament, the prerogatives of the king, and legislative representation; but, even the signers of the Declaration of Independence appreciated, perhaps more than we are aware, Blackstone's encomia on inalienable rights. The first chapter of the first book of the *Commentaries* is entitled, "Of the Absolute Rights of Individuals."

Blackstone, like Locke, presumed a state of nature in which men enjoyed, theoretically, a complete and natural liberty. When men emerged from the natural state to form a society, they gave up a part of their natural liberty "as the price of so valuable a purchase." [13] But, they retained certain rights, and these, says Blackstone, "may be reduced to three principal or primary articles; the right of personal security, the right of personal liberty, and the right of private property." [14] Blackstone insisted that the chief aim of society and its agent, government, was to protect individuals in the enjoyment of these absolute rights.

The writers of the Declaration underlined the "self-evident truth" which needed no proof, that men were "endowed by their Creator with certain unalienable Rights, that among these are Life, Liberty and the pursuit of Happiness." Later, in the Constitution of the United States, the "pursuit of happiness," became "property."

A study of that Constitution, including the first ten Amendments, will reveal the influence of the common law. A few manifestations of this influence may be mentioned. Blackstone holds that double jeopardy "is grounded on this universal maxim of the common law of England, that no man is to be brought into jeopardy of his life, more than once, for the same offence." [15] The Constitution provides that no person shall "be subject for the same offence to be twice put in jeopardy of life and limb." "A *general* warrant," says Blackstone, "to apprehend all persons suspected, without naming or particularly describing any person in special, is illegal and void for its uncertainty." [16] The Fourth Amendment declares that "The right of the people to be secure in their persons, houses, papers, and effects, against unreasonable searches and seizures, shall not be violated, and no Warrants shall issue, but upon probable cause, supported by oath or affirmation, and particularly describing the place to be searched, and the persons or things to be seized." "To refuse or delay to bail any person bailable," says Blackstone, "is an offence against the liberty of the subject . . . by the common law. . . . And, lest the intention of the law should be frustrated by the justices requiring bail to a greater amount than the nature of the case demands, it is expressly declared by statute . . . that excessive bail ought not to be required." [17] The Eighth Amendment provides, in part, that "Excessive bail shall not be required. . . ."

The struggle in England against arbitrary government was not lost upon the patriot lawyers in the colonies. They knew their Magna Carta and its famous section 39: "No freeman shall be taken or imprisoned or dispossessed, or outlawed, or banished, or in any way destroyed, nor will we go upon him, nor send upon him, except by the legal judgment of his peers or by the law of the land"—as we, today, know that provision of the Fifth and Fourteenth Amendments which forbids the Federal and state governments to deprive any person of life, liberty, or property, without due process of law. They knew their Petition of Right (1628) and the Bill of Rights (1689), which were, in part, simply a demand that the king recognize and respect certain requirements of the common law. And it may be presumed that they knew their common law, at least, in part, through Blackstone. That the first few chapters of the *Commentaries* became a "revolutionist's handbook" for the colonists in the conflict with England is understandable.

The chief problem of the fifty-five delegates to the Federal Convention, thirty-one of them lawyers, was how to create a governmental structure organizing thirteen independent states into a strong and stable whole. Jealous of their sovereignty, suspicious of power, wary of any experiment which might redound to their economic disadvantage, the states forced upon the framers, albeit unconsciously, a new structure—the Federal system. This structure, with its division of powers between the Federal government and the states, was new. But, freedom of the press, of petition and assembly, *habeas corpus,* indictment by grand jury, trial by jury, the power to pardon, the division of crimes into treasons, felonies and misdemeanors, all these and more, have their *roots* in the common law. And if the index of *The Records of the Federal Convention of 1787* [18] reveals but few references to the common law and but one to Blackstone, it must be remembered that the common law was part of the intellectual equipment of a majority of the framers. Perhaps, to those late eighteenth-century lawyers, the common law was like the barnyard to the farmers or the workshop to the turners; there was no need to cite volume and page of that with which they were all familiar.

Professor Boorstin sums up the achievement and influence of the *Commentaries* in these words:

since 1765, this work has . . . filled a place unique in the history of law in the English-speaking world. It is the first important and the most influential systematic statement of the principles of the common law. For generations of English lawyers, it has been both the foremost coherent statement of the subject of their study, and the citadel of their legal tradition. To lawyers on this side of the Atlantic, it has been even more important. In the first century of American independence, the *Commentaries* were not merely an approach to the study of law; for most lawyers they constituted all there was of the law. The influence of Blackstone's ideas on the framers of the Federal Constitution is well known. And many an early American lawyer might have said, with Chancellor Kent, that "he owed his reputation to the fact that, when studying law . . . he had but one book, Blackstone's *Commentaries,* but that one book he mastered." For generations of American lawyers from Kent to Lincoln, the *Commentaries* were at once law school and law library. In view of the scarcity of lawbooks during the earliest years of the Republic, and the limitations of life on the frontier, it is not surprising that Blackstone's convenient work became the bible of American lawyers.[19]

In fact, it is probably not too much to say that to American lawyers during the greater part of the nineteenth century, Blackstone was the common law, and the common law was Blackstone.

The English common law, as understood and modified either by judicial interpretation or by statute, was, explicitly or implicitly, taken over by the states. All of the states, except Louisiana, recognize the English common law. Maryland's constitution, for example, provides "That the inhabitants of Maryland are entitled to the Common Law of England, and the trial by jury, according to the course of that law. . . ." This law, modified and developed by American conditions and American needs, is still the basis for the settlement of controversies not governed by constitution or statute.

In the United States, the distinction between actions at law and suits in equity, and the complex forms of all such actions and suits, have been abolished. There is now but one form of action for the enforcement and protection of private rights and the redress of private wrongs, and this is called a civil action. The complicated writ system of the English common law is no more, and any action of a private nature begins with a summons and a complaint. This is true of both Federal and state courts. In general, it may be said that there are no longer any common law crimes. There are no offences against the United States except those made so by act of Congress; no offences against the State of New York except those made so by act of the legislature.

The common law is extremely important, and its modification in behalf of simplicity and security has not lessened this importance. Many of the situations of conflict which arise in everyday life are not the subject of legislative action and, perhaps, they could not be. Let us look at some of the situations in the field of *torts,* for here the common law reigns supreme.

The Common Law in Action

First, what is a tort? Professor Prosser defines "tort" as follows: it "is a term applied to a miscellaneous and more or less unconnected group of civil wrongs, other than breach of contract, for which a court of law will afford a remedy in the form of an action for damages. The law of torts is concerned with the compensation of losses suffered by private individuals in their legally protected interests, through conduct of others which is regarded as socially unreasonable." [20] Scholars in this area of the law do not agree as to a precise, iron-clad, watertight definition; in fact, even Professor Prosser asserts that a "really satisfactory definition of a tort has yet to be found." [21] The difficulty arises because, though an action for damages is the all-important remedy, there are other remedies, one of them being the injunction. If a plaintiff sues for damages for an alleged "nuisance," the defendant may be assessed damages *and* an injunction may be directed to him forbidding a continuation of the nuisance.

The term "tort" comes from the Latin, *tortus,* meaning "twisted." In England, the word came to mean "wrong." In the fourteenth century, Thomas Usk in *The Testament of Love* wrote "Than ever tort & forthe (force?) nought worthe an haw about"; and in 1585, James I of England in the *Essay on Poesie* wrote "So Job and Jeremie, preast with woes and wrongs, Did right descryue their joyes, their woes and torts." The word apparently lost its usefulness and disappeared from common English. The word, however, "remained in the law, and gradually acquired a technical meaning." [22]

In general, each individual has certain rights, legally protected interests, with which government as such has little to do. If the student will scan the table of contents of any casebook on torts, he will find, among other matters, that the individual is protected against assault and battery (a tort which is also a crime), the intentional infliction of mental disturbance, false imprisonment, misrepresentation, defamation, invasion of his privacy, and nuisance.

Tort liability rests upon one of the following fundamental grounds:

(1) the intent of the defendant to interfere with the plaintiff's interests; (2) strict liability where without wrongful intent or negligence the defendant is liable for reasons of policy; and (3) negligence. We shall discuss, at some length, the matter of negligence, but before doing so a word should be said of (1) and (2).

Intentional Tort

As a practical joke, the defendant informed a woman that her husband had been seriously injured, both his legs having been broken, and that she was to go to him in a cab as soon as possible. The effect of the so-called "joke" on the plaintiff "was a violent shock to her nervous system, producing vomiting and other more serious and permanent physical consequences at one time threatening her reason, and entailing weeks of suffering and incapacity to her as well as expense to her husband for medical attendance." A verdict for the plaintiff led to an appeal to the Court of Queen's Bench. Here the verdict was sustained, Wright, J., saying "The defendant has . . . wilfully done an act calculated to cause physical harm to the plaintiff—that is to say, *to infringe her legal right to personal safety*, and has in fact thereby caused physical harm to her." [23] This is but one example of an intentional tort.

Strict Liability

The second ground is that of strict liability, and involves neither negligence nor intent to do an injury. This ground is also called liability at peril. The Cohoes Corporation was digging a canal upon a strip of land of which the corporation was owner. In digging, blasting, and excavating in the neighborhood of Hay's property and home, it was alleged that the defendant corporation "wrongfully and unjustly blasted and threw large quantities of earth, gravel, slate, and stones, upon the dwelling house and premises of the plaintiff, and shut and darkened the windows . . . obstructed the light, and broke the windows, doors . . . to the damage of the said plaintiff." [24] The company pleaded not guilty. The company moved for a nonsuit and insisted "that to make them liable it was incumbent on the plaintiff both to *aver* and prove that there was negligence, unskilfulness, wantonness or delay. . . ." [25] The trial court —the Court of Common Pleas—nonsuited the plaintiff, a decision to which exception was taken. The Supreme Court reversed the judgment and ordered a new trial. From this decision, the company appealed to the Court of Appeals. This court sustained the judgment of the Supreme Court. "The defendants," said Gardiner, J., "had the right to dig the canal. The plaintiff the right to the undisturbed possession of his property.

If these rights conflict, the former must yield to the latter, as the more important of the two, since, upon grounds of public policy, it is better that one man should surrender a particular use of his land, than that another should be deprived of the beneficial use of his property altogether, which might be the consequence if the privilege of the former should be wholly unrestricted." [26] If without intent and without negligence of any sort, and building on their own property a lawful and useful canal, the defendants could "demolish the stoop of the plaintiff with impunity, they might, for the same purpose, on the exercise of reasonable care, demolish his house, and thus deprive him of all use of his property." [27] Thus, the right to use one's own land as one sees fit is not an absolute right "but qualified and limited by the higher right of others to the lawful possession of their property." [28]

One of the most famous cases of strict liability is the English case of *Rylands v. Fletcher*.[29] Rylands employed independent contractors to construct a reservoir on his land. The contractors came upon some old mine shafts and passages. These appeared to be filled with earth and no one suspected that the passages connected with the mines of Fletcher, Rylands' neighbor. The shafts and passages apparently were not blocked up so that when the reservoir was filled, the water ran through the connecting passages and flooded Fletcher's mines. Rylands had not been negligent but the contractors had been.

Fletcher sued Rylands for damages. At the Liverpool Assizes, a verdict was returned for Fletcher. On appeal to the Court of Exchequer, a majority held that Fletcher could recover nothing. This was unanimously reversed by the Court of Exchequer Chamber. The judgment of this court was given by Blackburn, J.: "We think that the true rule of law is, that the person who, for his own purposes, brings on his land and collects and keeps there anything likely to do mischief if it escapes, must keep it in at his peril; and if he does not do so, is *prima facie* answerable for all the damage which is the natural consequence of its escape." [30] This is the rule. Blackburn went on to say that a defendant "can excuse himself by showing that the escape was owing to the plaintiff's default; or perhaps, that the escape was the consequence of a *vis major,* or the act of God; but as nothing of this sort exists here, it is unnecessary to inquire what excuse would be sufficient." [31]

Suppose that a malicious third person stopped up the waste pipe of a lavatory basin on the premises of one person with the result that the premises of another person were flooded. Would the rule in *Rylands v. Fletcher* apply? Such a case came before the Judicial Committee of the Privy Council. It was held that the defendant was not liable and so added to the "plaintiff's default" and an act of God, another exception to the rule of *Rylands v. Fletcher*. "A defendant," said Lord Moulton, "cannot . . . be properly said to have caused or allowed the water to escape if the malicious act of a third person was the real cause of its escaping without any fault on the part of the defendant." [32]

Negligence

The third ground on which tort liability rests is negligence. Negligence for our purposes may be defined as a breach of a legal duty owed to the plaintiff to exercise the care of a reasonable, prudent man. Putting it another way, "negligence is the omission to do something which a reasonable man, guided upon those considerations which ordinarily regulate the conduct of human affairs, would do, or doing something which a prudent and reasonable man would not do." [33] There are questions we may ask. What is a legal duty? What is the care demanded? What is a reasonable man?

A. P. Herbert humorously defines the reasonable man as one who

invariably looks where he is going, and is careful to examine the immediate foreground before he executes a leap or a bound; who neither star-gazes nor is lost in meditation when approaching trap-doors or the margin of a dock; who records in every case upon the counterfoils of cheques such ample details as are desirable . . . who never mounts a moving omnibus and does not alight from any car while the train is in motion; who investigates exhaustively the *bona fides* of every mendicant before distributing alms, and will inform himself of the history and habits of a dog before administering a caress; who believes no gossip, nor repeats it, without firm basis for believing it to be true; who never drives his ball till those in front of him have definitely vacated the putting-green which is his own objective; who never from one year's end to the other makes an excessive demand upon his wife, his neighbours, his servants, his ox, or his ass; who in the way of business looks only for that narrow margin of profit which twelve men such as himself would reckon to be "fair," and contemplates his fellow merchants, their agents, and their goods, with that degree of suspicion and distrust which the law deems admirable; who never swears, gambles, or loses his temper, who uses nothing except in moderation, and even while he flogs his child is meditating only on the golden mean. Devoid, in short, of any human weakness, with not one single saving vice, *sans* prejudice, procrastination, ill-nature, avarice, and absence of mind, as careful for his own safety as he is for that of others, this excellent but odious creature stands like a monument in our Courts of Justice, vainly appealing to his fellow-citizens to order their lives after his own example.[34]

Obviously, the young man who drives a car eighty miles an hour, one arm about a girl, giving more attention to her than to the road ahead, is not a reasonable man. The man who drives in a crowded city street at fifty miles an hour is not reasonable. The man who gives the keys of his car to a friend who is reeling drunk is not a reasonable man. In each case mentioned there is implicit a standard of conduct—a standard of care. The standard of conduct or care of the reasonable man, the normal adult, is one thing; the standard of conduct of the reasonable child is another; the standard of care of the reasonable blind man is still another.

In *The Moral Decision*,[35] Edmond Cahn discusses a Pennsylvania case which relates to a blind man. *X,* a partially blind man, made a living as a door-to-door salesman in a part of Philadelphia which was familiar to him. He could get about well enough being guided by a dim skyline and the trees, poles, and hedges bordering the sidewalk. One day he approached a trench which had been dug across the sidewalk for the purpose of making a sewer connection. On one side of the trench there was a barricade; on the other, a pile of dirt two feet high which had been thrown up from the excavation. *X* approached the pile of dirt, unaware of the danger, slipped, and fell into the trench. *X* sued the plumber for damages. The trial jury awarded *X* $500. The defendant appealed to the Superior Court, the verdict of the jury was set aside, and *X*'s suit dismissed. This decision was upheld by the highest court in Pennsylvania, which said that *X* "was bound to take precautions which one not so afflicted need not take. In exercise of due care for his own safety it was his duty to use one of the common, well-known compensatory devices for the blind, such as a cane, a 'seeing-eye' dog, or a companion." [36] This is an example of the unreasonable blind man.

A little girl, ten years of age, was sent on an errand by her mother, which required her to cross the railroad tracks. The mother warned the child of the danger and told her to look both ways before crossing the tracks. The girl did look both ways as she approached the tracks and saw no train approaching either way. She walked onto the tracks and was struck by the rear end of a train which was backing at the rate of eight miles an hour. Fortunately, she was not killed. It was claimed by the railroad that she could not have looked both ways because, if she had, she would have seen the approaching train in time to escape the danger. This claim was based on measurements. The plaintiff was nonsuited. The Court of Appeals reversed: "It may be that this evidence would show the want of that care which the law would exact of an adult. But does it show the want of that care which is demanded of an infant of plaintiff's age? She cannot be supposed to have had that knowledge of the speed of trains and the importance of looking again, just before taking the step upon the track, which an adult would have. The law is not so unreasonable as to exact from an infant the same degree of care and prudence in the presence of danger as it exacts from adults. An infant, to avoid the imputation of negligence, is bound only to exercise that degree of care which can reasonably be expected of one of its age." [37]

Circumstances alter cases, however. Conduct which might be deemed unreasonable under ordinary circumstances might be deemed reasonable under other circumstances.

Arthur Wagner and his cousin, Herbert, boarded an electric car operated by the International Railway Company, connecting Buffalo and Niagara Falls. At one point it crossed the New York Central and Erie tracks by means of a trestle. Approaching the trestle, there was a gradual incline upwards to about twenty-five feet, then a curve and a bridge over the tracks below, another turn, and finally the car would descend to grade level. The car was crowded and the cousins had to hang on near the doors, which the conductor did not close. Moving upwards at a speed of six to eight miles an hour, the car reached the curve. Without slowing down, there was a violent lurch on the curve and Herbert Wagner was thrown out. The car went on, down the incline on the farther side and stopped. Arthur walked back up the incline and across the trestle hoping to find his cousin's body. Other people walked under the trestle and found the body of Herbert. "As they stood there, the plaintiff's body struck the ground beside them." [38] In the darkness which had come on, Arthur had missed his step and fallen. He sustained serious injuries.

"The trial judge," said Cardozo, "held that negligence toward Herbert Wagner would not charge the defendant with liability for injuries suffered by" Arthur "unless two other facts were found: First, that the plaintiff had been invited by the conductor to go upon the bridge; and second, that the conductor had followed with a light." The conductor denied, as Arthur claimed, that he invited the plaintiff to ascend the trestle or that he had followed with a lantern. "Thus limited, the jury found in favor of the defendant." [39] The Appellate Division affirmed the judgment of the trial court. The Court of Appeals reversed and ordered a new trial.

"Danger invites rescue," declared Cardozo.

The cry of distress is the summons to relief. The law does not ignore these reactions of the mind in tracing conduct to its consequences. It recognizes them as normal. It places their effects within the range of the natural and probable. The wrong that imperils life is a wrong to the imperilled victim; it is a wrong also to his rescuer. The state that leaves an opening in a bridge is liable to the child that falls into the stream, but liable also to the parent who plunges to its aid. . . . The railroad company whose train approaches without signal is a wrongdoer toward the traveler surprised between the rails, but a wrongdoer also to the bystander who drags him from the path . . . the risk of rescue, if only it be not wanton, is born of the occasion. The emergency begets the man. The wrongdoer may not have foreseen the coming of a deliverer. He is accountable as if he had.[40]

If the defendant is found negligent, the plaintiff will usually recover. Still, it often happens that the defendant countercharges contributory negligence on the part of the plaintiff. The defendant alleges that the plaintiff himself was negligent and that without that negligence, however slight, the accident would never have occurred. This is the common law rule and in some jurisdictions the doctrine of comparative negligence has been substituted for it; but it is still important and still plays a role in our courts.

In the Wagner case, Arthur, in going up the trestle and crossing the bridge in the darkness, was clearly negligent. The question was whether, considering the circumstances, that negligence was to be excused. The two lower courts thought not, but the Court of Appeals thought otherwise.

One of the most difficult problems in connection with the duty to take care is the problem of the unforeseeable plaintiff. If the defendant's conduct threatens harm to X which a reasonable man would foresee, then he is negligent towards X, and he is liable for all injury to X even if the injury was not to be anticipated. But what if harm comes to Z who stands outside the area of any apparent danger and to whom no injury could reasonably have been foreseen?

Intending to take a train, Helen Palsgraf stood close by some scales, on the platform of the East New York passenger station of the Long Island Railroad. A train came in and stopped but it was not the train which would carry Mrs. Palsgraf to her destination. As this train slowly started on its way, two young men, one of them carrying a bundle, undertook to board it. The guard did not close the car door and one of the men got aboard without trouble. The second man, bundle under his arm, apparently had some difficulty boarding the train, but with the assistance of the guard on the moving train and a platform guard, he made it safely. However, during their efforts to assist the passenger, somehow, the bundle was knocked from under the passenger's arm; it fell under the train; there was an explosion which caused the scales near which Mrs. Palsgraf was standing, twenty-five or thirty feet away from the scene of the incident, to be thrown against her, injuring her severely. Mrs. Palsgraf sued the railroad for damages, alleging the negligence of the company's servants. The railroad, of course, contended that the injury to Mrs. Palsgraf was not caused by its negligence.[41]

At the trial, the sole question of the defendant's negligence submitted to the jury was whether the railroad's employees were "careless and negligent in the way they handled this particular passenger after he came upon the platform and while he was boarding the train." [42] The jury found for Mrs. Palsgraf and damages were awarded.

The Long Island Railroad then appealed to the Appellate Division of the Supreme Court. Here the judgment of the trial court was affirmed. "While there seems to be," said the Court, "no precedent for this case, every case must stand upon its own facts." In effect, the Court was saying that the facts could not be altered in order to conform to a certain precedent. But, said the Court, the principles surrounding the injury to Mrs. Palsgraf were not too unlike those of the squib case, the tap case, and the balloon case.

In the English case of *Scott v. Shepard,* the defendant threw a lighted squib into a crowded market-house. It fell into the gingerbread stall of one Yates. Willis instantly, in order to prevent injury to himself and to the wares of Yates, picked up the squib and tossed it across the market. The squib fell into the stall of one Ryal, who, to save his goods, threw it into another part of the market where it exploded and put out the plaintiff's eye. "The true question is," said De Grey, C. J., "whether the injury is the direct and immediate act of the defendant, and I am of opinion that in this case it is. The throwing of the squib was an act unlawful, and tending to affright the bystander. So far mischief was originally intended; not any particular mischief, but mischief indiscriminate and wanton. Whatever mischief therefore follows, he [the defendant] is the author of it. . . . It has been urged that the intervention of a free agent will make a difference: but I do not consider Willis and Ryal as free agents in the present case, but acting under a compulsory necessity for their own safety and self-preservation." [43] The defendant was held liable.

In *Vandenburgh v. Truax*[44] a boy, in escaping a threatened attack by a man pursuing him with an ax, ran into the plaintiff's store, overturned a cask of valuable wine and knocked out the tap. The pursuing party was held liable for the loss of the wine.

In *Guille v. Swan,*[45] the defendant, while in a balloon, descended into the plaintiff's garden under circumstances which tended to invite some 200 people to go to his assistance, thereby destroying the plaintiff's potatoes and radishes. The defendant contended that he was liable only for the damage to the crops done by the balloon, which was estimated at fifteen dollars, and not for the damage done by the crowd, an amount of ninety dollars. The trial court judge instructed the jury that Guille was answerable for all the damage done, and the jury agreed. On appeal to the Supreme Court, this judgment was affirmed.

The facts in these three cases were unlike the facts in the Palsgraf case, but a majority of the appellate court thought that in principle there was a similarity; in each, the defendant was the proximate cause of the damage; as a consequence, the judgment of the Palsgraf trial court was affirmed.

There was a dissent, however. The facts may have warranted the jury in finding that the defendant's servants were negligent in assisting a passenger in boarding a moving train since the door should have been closed before the train started. There was also warrant for a finding by the jury that as a result of the defendant's negligence a package was thrown under the train and exploded causing injury to the plaintiff. But, said the dissenting judge,

In my opinion, the negligence was not a proximate cause of the injuries to plaintiff. Between the negligence of defendant and the injuries, there intervened the negligence of the passenger carrying the package containing an explosive. This was an independent, and not a concurring act of negligence. The explosion was not reasonably probable as a result of defendant's act of negligence. The negligence of defendant was not a likely or natural cause of the explosion, since the latter was such an unusual occurrence. Defendant's negligence was a cause of plaintiff's injury, but too remote.[46]

A final decision was yet to come. The Long Island Railroad appealed for a second time, this time to the New York Court of Appeals, the highest court in the state. Here, by a four-three decision, the judgment of the Appellate Division and that of the trial court was reversed and the complaint dismissed. There was a dissenting opinion and both opinions, the majority and the dissenting, are worth consideration.

Chief Judge Cardozo, speaking for the majority, held that since there was no negligence toward the plaintiff, there was no liability. Negligence, he said, is a matter of relationship between parties; some duty is involved, and duty can be established only on the foreseeability of injury to the plaintiff who is in fact harmed. "The conduct of the defendant's guard," said Cardozo, "if a wrong in its relation to the holder of the package, was not a wrong in its relation to the plaintiff, standing far away. Relatively to her it was not negligence at all." [47]

The man carrying the bundle was not injured nor was his life endangered. What the guards did was to safeguard his life. "If there was a wrong to him at all, which may very well be doubted, it was a wrong to a property interest only, the safety of his package." [48] But, "out of this wrong to property, which threatened injury to nothing else, there has passed, we are told, to the plaintiff by derivation or succession a right of action for the invasion of an interest of another order, the right to bodily security." [49]

Cardozo gives the hypothetical situation of a man who jostles his neighbor in a crowd, causing a bomb to fall to the ground. Has the man who jostled his neighbor invaded the rights of others standing on the outer fringe of the crowd? "As to them," said Cardozo, the wrongdoer "is the man who carries the bomb, not the one who explodes it without suspicion of the danger." [50] Life, he goes on to say, "will have to be made over, and human nature transformed, before prevision so extravagant can be accepted as the norm of conduct, the customary standard to which behavior must conform." [51]

Judge Andrews who read the dissenting opinion disagreed four-square with Cardozo. He rejected the idea that negligence is a relative concept, "the breach of some duty owing to a particular person or to particular persons." To Judge Andrews, negligence is a wrong to anyone who is in fact injured by the negligent act. "Every one owes to the world at large," said Judge Andrews, "the duty of refraining from those acts that may unreasonably threaten the safety of others. Such an act occurs. Not only is he wronged to whom harm might reasonably be expected to result, but he also who is in fact injured, even if he be outside what would generally be thought the danger zone. . . . All those in fact injured may complain." [52] The plaintiff in this case was therefore not suing by "derivation or succession"; her action was "original and primary."

There are limitations to such widespread liability but they are limitations of proximate cause, and the remoteness of damage. Proximate cause may be defined as follows: "That which, in a natural and continuous sequence, unbroken by any intervening cause, produces the injury, and without which the injury would not have occurred." [53] Damage is said to be too remote to be actionable when it is not the legal and natural consequence of the act complained of. Judge Andrews, in the words of Professor Prosser, was saying that "The injury here was direct and immediate; the distance was short; there was no remoteness in time, little in space. It cannot be said as a matter of law that the plaintiff's injuries were not the proximate result of the negligence." [54]

The student will note that the problem to both Cardozo and Andrews and on which they differed was that of "transferred negligence"; whether "Mrs. Palsgraf, who was in no way foreseeably endangered, could base her cause of action upon the railroad's negligence toward the man with the package." [55]

"The plaintiff," said Cardozo, "sues in her own right for a wrong personal to her, and not as the vicarious beneficiary of a breach of duty to another." [56] Any other conclusion, he said, would lead to a maze of contradictions. "A guard stumbles over a package which has been left upon a platform. It seems to be a bundle of newspapers. It turns out to be a can of dynamite. To the eye of ordinary vigilance, the bundle is abandoned waste, which may be kicked or trod on with impunity. Is a passenger at the other end of the platform protected by the law against the unsuspected hazard concealed beneath the waste? If not, is the result to be any different, so far as the distant passenger is concerned, when the guard stumbles over a valise which a truckman or a porter has left upon the walk?" [57]

Judge Andrews looked upon the matter from the view of proximate cause and was of the opinion that negligence was transferrable and that it was transferred in Mrs. Palsgraf's case. It is important to remember that in this regard the word "cause" is not used alone. The cause of an event or incident, say an automobile accident, could be traced back to the invention of the wheel; there must be some limitation and so to the word "cause" the courts have added the qualifying word, "proximate."

But, as Professor Prosser says, "The quest of the 'proximate' does not solve the problem. It adds nothing in the way of certainty or convenience; if anything, it only increases our difficulties . . . All that it does is to direct attention to the plaintiff as well as the defendant, to the role of the consequences as well as that of the fault." [58]

It will be remembered that one judge of the Appellate Division dissented.[59] He was of the opinion that between the negligence of the defendant and the injuries sustained by Mrs. Palsgraf there was the negligence of the passenger who carried the bundle of explosives. The idea was that the passenger's negligence broke the line of direct cause and effect. This is spoken of as a *novus actus interveniens,* a new intervening action.

A simple situation, noted in one or two textbooks, is that of a hide which fell from the upper story of a tannery. It was allowed to remain in the street. A gust of wind hurled the hide against a passerby and injured him. He was not allowed to recover from the tannery because a new force, a new action, had intervened which broke the line of cause and effect. Another situation was that of a woman who, by mistake, was put off of a train at the wrong station so that she was compelled to spend the night in a hotel and the next day get a train which would take her to her intended destination. Due to a defective light in her hotel room she received a shock and was slightly injured. She sued the railroad unsuccessfully. New factors had intervened. Still another situation was that of the engineer of a locomotive hauling tanks of crude oil. He negligently failed to keep his eyes on the track ahead and ran into a landslide; some of the tanks turned over and fell into an adjoining stream. The oil escaped, ignited, and was carried downstream and set fire to a man's home. The homeowner sued the railroad, but without success. The court held that to allow recovery would extend liability too far. Who could foresee all the consequences? Certainly the chance of such an event is slight. The burning of the man's home was not reasonably foreseeable. The court referred to the water which carried the burning oil as an intervening force which broke the chain of causation.

If the student will analyze these cases, he will understand that causation is not an easy thing with which to deal. Many years ago when coal-burning locomotives brought passengers into New York on elevated tracks, care was exercised by the railroad to prevent the falling of cinders and hot coals to the streets below. It so happened that a horse-drawn delivery wagon was standing by the curb, and the driver of the horse was sitting with the reins in his hands, awaiting the return of his assistant. A train passed overhead and a hot coal fell on the horse which was shocked into violent action. The driver tried to run the horse into one of the piers but without success. He did turn the horse around and tried to run the wagon close to the curb in hopes that the friction of the wheels against the curb would slow him down. At this point, the wagon tipped over and fell upon a man who happened to be standing near the curb. He sued the railroad and won his case. Is there a clearcut difference between this case and the case of the burning crude oil?

We have said enough to suggest the importance of the common law in America, of the role it can play in our lives, and, implicitly, of the wisdom that is required of judges in the resolution of conflict under the common law. This law is not complete; and as long as it is challenged by new conditions and new situations, it will never be complete. It is a living law and as such reveals a flexibility which makes difficult a certain prediction of what a court will do in a given case. Be that as it may, one can begin to see that the judging process is not a mechanical application of rules to concrete situations. It is a very human process and one which requires that our judges be men of integrity and intelligence, men who know and understand other men and their ways, and above all, men who are imbued with a spirit of justice and fair-dealing.

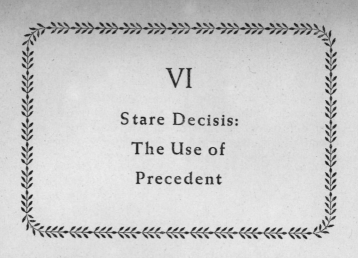

VI

Stare Decisis:
The Use of
Precedent

In the resolution of conflicts a court invokes and applies rules of law to proven facts. A question arises: Just where does a court find these rules?

There are two *chief* sources of law: *statutes* and *precedents*. The former, of course, come from the legislature which consists of the elected representatives of the people. The latter come from the courts; precedents are the products of earlier decisions. To the latter, we should add the decisions of an increasing number of administrative bodies and the precedents established thereby, but of this matter we shall speak later.

Most everybody knows what a statute is, but what is a precedent? In a general, nonlegal way, precedent plays an important role in our lives. Often, we do things as our parents did them and cite their experience as precedent for what we do now; out of some continuing or repetitive situation there comes a rough rule of thumb. When a father is questioned as to why he spanked his son for some infraction of the household rules, he might reply that as a boy in like circumstances he had been spanked as had his father before him. He might go on to explain that such treatment was an application of the rule of experience, "Spare the rod and spoil the child."

When a mother solicits the aid of her protesting children in doing the household chores, she might declare that children have always helped their parents, and in support of this experience she quotes the rule, "Many hands make light work." On the other hand, when the children clamor to help her make a cake for a church bazaar, she more than likely will decline the proffered aid and repeat the ancient adage, "Too many cooks spoil the broth."

A young man, intending a change from one job to another, is cautioned by his father, who tries to dissuade him with the rule, hoary with time, that "A rolling stone gathers no moss," or no money, as the case may be.

The son, wanting a change of work, answers with another ancient rule, "Nothing ventured, nothing gained."

In all of these instances, there is the application of a rule of experience to a given situation. These are homely examples. Clubs, business organizations, boards of trustees, student groups—all have their rules, some written, some unwritten, which are often invoked as precedent for doing, or not doing, one thing or another. And a precedent here is defined by Webster as "something done or said that may serve as an example or rule to authorize or justify a subsequent act of the same or analogous kind."

Judicial Precedent

A judicial precedent is defined in the same dictionary as "a judicial decision, a form of proceeding, or course of action that serves as a rule for future determinations in similar or analogous cases."

The driver of a wagon loaded with buckskin goods stopped for the night at a certain inn. He was received as a guest and the innkeeper took charge of his property. During the night a fire broke out which resulted in the destruction of horses, wagon and goods. The owner of the property thus destroyed sued the innkeeper for damages.

Let us suppose that this was a case of first impression, that is, a situation which is before an American court for the first time. After hearing the evidence from both sides, the judge does not simply say "I decide for the plaintiff," or "I decide for the defendant." He decides for one or the other and gives his reasons. He will speak as follows: "An innkeeper is responsible for the safe keeping of property committed to his custody by a guest. He is an insurer against loss, unless caused by the negligence or fraud of the guest, or by the act of God or the public enemy." [1] The judge looks to the English common law and finds that the liability of innkeepers was expressed tersely in *Cross v. Andrews:* "The defendant, if he will keep an inn, ought, *at his peril,* to keep safely his guests' goods";[2] and at greater length by Coke in *Calye's Case*:[3] "If one brings a bag or chest, etc., of evidences into the inn as obligations, deeds, or other specialties, and by default of the innkeeper they are taken away, the innkeeper shall answer for them."

The judge will go on to explain the reason for the rule. He will say that the rule has its origins in public policy.

Every facility should be furnished for secure and convenient intercourse between different portions of the kingdom. The safeguards, of which the law gave assurance to the wayfarer, were akin to those which invested each English home with the legal security of a castle. The traveller was peculiarly exposed to depredation and fraud. He was compelled to repose confidence in a host, who was subject to constant temptation, and favored with peculiar opportunities, if he chose to betray his trust. The innkeeper was at liberty to fix his own compensation, and enforce summary payment. His lien, then as now, fastened upon the goods of his guest from the time they came to his custody. The care of the property was usually committed to servants, over whom the guest had no control, and who had no interest in its preservation, unless their employer was held responsible for its safety. In case of depredation by collusion, or of injury or destruction by neglect, the stranger would of necessity be at every possible disadvantage. He would be without the means either of proving guilt or detecting it. The witnesses to whom he must resort for information, if not accessories to the injury, would ordinarily be in the interest of the innkeeper. The sufferer would be deprived, by the very wrong of which he complained, of the means of remaining to ascertain and enforce his rights, and redress would be well-nigh hopeless, but for the rule of law casting the loss on the party entrusted with the custody of the property, and paid for keeping it safely.[4]

Stare Decisis

Let us suppose that a year or so later, another driver with a wagon load of hides spends the night at an inn. Again, the horses, the wagon, and the hides, are turned over to the innkeeper; and again, a fire occurs during the night and the property of the guest is burned up. The owner of the property then sues the innkeeper for damages. The situation here is exactly the same as in the earlier case.

The judge in the second case, according to the theory, will apply the rule or principle (which is the precedent) and decide in favor of the plaintiff. The precedent or authority of the first case is precise and fits the facts of the second case very nicely. This application by courts of rules announced in earlier decisions is spoken of as *stare decisis,* which means "let the decision stand." This has been, and is, a fundamental characteristic of the common law, although in American jurisdictions it is the practice upon occasion for a high court to overrule its own precedents.

Obviously, a legal system in which judges could decide cases any which way, manifesting prejudice, whimsy, ignorance and venality, each decision being an entity in itself unconnected with the theory, practices and precedents of the whole, would be a sorry system, or, one might say, no system at all, and a source of little comfort either to attorneys or litigants. Speaking of *stare decisis* many years ago, Judge Maxwell of the Supreme Court of Nebraska said: "In the application of the principles of the common law, where the precedents are unanimous in the support of a proposition, there is no safety but in a strict adherence to such precedents. If the court will not follow established rules, rights are sacrificed, and lawyers and litigants are left in doubt and uncertainty, while there is no certainty in regard to what, upon a given state of facts, the decision of the court will be." [5]

One concludes, after a little thought, that *stare decisis* is "the instrument of *stability* in a legal system," that it "furnishes a legal system with *certainty* and *predictability*," and "clothes a legal system with *reliability*"; in addition, it "assures all persons of *equality and uniformity of treatment*" and judges with "an instrument of *convenience and expediency*." In short, "*Stare decisis* preserves the judicial *experience* of the past." [6]

After a little more thought, however, one also sees that *stare decisis* is an instrument of conservatism, of immobility, of eyes-in-the-back-of-the-head, of stultification. The application of the same rule, decade after decade, long after changed conditions have robbed the rule of its validity, makes the rule a troublesome fiction.

But, American high courts do not hesitate to overrule their own precedents when social, economic, or political change demand a corresponding change in the law. Cardozo has said that "If we figure stability and progress as opposite poles, then at one pole we have the maxim of *stare decisis* and the method of decision by the tool of a deductive logic; at the other we have the method which subordinates origins to ends. The one emphasizes considerations of uniformity and symmetry, and follows fundamental conceptions to ultimate conclusions. The other gives freer play to considerations of equity and justice, and the value to society of the interests affected. The one searches for the analogy that is nearest in point of similarity, and adheres to it inflexibly. The other, in its choice of the analogy that shall govern, finds community of spirit more significant than resemblance in externals. 'Much of the administration of justice,' says Pound, 'is a compromise between the tendency to treat each case as one of a generalized type of case, and the tendency to treat each case as unique.' Each method," concludes Cardozo, "has its value, and for each in the changes of litigation there will come the hour for use. A wise eclecticism employs them both." [7]

Precedent and Facts

In the two cases outlined above, it has been assumed that the facts were identical, but only rarely are fact situations exactly alike. And from a different fact situation there may arise a different precedent or rule of law. Professor Rodell, taking as an example a collision of two automobiles, points out the difficulties:

Suppose a man driving a 1939 Cadillac along the Lincoln Highway toward Chicago runs into a Model T Ford, driven by a farmer who has just turned onto the Highway from a dirt road, and demolishes the Ford but does not hurt the farmer. The farmer sues, and a local judge, on the basis of various principles of Law which are said to "control" the case, awards him $100.

A week later, another man driving a 1939 Cadillac along the Lincoln Highway toward Chicago runs into a Model T Ford driven by another farmer
who has just turned onto the Highway from the same dirt road, and demolishes the Ford but does not hurt the farmer. This farmer also sues. The
facts, as stated, seem to make this case quite familiar to the previous case. Will
it then fall into the same group of fact situations? Will it be "controlled" by
the same principles of Law? Will the second farmer get $100?

That all depends. For of course [as in the innkeeper's case] there will be
other facts in both cases. Some may still be similar. Others, inevitably, will
be different. And the possibilities of variation are literally endless.

Maybe the first Cadillac was doing sixty miles an hour and the second
one thirty. Or maybe one was doing forty-five and the other one forty. Or
maybe both were doing forty-five but it was raining one week and clear the
next. Maybe one farmer blew his horn and the other didn't. Maybe one
farmer stopped at the crossing and the other didn't. Maybe one farmer had
a driver's license and the other didn't. Maybe one farmer was young and
the other was old and wore glasses. Maybe they both wore glasses but one
was nearsighted and the other farsighted.

Maybe one Cadillac carried an out-of-state license plate and the other
a local license plate. Maybe one of the Cadillac drivers was a bond salesman
and the other a doctor. Maybe one was insured and the other wasn't. Maybe
one had a girl in the seat beside him and the other didn't. Maybe they both
had girls beside them but one was talking to his girl and the other wasn't.

Maybe one Cadillac hit its Ford in the rear left wheel and the other in
the front left wheel. Maybe a boy on a bicycle was riding along the Highway at one time but not the other. Maybe a tree at the intersection had
come into leaf since the first accident. Maybe a go-slow sign had blown
over.[8]

In the second case of the innkeeper and the guest a difference in the
fact situation, no matter how similar it may be to that of the first case,
may lead a court to *distinguish* the one case from the other and to
apply therefore a different precedent or rule.

James P. Tallon was employed as a guard on one of the trains of the
Interborough Rapid Transit Company. He lived at 146th Street in Manhattan and it was his duty to report for duty each morning at the Transit
Company's station at 177th Street and Third Avenue. To get to and
from work, he was provided with a pass by the company which allowed
him free passage. One morning on his way to work and in the uniform
of a guard, a collision of trains occurred which resulted in Tallon's death.

Tallon's wife brought suit against the company for damages, alleging
negligence on the part of the company, and claiming that her husband
was a passenger on one of the defendant's trains and not an employee
within the meaning of the Workmen's Compensation Law.

The defendant insisted on the trial that, "Tallon was injured in an
accident arising out of and in the course of his employment and that this
action could not be maintained." [9] The trial judge ruled as a matter of

law that Tallon had been a passenger and "the negligence being admitted, left to the jury solely the question of damages." [10]

The Appellate Division reversed the judgment of the trial court and dismissed the complaint on the ground that the only relief for Mrs. Tallon was under the Workmen's Compensation Law, since Tallon, at the time of his death, was within the terms of that law in that "he was injured in an accident arising out of and in the course of his employment." [11]

The Court of Appeals, speaking through Judge Crane, reversed the Appellate Division and affirmed the judgment of the trial court. Judge McLaughlin, dissenting, and supporting the judgment of the intermediate court, was of the opinion that "at the time of the collision Tallon occupied the status of an employee and, therefore, relief should have been sought under the Workmen's Compensation Law. At the time of the accident he was riding on a pass which entitled him to free transportation to and from his work. Such transportation was an incident of the employment. It was a part of the contract of employment and enforcible by him as such. The facts bring the case directly within the principle laid down in *Matter of Littler v. Fuller Co.*" [12]

Littler was a bricklayer. He worked for the Fuller Co. which was constructing a residence in Great Neck, some two miles from the railroad station. The workmen who came out to Great Neck by train had refused to continue to work unless the employer would furnish them with free transportation from the railroad station and back again at the end of a day's work. The employer hired a truck to transport the men. Littler was injured when the truck, making its way back to the station, turned over in a ditch.

Littler sued the Fuller Company, arguing that his injury did not arise out of or in the course of employment. The Court of Appeals thought otherwise. "The vehicle," said Judge Pound, "was provided by the employer for the specific purpose of carrying the workmen to and from the place of the employment and in order to secure their services. The place of injury was brought within the scope of the employment because Littler, when he was injured, was 'on his way . . . from his duty within the precincts of the company.' . . . The day's work began when he entered the automobile truck in the morning and ended when he left it in the evening. The rule is well established that in such cases compensation should be awarded." Judge Pound goes on to say that the "case would be different if at the time of the accident" Littler "had been on the railroad train on his way to or from Great Neck." [13]

Judge Crane, speaking for the majority in the Tallon case, *distinguished* the Littler case from the matter at hand. He said,

The cardinal underlying fact is that Tallon's employment did not actually begin until he reported for work at One Hundred and Seventy-seventh Street and Third avenue. He had to get there, and get there on time, and to facilitate his arriving on time the defendant gave him the right to ride in its passenger trains free of charge, but I cannot see how this in any way changes the reality, the existing fact, that the employment commenced at One Hundred and Seventy-seventh Street and Third avenue at the time of reporting. It would cause no such change, had Tallon paid his fare on defendant's train or had ridden in another conveyance, the defendant paying his fare. The pass alone, even though it be a part of his compensation, cannot create a fictitious relationship.[14]

But there is still the Littler case to be considered, which Judge McLaughlin in his dissent thought applicable in this matter. Judge Crane, therefore, *distinguished* the Littler case as follows: "Now this case differs materially from those cases where the employer in order to get his employees to and from their work, provide conveyances exclusively for their use which in no sense are public conveyances and in which the employees undertake to ride as part of their contract of employment in going to and from their work. Such a case was *Matter of Littler v. Fuller Co.*" [15]

Thus, Littler had to accept an award under Workmen's Compensation while Mrs. Tallon would receive damages from the wealthy construction company. Between the majority view and the dissenting view of the facts there was a decided difference; each view elicited a different precedent and each produced a different result.

Imprecise Precedents

The Tallon matter might be called a run-of-the-mill case, and it is an example of the kind of thing courts do every day. They "distinguish" or they "follow" precedents. But what happens when the precedents do not fit the facts or two precedents might well and equally, but not exactly, cover a situation?

It was customary some years ago for young boys to swim in the United States Ship Canal, a narrow body of water separating Manhattan and the Bronx. They would cross from the Manhattan side and climb the bulkhead belonging to the New York Central Railroad and to which was attached, by whom or when no one knew, a rough plank which served as a diving board. This plank extended several feet beyond the line of the railroad's property. As sixteen-year-old Harvey Hynes stood poised on the board ready to dive, a high tension wire belonging to the railroad fell upon him and swept him to his death below. Hynes' mother brought an action for damages against the company.

The complaint brought by Mrs. Hynes alleged that the defendant's neglect in improperly erecting, constructing, and maintaining its poles and appurtenances and the wires attached thereto was responsible for the death of her son.

In the court of first instance, a jury awarded the plaintiff, Mrs. Hynes, eight thousand dollars. The defendant, the railroad, at once appealed to the Supreme Court of New York to set aside the verdict of the jury and to grant a new trial, and the Supreme Court so ordered. Mrs. Hynes then appealed from this order to the Appellate Division of the Supreme Court.[16]

Before the Appellate Division, the defendant argued that Hynes, in climbing the bulkhead and standing in readiness to plunge from the diving board into the water, was a trespasser. True, the railroad was duty bound "to use reasonable care that bathers swimming or standing in the water should not be electrocuted by wires falling from its right of way," but that there was no duty to a boy on the springboard unless any injury he might receive was "the product of mere wilfulness or wantonness."

The court accepted his argument. The majority held that one who trespasses on a riparian owner's land and goes from there onto a springboard extending out over public waters is still a trespasser even though he is on that part of the board beyond the technical boundary of the riparian owner.

Two of the Appellate Division judges did not agree with the majority and one of them wrote a dissenting opinion. His argument was that Hynes was not a trespasser in the usual sense. Ordinarily, in like cases, the accident would not have happened but for the trespass. In this case, however, the falling wires would have been as fatal to the boy swimming in the river at that point as standing upon a plank attached to the defendant's premises. "If a wagon of the defendant," he said, "had been left standing in the highway" and young Hynes "had climbed into that wagon and while there had been killed by the defendant's wires falling into the highway, there would have been no question as to the plaintiff's right to recover. The situation," he continued, "is exactly analogous to the situation involved in this action. The boy's death was not caused by a defect in the premises upon which he trespassed, but by the negligence of the defendant which permitted its wires to fall into the navigable waters of the river." [17]

Finally, Mrs. Hynes appealed to the Court of Appeals, the highest court of the State of New York. Here, the decision of the Appellate Division was reversed.[18]

In the lower courts, the judges emphasized the concept of the trespasser. Hynes was a trespasser pure and simple and therefore his mother could not recover. The Court of Appeals, speaking through Judge Cardozo, gave equal emphasis to another concept, namely, the concept of the traveller on the highway. This concept had its beginnings at a time when roads were not lighted and when it was quite possible on a moonless night for the traveller to stray from the highway. If, for example, a landowner dug a hole four or five feet from the highway and the traveller strayed a little off the road at night, fell into the hole, and was injured, the landowner would be liable in damages even though the traveller was an inadvertent trespasser. To this day, one sees with the coming of darkness red lanterns and planks surrounding any kind of excavation near the highway. If the wayfarer fell into a hole three hundred yards from the road, it might be surmised that the luckless one was there for no good reason or that he was in such a state as not to know the difference between a highway and a melon patch. The traveller concept would hardly apply.

"Landowners," said Judge Cardozo, "*are* bound to regulate their conduct in contemplation of the presence of travelers upon the adjacent public ways." [19] Hynes, until the moment of his death, was in the enjoyment of the public waters and when he climbed the bulkhead and stood on the board poised to dive, he had not abandoned his "rights as a bather." The court chose to look upon the use of the springboard as "a mere byplay, an incident, subordinate and ancillary to the execution of his primary purpose, the enjoyment of the highway. The byplay, the incident, was not the *cause* of the disaster. Hynes would have gone to his death if he had been below the springboard or beside it." [20]

The railroad would have been liable if the wires had fallen upon a bather in the water, or upon a fisherman in a rowboat, or upon the pilot of an airplane skimming a few feet above the public waters. But because the board was attached to land belonging to the railroad, it was deemed in the lower court to be an extension of the company's property and the use of it by the boy, a trespass. The Court of Appeals could not accept this view. "Two boys walking in the country or swimming in a river," said Judge Cardozo, "stop to rest for a moment along the side of the road or the margin of the stream. One of them throws himself beneath the overhanging branches of a tree. The other perches himself on a bough a foot or so above the ground. . . . Both are killed by falling wires. The defendant would have us say that there is a remedy for the representatives of one, and none for the representatives of the other." [21]

Cardozo stated the problem succinctly: in one sense, Hynes standing on the springboard was a trespasser; in another sense, he was still on the public waters in the enjoyment of public rights. "The law," said Cardozo, "must say whether it will subject him to the rule of the one field or of the other. . . ." [22]

Considerations "of analogy, of convenience, of policy, and of justice," led the Court of Appeals to hold the railroad "in the field of liability and duty."

Commenting later on the analogy of the trespasser and the analogy of the traveller on the highway, Cardozo said that "as a mere bit of dialectics, these analogies would bring a judge to an impasse. No process of merely logical deduction could determine the choice between them. Neither analogy is precise, though each is apposite. There had arisen a new situation which could not force itself without mutilation into any of the existing moulds. When we find a situation of this kind," he continued, 'the choice that will approve itself to this judge or to that, will be determined largely by his conception of the end of the law, the function of legal liability; and this question of ends and functions is a question of philosophy." [23]

The Creation of New Precedents

Stare decisis is a characteristic of the common law; but it is true that in American jurisdictions high courts will, when conditions change or necessity demands, overrule their own precedents.

Robert C. Woods was *en ventre sa mere* in the ninth month of his mother's pregnancy when she fell down a stairway in a multiple dwelling house, causing injuries to herself and to the child who was born thirteen days after the accident. The child came into the world permanently maimed and disabled. The mother, in behalf of her infant son, sued the owner of the multiple dwelling, the complaint alleging negligence.

The suit was brought in the Supreme Court for Bronx County. The defendant moved for a dismissal of the complaint on the ground that it failed to state a cause of action. The court sustained the motion and dismissed the complaint. From this order, the plaintiff appealed to the Appellate Division of the Supreme Court which affirmed (four to one) the order of the lower court.[24]

The four judges who affirmed the order wrote no opinion, except for Judge Shientag, who concurred but would have allowed recovery provided the causal relation between the negligence and the damage to the child be established by competent medical evidence"; he concurred with the majority because thirty years earlier the Court of Appeals had squarely decided against the plaintiff.

This was in the case of *Drobner v. Peters*,[25] decided in 1921. The defendant negligently permitted a coal hole in the sidewalk in front of his premises to remain uncovered and the plaintiff's mother fell into it. The child was born eleven days later. He had sustained injuries as a result of the accident. The question before the Court of Appeals was: "Does the complaint herein state facts sufficient to constitute a cause of action?" It was contended by the defendant that at the time of the injury the child was not a person but was a part of the body of his mother and that, as the injury was to his mother, he has no cause of action." [26] The Court of Appeals answered the question in the negative.

To return to *Woods v. Lancet,* Judge Heffernan (in the Appellate Division of the Supreme Court) dissented. He referred to *Drobner v. Peters* and admitted that no case could be found in New York wherein a plaintiff had been awarded damages for injuries inflicted upon his person while *in utero*. He said, however, that "an adjudicated case is not indispensable to establish a right to recover under the rules of the common law.

Precedent is merely a guide; its absence never a bar. The fact that ther
is no precedent is not conclusive. The law would be an absurd scienc
were it founded on precedents only. The absence of precedent shoul
give no immunity to one who by his wrongful act has invaded the rigl
of an individual. No right is more inherent, more sacrosanct, than that c
an individual in his possession and enjoyment of his life, his limbs an
his body. The law is not static and inert, but is sufficiently elastic to mee
changing conditions. It is presumed to keep pace with present day cor
cepts. To deny the infant relief in this case is not only a harsh result, bu
its effect is to do reverence to an outmoded, timeworn fiction not founde
on fact and within common knowledge untrue and unjustified." [27]

Judge Heffernan referred to the fact that courts in other jurisdictior
had held "that an unborn viable child is capable of independent existenc
and" hence "should be regarded as a separate entity." He quoted wit
approval from the dissenting opinion of Mr. Justice Boggs in *Allaire v. S
Luke's Hospital,* an Illinois case: "The argument is, that at the commo
law an unborn child was but a part of the mother, and had no existenc
or being which could be the subject matter of injury distinct from th
mother, and that an injury to it was but an injury to the mother; that i
such case there was but one person—one life—that of the mother." :
Mr. Justice Boggs went on to say,

but if, while in the womb, it reaches that prenatal age of viability whe
the destruction of the life of the mother does not necessarily end i
existence also, and when, if separated prematurely and by artificial mear
from the mother, it would be so far a matured human being as that
would live and grow, mentally and physically, as other children generall'
it is but to deny a palpable fact to argue there is but one life, and th;
the life of the mother. Medical science and skill and experience hav
demonstrated that at a period of gestation in advance of the period c
parturition the foetus is capable of independent and separate life, and th;
though within the body of the mother it is not merely a part of her bod'
for her body may die in all of its parts and the child remain alive ar
capable of maintaining life when separated from the dead body of th
mother. If at that period a child so advanced is injured in its limbs or men
bers and is born into the living world suffering from the defects of th
injury, is it not sacrificing truth to a mere theoretical abstraction to s;
the injury was not to the child, but wholly to the mother? [29]

The Court of Appeals in *Woods v. Lancet* reversed both lower courts.
Speaking through Judge Desmond, a majority held that recovery shoul
be allowed. In his opinion, Judge Desmond reviewed the history of pr
natal injury, going back no further than *Dietrich v. Northampton,*[31] d
cided in 1884, and "apparently, the first American case." In an opinio
by Justice Holmes, the Massachusetts Supreme Court denied recover
on the grounds that "the unborn child was a part of the mother at th

ime of the injury," and that any damage to it which was not too remote
ɔ be recovered for at all was recoverable by her. Judge Desmond cited
ther cases where courts had refused to allow a suit to be brought on
•ehalf of a child who sustained an injury prior to birth.

In *Drobner v. Peters,* the Court of Appeals, finding no precedent for
llowing the suit, had adopted the general theory of *Dietrich v. Northamp-
on.* Judge Desmond went on to say that since 1921, "numerous and im-
•ressive affirmative precedents have been developed." The highest courts
n California, Ohio, Minnesota, Maryland, and Georgia, had all upheld
he right of an infant to bring an action for prepartum injuries tortiously
nflicted. "What, then, stands in the way of reversal here?" asked Judge
)esmond. "Surely," he said, "as an original proposition, we would, today,
•e hard put to it to find a sound reason for the old rule. Following Drobner
*. Peters . . . would call for an affirmance but the chief basis for that
tolding (lack of precedent) no longer exists." [32]

The argument as to the supposed difficulty of proving or disproving
hat certain injuries befell the unborn child is a valid one but does not
>resent an insuperable obstacle since "Every day in all our trial courts
and before administrative tribunals, particularly the Workmen's Com-
>ensation Board), such issues are disposed of, and it is an inadmissible
:oncept that uncertainty of proof can ever destroy a legal right." [33]

Thus *Drobner v. Peters* was overruled and recovery was allowed. Any-
ɔne bringing suit for injuries before birth must still *prove* that the injuries
vere the result of the accident and tortiously inflicted.

Certainty and the Law

The overruling of ancient precedents is a cause of dismay to many
awyers; and those who are not lawyers tend to look askance at a much-
ʲaunted legal system which allows such a degree of uncertainty. "The
aw ought to be certain," is a remark often heard. "How can I know my
·ights if the law itself is uncertain?"

The desire for certainty is all-important. We like to feel certain of an
:conomic system which gives us security and a political system which
;afeguards that security. We like the comfort of the absolute.

Yet individuals too readily forget that their forefathers once subscribed
vith absolute certainty to astrology, the existence of witches and bogey-
nen, and the notion that the earth was a flat body; individuals also forget
·hat the present is very much a part of the historical process and look
ɪpon society, though turbulent in its development, as static.

If history teaches us anything, it is that society is not static. This lesson,
;imple as it is, and implied on every page of the most elementary text-
ɔook, is seemingly lost, as it always has been lost, in the illusion that as
·hings are so shall they ever be; we wait until new social conditions, long

unrecognized or ignored, pull the rug from under our feet and force us to a revision of our theories, or our precedents. "The logical method and form," declared Mr. Justice Holmes, "flatter that longing for certainty and for repose which is in every human mind. But certainty generally is an illusion, and repose is not the destiny of man." [34]

Early in the present century, the philosophical scientists rejected the classical conception that "science deals with a determinate universe and must therefore aim at propositions that are demonstrably true." [35] In its place they have substituted the notion of probability. "However solidly founded," said Poincaré, "a prediction may seem to us to be, we are never absolutely sure that experiment will not prove it false." [36] Gilbert N. Lewis has said that the search for ultimate truths is no longer useful to science "except in the sense of a horizon toward which we may proceed, rather than a point which may be reached." [37] After all, Lewis continued, "is it necessary to decide as to the existence of all these ultimates and absolutes, and especially as to the existence of an absolute truth? If we once overcome the childlike notion that every act is either right or wrong, that every statement is either true or false, that every question may be answered by a 'yes' or 'no,' we still recognize that with our present knowledge there are some statements which are more probable than others." [38]

No one yearned more for certainty in the law than Cardozo. The opening paragraphs of *The Paradoxes of Legal Science* testify to the disappointment engendered by an awareness that he, as a judge, could not do with his rules of law what the engineer can do with his slide rule and logarithms. The latter can build his bridge safe in the knowledge that he has wrought "a highway to carry men and women from shore to shore, to carry them secure and unafraid, though the floods rage and boil below." Cardozo laments that though he has given his life to the law, as have generations of judges before him, "yet unwritten is my table of logarithms, the index of the power to which a precedent must be raised to produce the formula of justice. My bridges are experiments." "Until deeper insight is imparted to us," said the gentle Cardozo, "we must be content with many a makeshift compromise, with many a truth that is approximate and relative. . . ." [39]

Reasoning by Analogy

Donald MacPherson had bought a Buick automobile from a dealer in Schenectady, New York. While in the car with two friends and travelling at the rate of about eight miles an hour, the spokes of the left rear wheel collapsed and Mr. MacPherson was thrown into a ditch and injured. He brought suit, not against the dealer with whom he had entered into a contract for the purchase of the car, but against the Buick

Motor Company with whom he had no contractual relationship whatever. The general rule was well expressed by Chief Justice Cooley of Michigan many years ago: "The general rule is that a contractor, manufacturer, vendor or furnisher of an article is not liable to third parties who have no contractual relations with him for negligence in the construction, manufacture or sale of such article." [40] And the exceptions to the general rule recognized in New York are cases in which the article sold "was of such a character that danger to life or limb was involved in the ordinary use thereof; in other words, where the article sold was inherently dangerous." [41]

The trial judge instructed the jury that an automobile was not an inherently dangerous vehicle but that it may become so if it is equipped with a defective wheel; and that "if the motor car in question, when it was put upon the market was in itself inherently dangerous by reason of its being equipped with a weak wheel, the defendant was chargeable with a knowledge of the defect so far as it might be discovered by a reasonable inspection and the application of reasonable tests." [42] The jury returned a verdict for the plaintiff for $5,025.

The Buick Company then appealed to the Appellate Division of the Supreme Court. This court affirmed the judgment of the lower court.

The Buick Company had purchased the wheel from the Imperial Wheel Company. When received by the defendant, it was ironed and primed with one coat of paint. No examination of the wheel was made by the defendant except to see that it ran true and that it had not been marred in shipment. "The evidence," said Judge Kellogg, "indicates quite clearly that many other automobile manufacturers, prior to 1909, exercised no greater care as to wheels bought by them than the defendant exercised with reference to its wheels, and that no accident had resulted therefrom. This evidence indicated, not that the defendant was careful, but that the manufacturer had been very lucky." [43]

Judge Kellogg stressed the fact that a defective wheel is liable to cause serious damage not only to the people using the car but to others as well; an automobile, he said, "equipped with weak wheels" is an "imminently dangerous machine."

Speaking *obiter,* Judge Kellogg said that

> In the old days a farmer who desired to have wheels made for an ox-cart would be apt to inspect the timber before it was painted, before the wheel was ironed and the defects covered up, in order that he might know what he was buying. He would realize that the oxen, in case of an accident or fright, as he would say, "might go pretty fast," and that if a wheel broke serious damage might occur to him or to others. . . . An ordinary man, in buying a pitchfork, a golf club, an axe-helve, or an oar for a boat, will look at the timber, "heft it," and otherwise endeavor to ascertain whether it is made of suitable material. [44]

Since the ultimate purchaser is not qualified to make such an examination, or even to examine the quality of the wood, it is incumbent upon the manufacturer to do it for him.

The court held that under the circumstances, the Buick Company "owed a duty to all purchasers of its automobiles to make a reasonable inspection and test to ascertain whether the wheels purchased and put in use by it were reasonably fit for the purposes for which it used them, and if it fails to exercise care in that respect it is responsible for any defect which would have been discovered by such reasonable inspection and test." [45]

The Buick Company appealed to the New York Court of Appeals. The sole question to be determined was "whether the defendant owed a duty of care and vigilance to anyone but the immediate purchaser," that is, the retail dealer.

For the appellant—the Buick Company—it was argued that an automobile "is not an inherently dangerous article" and that therefore "the defendant was not liable to a third party in simple negligence—that is, for negligence as contradistinguished from willful or knowing negligence, or in a negligence action as distinguished from an action for deceit, fraud or misrepresentation, to third parties not in contractual relations with it." [46]

For the respondent, it was argued that an automobile "propelled by explosive gases" and capable of "a speed of fifty miles an hour" is an inherently dangerous machine and that therefore the manufacturer was liable to a third party with whom he had no contractual relations. [47]

The general rule, you will remember, was well expressed by Judge Cooley. An exception to the general rule is the doctrine, if such it may be called, of the "inherently dangerous instrument." If the article is "inherently" or "imminently" dangerous, then the manufacturer is liable to third parties; if it is not within the category of "inherently dangerous," then the manufacturer is not liable to third parties. The Buick Company struggled to the bitter end to persuade the court not to include an automobile in this category, while the respondent sought to persuade the court to keep the car in the category in line with the lower court opinion.

The Court of Appeals, speaking through Judge Cardozo, affirmed the judgment of the Appellate Division. First he reviewed the precedents. That a manufacturer may be liable to a third party was established in New York in the case of *Thomas v. Winchester*,[48] decided in 1853. A druggist had purchased a bottle of what was supposedly extract of dandelion from Winchester, who operated a pharmaceutical business in New York City. The bottle, through the negligence of one of Winchester's employees, had been incorrectly labeled extract of dandelion although the bottle did in fact contain belladonna, a poison. A Mr. Thomas bought a small quantity of this liquid from the druggist for his wife, who, after taking a few spoonfuls, became violently sick. Mrs. Thomas sued Winchester, not the druggist, and recovered damages. "The defendant's negligence," said the Court, "put human life in imminent danger." With regard to this early case, Cardozo said, "A poison falsely labeled is likely to injure anyone who gets it. Because the danger is to be foreseen, there is a duty to avoid the injury." [49]

In 1882, in *Devlin v. Smith*,[50] the Court of Appeals had under consideration a case in which the defendant, a contractor, contracted to build a scaffold for a painter. The painter's workmen were injured when the scaffold collapsed, and the contractor was held liable although there was no privity of contract between him and the workmen. The defendant, said Cardozo, "knew that the scaffold, if improperly constructed, was a most dangerous trap. He knew that it was to be used by the workmen. . . . Building it for their use, he owed them a duty, irrespective of his contract with their master, to build it with care." [51]

Cardozo then considers another case in which the rule of *Thomas v. Winchester* was followed: *Statler v. Ray Manufacturing Company*.[52] Here the manufacturer of a coffee urn was held liable when one of his urns, installed in a restaurant, exploded and injured the plaintiff. The court declared that the urn "was of such a character inherently that, when applied to the purposes for which it was designed, it was liable to become a source of great danger to many people if not carefully and properly constructed." [53]

To the argument that things imminently dangerous to life were poisons, explosives, and deadly weapons, and that (reasoning by analogy) the automobile was not like any of these, Cardozo said: "Whatever the rule in *Thomas v. Winchester* may once have been, it has no longer that restricted meaning. A scaffold . . . is not inherently a destructive instrument. It becomes destructive only if imperfectly constructed. A large coffee urn . . . may have within itself, if negligently made, the potency of danger, yet no one thinks of it as an implement whose normal function is destruction." [54] After a review of New York court decisions, Judge Cardozo declared that the rule of *Thomas v. Winchester* was not limited to "poisons, explosives, and things of like nature. . . ." He goes on to state the rule: "If the nature of a thing is such that it is reasonably certain to place life and limb in peril when negligently made, it is then a thing of danger. Its nature gives warning of the consequences to be expected. If to the element of danger there is added knowledge that the thing will be used by persons other than the purchaser, and used without new tests, then, irrespective of contract, the manufacturer of this thing of danger is under a duty to make it carefully. That is as far as we are required to go for the decision of this case." [55]

Cardozo then goes on to clarify the rule. "There must be knowledge of a danger," he said, "not merely possible, but probable. It is *possible* to use almost anything in a way that will make it dangerous if defective. That is not enough to charge the manufacturer with a duty independent of his contract." [56]

In a later case of *Smith v. Peerless Glass Company*,[57] the plaintiff, a waitress at a soda water and cigar stand, lost the sight of one eye through the explosion of a soda water bottle. She sued not only the manufacturer of the bottle but the bottler, Minck Brothers and Company. The trial court's finding for the plaintiff against both defendants was upheld by the Appellate Division. On appeal, the Court of Appeals affirmed the judgment against the glass company; that against the bottler was reversed and a new trial ordered.

"If the filled bottle," said Crouch, J., "may be regarded as an assembled product of which the bottle itself was a component part, the approach to the applicable rule of law may be made by way of *MacPherson v. Buick Motor Co.* By analogy, the bottler will be in the position of the defendant in that case and the maker of the bottle in that of the . . . maker of the wheel. The liability of the bottler will then be ruled clearly enough by the law of that case and the evidence only need be considered." [58] As to the maker of the bottle, Cardozo had said in the MacPherson case, "We are not required at this time to say that it is legitimate to go back of the manufacturer of the finished product and hold the manufacturers of the component parts"; and Judge Crouch said that "The doubt seemed to hang on the problem of causation" but that the doubt had vanished "in the light of subsequent decisions." Thus, he says, "There emerges . . . a broad rule of liability applicable to the manufacturer of any chattel, whether it be a component part or an assembled entity." With reference to the instant case, "it is that if either defendant was negligent in circumstances pointing to an unreasonable risk of serious bodily injury to one in plaintiff's position, liability may follow though privity [of contract] is lacking." [59]

The evidence sustained the finding of the jury that the manufacturer of the bottle had failed to use the ordinary or the customary tests to detect defects in his product; therefore, the judgment against him was upheld. As to the bottler, there was no proof that he was negligent; as a consequence, the judgment against him was reversed and a new trial ordered.

The MacPherson and Smith cases, as compared with *Thomas v. Winchester*, reveal an enlargement of a rule of society as manifested by the courts. Certainly, in this area the law was brought more "in line with social considerations." Unlike a hundred years ago, the enlarged ruling recognized the new position of the buyer vis-à-vis the manufacturer. The meat, the canned or frozen fruits and vegetables, the bottled waters—these come from distant places and merely pass through the hands of the retailer to the consumer. If a young man buys a bottle of ginger beer from a retailer for his girl and she drinks the concoction only to find the remains of a decomposed snail in the bottom of the bottle and becomes deathly sick, are we, in this day and age, to say that the poisoned consumer has no remedy against the negligent manufacturer? [60]

As Mr. Holmes said, with some tenderness for a felicitous statement, the life of the law has not been logic, it has been experience. Perhaps this is not altogether true, but the cases do reflect the changing attitudes of courts to the changing facts of social life. And, as Professor Levi says, to contrast "logic and the actual legal method [reasoning by example] is" to do "a disservice to both. Legal reasoning has a logic of its own. Its structure fits it to give meaning to ambiguity and to test constantly whether the society has come to see new differences or similarities. Social theories and other changes in society will be relevant when the ambiguity has to be resolved for a particular case." [61]

Statutes and Common Law Precedents

Since before the turn of the century, a good part of the labors of Congress and the state legislatures has been devoted to the resolution of conflicts relating to such matters as wages, working conditions, farm income, taxes, health, old age, securities, and rights, to give but a few examples. The National Labor Relations Act of 1935, the Social Security Act of the same year, the Fair Labor Standards Act and the second Agricultural Adjustment Act, both of 1938, the Labor-Management Act of 1947—all reflect deep-seated conflicts within our society. These enactments were designed to abolish old practices which had worked to the disadvantage of a particular group, to institute new practices, and to provide ways and means whereby the more or less peaceful settlement of disputes between groups might be effected.

Prior to 1908, if an employee of an interstate railroad were injured, the common law armed the employer with defenses by which he could escape liability. To be sure, the common law did impose obligations and attendant liabilities upon the employer: the master had to provide his servants with a safe place to work, and with tools, appliances and machinery which might be used with safety; he was to instruct his servants in the use of new or unusual tools, especially those involving possible and unexpected danger; the master had to provide trustworthy, reliable, and competent co-workers and to make rules and regulations for the protection of employees in line of work. These demands upon the employer, however, were not absolute, nor could they have been, for all of them were modified by the word "reasonable." The railroad was "to use all reasonable care" in keeping its tracks and roadbed in safe condition. The best and latest improved machinery is not required of the employer but "only such as is reasonably safe and suitable." The rules and regulations for the government of employees must give them "reasonable protection." If the employer failed in any of the requirements of the common law and his servant was injured, he would be liable in damages.

There were three common law doctrines behind which the employer could protect himself from employee attack in case of injury. These were (1) the fellow-servant rule; (2) assumption of risk; and (3) the doctrine of contributory negligence.

In 1837 in England, there was decided the case of *Priestley v. Fowler*.[62] The plaintiff was a butcher's driver's helper. In the course of his duty the helper was injured when the butcher's van collapsed. He sued the butcher for negligence in that his servant, the driver, had overloaded the van. The helper and the driver were fellow-servants. This was a case of first impression since there was no precedent for such an action by a servant against a master.

In the court of first instance, the jury returned a verdict for the plaintiff. The Court of Exchequer reversed. Said Lord Abinger,

> If the master be liable to the servant in this action, the principle of that liability will be found to carry us to an alarming extent. . . . The mere relation of the master and the servant never can imply an obligation on the part of the master to take more care of the servant than he may reasonably be expected to do of himself. He is, no doubt, bound to provide for the safety of his servant in the course of his employment, to the best of his judgment, information, and belief. The servant is not bound to risk his safety in the service of his master, and may, if he thinks fit, decline any service in which he reasonably apprehends injury to himself: and in most of the cases in which danger may be incurred, if not in all, he is just as likely to be acquainted with the probability and extent of it as the master.[63]

The helper, continued Lord Abinger,

> must have known as well as his master, and probably better, whether the van was sufficient, whether it was overloaded, and whether it was likely to carry him safely. In fact, to allow this sort of action to prevail would be an encouragement to the servant to omit that diligence and caution which he is in duty bound to exercise on the behalf of his master, to protect him against the misconduct or negligence of others who serve him, and which diligence and caution, while they protect the master, are a much better security against any injury the servant may sustain by the negligence of others engaged under the same master, than any recourse against his master for damages could possibly afford.[64]

This is spoken of in England as the doctrine of common employment.

The doctrine was in no time adopted by American courts, and the leading case on the subject is *Farwell v. The Boston and Worcester Railroad*,[65] decided in 1842 by the Supreme Judicial Court of Massachusetts. The opinion of Chief Justice Shaw was an elaborate presentation of the English doctrine.

The plaintiff, an engineer, was injured through the negligence of another servant of the railroad company. As Chief Justice Shaw pointed out, he had voluntarily accepted the job as engineer and he had full knowledge of the risks of such employment. "The general rule," said Shaw, "resulting from considerations as well as justice as of policy, is, that he who engages in the employment of another for the performance of specified duties and services, for compensation, takes upon himself the natural and ordinary risks and perils incident to the performance of such services. . . ." And the Chief Justice was "not aware of any principle which should except the perils arising from the carelessness and negligence of those who are in the same employment." [66]

The fellow-servant rule, although later limited in its application by the courts because of the hardship it worked on employees injured through the negligence of co-workers, was widely adopted by state and Federal courts and served the corporations as a powerful defense against suits by employees.

A second defense was the doctrine of the assumption of risk. Professor Prosser defines this concept as follows: "In its primary and proper sense, it means that the plaintiff has consented to relieve the defendant of an obligation of conduct toward him, and to take his chance of injury from a known risk." [67]

Willis Parker, an employee of the Erie Railroad, was a freight conductor in charge of a train going east from Buffalo. The freight stopped at Attica and Parker went into the depot. The freight started to move, Parker came out, caught hold of a passing car and began to climb a ladder at the side. He was struck by the projecting roof of the depot and killed.

In the court of first instance, there was a verdict for the plaintiff and this was affirmed by the General Term of the Supreme Court. The defendant appealed to the New York Court of Appeals, arguing that the trial court should have nonsuited the plaintiff on the ground that there was no actionable negligence on the part of the defendant and that the evidence showed negligence on the part of the deceased. The Court of Appeals reversed both lower courts and ordered a new trial. Judge Allen said, "When the deceased

> entered the employment of the defendant he assumed the usual risks and perils of the service, and also the risks and perils incident to the use of the machinery and property of the defendant as it then was, so far as such risks were apparent. Accepting service with a knowledge of the character and position of the structures from which the employes (*sic*) might be liable to receive injury, he could not call upon the defendant to make alterations to secure greater safety, or in case of injury from risks which were apparent, he could not call upon his employer for indemnity.[68]

Parker lived in Attica, he knew the peculiarities of the depot if such they were, he had worked for the railroad for seven years as brakeman and conductor, passing over the road once or twice a day, and he knew that the usual place for him to ride between stations was in the caboose.

The Supreme Court of the United States, in part, accepted the doctrine of the assumption of risk in 1879, in the case of *Hough v. Railway Company*.[69]

In addition to the fellow-servant rule and assumption of risk, a third defense at hand for the employer was the doctrine of contributory negligence. Let us suppose that due to the negligence of the employer an employee is injured. If the employee has been in no way negligent himself, he may recover damages from the employer; but, if the employee has been negligent, no matter how slight the negligence and without which the accident would never have occurred, he is barred from recovery.

In the case discussed above—*Gibson v. Erie Ry. Co.*—the Court of Appeals had something to say about contributory negligence. Not only had the deceased "assumed the risk" of the employment, he was more than likely negligent in that "of his own volition and without any necessity connected with his duties as conductor of the train, so far as the evidence discloses, undertook to climb the cars when under way, and just at the point of danger, and, so far as appears, at the only point of especial risk. This he did at his peril. He did not incur the peril at the request of the defendant or its officers or agents, or in pursuance of any general or special orders of the company." [70]

In railroad cases before the Federal courts, contributory negligence was accepted and enforced in many cases with harsh results. If, for example, an engineer discovered a defect in his engine and "had continued to use the engine, without giving notice thereof to the proper officers of the company, he would undoubtedly have been guilty of such contributory negligence as to bar a recovery, so far as such defect was found to have been the efficient cause of the death." [71]

Now we may turn to *statutes* as a source of law and consider their relationship to common law precedents. The chief common law bulwarks against an attack for damages (by an employee injured through the negligence of the employer) were the rules or precedents which have been touched upon above: the fellow-servant rule, assumption of risk, and contributory negligence. The men of labor recognized the potency of these weapons in the hands of courts and judges whose sympathies and understandings appeared to favor business and industry. Perhaps the judges were reflecting a rugged individualism which theoretically was the quality not only of the most unscrupulous robber baron but of the laborer earning seventy-five cents a day working on the railroad. At any rate, labor set out to abolish these three defenses. They succeeded, to a degree.

In 1908, Congress, exercising its power to regulate foreign commerce and commerce among the states, passed the second Employers' Liability Act, which related solely to the interstate railroads. Section One provided that a common carrier in interstate commerce was liable in damages to any employee suffering injury or death "resulting in whole or in part from the negligence of any of the officers, agents, or employees of such carrier, or by reason of any defect or insufficiency, due to its negligence, in its cars, engines, appliances, machinery, track, roadbed, works, boats, wharves, or other equipment." [72] This section abolished the fellow-servant rule in interstate commerce as far as the railroads were concerned.

Section Three provided that "the fact that the employee may have been guilty of contributory negligence shall not bar a recovery, but the damages shall be diminished by the jury in proportion to the amount of negligence attributable to such employee";[73] and where the employee was injured or killed due to a "violation by such common carrier of any statute enacted for the safety of employees" and which "contributed to the injury or death," he shall be held not to have been guilty of contributory negligence. Thus, the old doctrine of contributory negligence as a carrier defense was modified and in its place there was substituted the rule of *comparative negligence.*

Section Four only to a limited extent abolished the doctrine of the assumption of risk. An injured employee "shall not be held to have assumed the risks of his employment in any case where the violation by such common carrier of any statute enacted for the safety of employees contributed to the injury or death of such employee." [74]

One might suppose that thus the matter was settled. Certainly, in theory, a statute in conflict with a rule of the common law will overrule the latter. Indeed, "the great office of statutes is to remedy defects in the common law as they are developed, and to adapt it to the changes of time and circumstances." [75] But let us see what happened to Section Four of the Act.

In 1914 one Horton sued the Seaboard Air Line[76] railroad in a North Carolina court to recover damages for injuries sustained by him while in the defendant's employ as a locomotive engineer. The action was brought under the second Employers' Liability Act, as amended.

The facts, as revealed by the plaintiff's evidence, were as follows: Horton was placed in charge of one of the defendant's locomotives which "was equipped with a Buckner water gauge, a device attached to the boiler head for the purpose of showing the level of the water in the boiler, and consisting of a brass frame or case inclosing a thin glass tube. . . . In order to shield the engineer from injury in case of the bursting of the tube, a piece of ordinary glass 2 or 3 inches wide, 8 or 9 inches long, and about half an inch thick, known as a guard glass, should have been provided, this being a part of the regular equipment of the Buckner water gauge." Horton reported the absence of the glass shield quite properly to the roundhouse foreman who had no such glass on hand. Apparently, it would be necessary for the foreman "to send to a distance to get one." The foreman appears to have told Horton to "run the engine without" [77] the glass guard, unfortunately as it turned out, for the glass tube exploded and flying fragments struck Horton in the face causing the injuries for which he asked damages.

Three issues were decided by the jury: (1) the plaintiff was injured by the defendant's negligence; (2) the plaintiff did not assume the risk of injury; and (3) the plaintiff did contribute by his own negligence to his injury. Substantial damages were awarded. And the Supreme Court of North Carolina affirmed the judgment of the trial court. The case then went to the Supreme Court of the United States "upon questions arising out of instructions given and refused to be given to the jury as to the nature of the duty of the employer and the rules respecting assumption of risk and contributory negligence under the Federal Employers' Liability Act." [78]

The Supreme Court of the United States reversed the North Carolina court and perpetuated the defensive use of assumption of risk. Section Four, you will remember, provided that employees shall not be held to have assumed the risks of their employment in any case "where the violation by such common carrier of any statute enacted for the safety of employees contributed to the injury or death of such employe." Assumption of risk was eliminated only in case of violation of such Federal statutes as the Safety Appliance Act; in all other cases, the Court declared assumption of risk "shall have its former effect as a complete bar to the action." [79] And the 1908 Congress never "dreamed, when it passed this former law [Employers' Liability Act], that this defense [assumption of risk] would ever be raised by the use of" §4 of the act. [80]

Twenty-five years passed before Congress again acted with regard to the doctrine of assumption of risk. It was in 1939 that the Employers' Liability Act, §4, was amended as follows: in any action brought by an employee, he "shall not be held to have assumed the risks of his employment in any case where such injury or death resulted in whole or in part from the negligence of any of the officers, agents, or employees of such carrier. . . ." [81] This does not entirely remove assumption of risk from the scene. "Once the negligence of the carrier is established, it cannot be relieved of liability by pleading that the employee 'assumed the risk.'" Where there has been no negligence on the part of the employer, would then the doctrine be operative?

John Lewis Tiller worked for a long time as a policeman employed by the Atlantic Coast Line. One of his duties was to inspect seals on cars in railroad yards to make sure that they had not been tampered with. The facts assumed by the Circuit Court of Appeals were as follows:

Tiller was standing between two tracks in the respondent's switch yards, tracks which allowed him three feet, seven and one-half inches of standing space when trains were moving on both sides. The night was dark and the yard was unlighted. Tiller, using a flashlight for the purpose, was inspecting the seals of the train moving slowly on one track when suddenly he was hit and killed by the rear car of a train backing in the opposite direction on the other track. The rear of the train which killed Tiller was unlighted although a brakeman with a lantern was riding on the back step on the side away from Tiller. The bell was ringing on the engine but both trains were moving, and the Circuit Court found that it was "probable that Tiller did not hear cars approaching" from behind him. No special signal or warning was given.[82]

Tiller's wife brought suit to recover damages under the Federal Employers' Liability Act. The complaint alleged negligent operation of the train which killed Tiller, and failure to provide a reasonably safe place to work. The railroad company, the respondent, denied negligence, pleading contributory negligence on the part of Tiller, and set up as a separate defense that Tiller had assumed all the risks "normally and necessarily incident to his employment."

The trial court granted a motion of the railway for a directed verdict (a judge's binding instruction to the jury that its verdict must be for the defendant) after the plaintiff's evidence had been heard, on two grounds: (1) that the evidence disclosed no actionable negligence; and (2) that the cause of the death was speculative and conjectural. Against this verdict, the plaintiff appealed to the Circuit Court of Appeals. This court affirmed "interpreting the decision of the district court as resting on a conclusion that the evidence showed no negligence" on the part of the railway company. This result was based "on a holding that the deceased had assumed the risk of his position and that therefore there was no duty owing to him by respondent." [83]

Finally, the plaintiff carried his case to the Supreme Court of the United States because of the interpretation put upon the 1939 amendment to the Federal Employers' Liability Act by the lower courts.

What the Circuit Court did was to distinguish between two concepts of assumption of risk: (1) as a defense by employers against the consequence of their own negligence; this, the Circuit Court asserted, was abolished by the 1939 amendment; and (2) assumption of risk as negating any conclusion that negligence existed at all. If, for example, the railway company had provided a workman with a defective tool and the workman was thereby injured, the company under the 1939 amendment could not claim that he had "assumed the risk." However, if a workman were injured in the ordinary course of his work, "assumption of risk might still be relied upon to prove that the respondent had no duty to protect him from accustomed danger" as in this switching operation. As the opinion of the Circuit Court reads, "The conclusion is inescapable that Congress did not intend to enlarge the obligation of carriers to look out for the safety of their men when exposed to the ordinary risks of the business, and that in circumstances other than those provided for in the amended section of the statute, the doctrine of the assumption of the risk must be given its accustomed weight." [84]

The Supreme Court, speaking through Mr. Justice Black, held "that every vestige of the doctrine of assumption of risk was obliterated from the law by the 1939 amendment, and that Congress, by abolishing the defense of assumption of risk in that statute, did not mean to leave open the identical defense for the master by changing its name to 'non-negligence.' " [85]

One may question this conclusion. The amendment specifically says that an "employee shall not be held to have assumed the risks of his employment in any case where such injury or death resulted in whole or in part from the negligence of any of the officers, agents, or employees of such carrier." But suppose that there is *no* negligence on the part of the officers, *et al.* of such carrier?

In the majority opinion, Mr. Justice Black declared categorically "that every vestige of the doctrine of the assumption of risk was obliterated from the law by the 1939 amendment. . . ." [86] Mr. Justice Frankfurter in a concurring opinion said that assumption of risk "as a defense *where there is negligence* has been written out of the Act," but assumption of risk "in the sense that the employer is not liable for those risks which it could not avoid in the observance of its duty of care, has not been written out of the law." Mr. Justice Frankfurter was "not at all certain that the Circuit Court of Appeals misconceived the nature and extent of the carrier's liability after the 1939 amendment, rather than merely obscured its understanding by beclouding talk about 'assumption of risk.' " [87]

A precedent is a principle, a doctrine, or rule of decision in a given case, which is deemed to be a controlling authority in identical situations coming before a court at a later time. The practice of applying precedent to later cases is called *stare decisis*. But only seldom are the facts of a later case identical with those of an earlier one. Of necessity, courts are thus concerned with similarities, differences, and approximations. The courts must meet a new situation which is both similar to, and different from, the precedent situation, and apply a doctrine which is in no sense precise. It is here that courts expand, refine, or restrict, and in some cases, even nullify the earlier doctrine. If the law has a living quality, it is to be found in the way judges mould precedent to meet the challenge of new, varied, subtle, and oftentimes complicated human relationships.

In the absence of statute, courts as a general rule will follow precedent or the rules announced by judges in earlier cases. As often as not, new facts do not adapt themselves precisely to existing precedent and, therefore, courts must make distinctions, analogies must be drawn, and in some cases precedents are overruled and new ones created. Where the legislature by statute moves in on territory occupied by precedent, the statute prevails, as we have seen in the labor cases. But statutes are not always crystal-clear and admit of various interpretations which may even allow the continuance of a common law rule it was presumably the intention of the legislature to abolish.

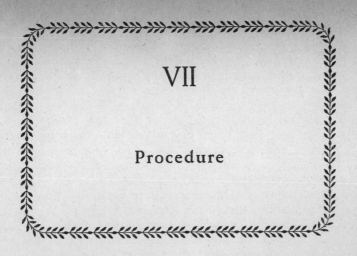

VII

Procedure

How does a court determine whether or not a man is guilty of robbery as alleged in the indictment (accusation)? How does a court determine whether a defendant is in fact maintaining a nuisance on his property to the discomforture of his neighbors? How does a court determine the truth, if it be the truth, of the plaintiff's complaint that the defendant has maliciously injured his reputation? Here we enter the realm of procedure.

Simply stated, the term procedure relates to the machinery of justice, to the form, manner, and order of conducting suits and prosecutions. In this chapter, the main emphasis will be upon criminal procedure.

A crime, as defined in the Penal Law of New York, is an act or omission forbidden by law and punishable upon conviction by death, or imprisonment, or fine, or removal from office, or disqualification to hold any office of trust, honor or profit under the state or other penal discipline. The Penal Law recognizes two categories of crime, felonies and misdemeanors.[1] The former comprise such infractions of the law as murder, burglary, arson, rape, robbery, and grand larceny; the latter include such offenses as petty larceny, libel, maintaining a nuisance, using false weights and measures, tatooing a child under sixteen, and exciting groundless judicial proceedings. The Penal Law succinctly defines a felony as a crime which is or may be punishable by death or imprisonment in a state prison for one year or more; misdemeanors comprise all other crimes. In the case of misdemeanors, imprisonment (if that is the punishment) is for a year or less in a county or city jail.

Arrest

The distinction between a felony and a misdemeanor is important in connection with the problem of arrest. An officer may arrest anyone who commits a misdemeanor in his presence; otherwise, he must first secure a warrant. In connection with a felony, an officer may have a warrant for the offender's arrest, but the law allows him, without a warrant, to arrest a man, if he has reasonable grounds for believing that a felony has been committed and that a certain person is the offender.

This question arose in the case of *People v. Wilson,*[2] decided by the New York Court of Appeals in 1894. On the night of June 5, 1893, a shoe store in Syracuse was entered by burglars and several hundred dollars worth of property and some money were stolen. For three days prior to the theft, and the day succeeding it, three men had taken meals at Palmer's restaurant and the proprietor and his head waiter were led to believe from overheard conversations that these men were connected with the theft of the shoes. Palmer communicated his suspicions to the police. The chief of detectives told Palmer to telephone headquarters should the suspected persons appear again in his restaurant; and he informed Detective Harvey that should such a call come from the proprietor that he, Harvey, should go to the restaurant, arrest the men, and bring them to the police station. The men did return to the restaurant, Palmer did call the police, and Harvey did go to the restaurant and arrest Charles and Lucius Wilson. The detective walked between the two prisoners, holding their arms, as they made their way by the most direct route to the police station. As they approached some obstacle on the sidewalk which made it necessary for them to turn into the street, Charles Wilson drew a revolver and struck Harvey with the butt; Lucius Wilson also drew a gun and from a distance of eight or ten feet shot and killed the dazed detective. The gunmen were soon captured and indicted for murder in the first degree. They were tried and found guilty.

The important issue on the appeal was the use made of the burglary of the shoe store by the district attorney at the trial. The defense objected strongly to the introduction of such evidence. Counsel for the defendant insisted that it was "fatal error" for the trial court to admit this evidence and urged that it was an attempt on the part of the prosecution "to prove a crime not alleged in the indictment." He argued, too, that such evidence "was calculated to greatly prejudice the minds of the jury." At the close of the People's case, the defense counsel moved to strike all this evidence from the record and the Court denied the motion. "The evidence was not received," said the trial judge, "so stated at the time, for the purpose of showing the fact that this defendant committed the burglary, but for the purpose of showing that a felony was committed, and that certain facts, whether true or otherwise, were brought to the knowledge of Detective Harvey, tending to show that he had reasonable ground, or cause, if it has that tendency, for making the arrest, if he did make the arrest, all of which are questions for the jury, of the defendant here; and the evidence is admitted in the case and allowed to stand for no other purpose." [3]

The district attorney was equally explicit. The purpose of the proof of the burglary, he said, "is to justify the officer; to show, in accordance with the provision of the Code, that a felony had been committed, and that he had reasonable cause to believe that the defendant had committed it, and that the persons arrested had committed it." [4] Asked by defense counsel if he intended to prove the burglary, the district attorney said, "Certainly, I propose to prove it was committed." "And to trace it to this defendant?" he was asked; and the district attorney answered, "Not at all." The trial judge, at the close of the case, struck out a portion of the evidence objected to by the defendant. Any evidence, he said, "tending to show that this defendant, or any other party, was guilty of this burglary, is stricken from the case and you must give it no consideration." [5]

Proof of the burglary was introduced "to justify the officer." This was necessary since the arrest was made without a warrant. If the defense could have prevailed upon the Court to exclude all evidence that a burglary had been committed, then the prosecution could not have argued justification and Detective Harvey should not have made the arrest.

The defendant, facing the death penalty, was seeking a new trial in the hope that the charge against him might be reduced to murder in the second degree or even manslaughter. He was unsuccessful, for the Court of Appeals affirmed the conviction. Even if the arrest were illegal, the defendant was not justified in shooting the detective; it was, said the Court, "a ruthless assassination."

"Suspects," however, are picked up every day by the police and taken to the station house without a warrant. They are held for a brief but indefinite time and then either arrested or freed. Holding a suspect is not in itself an arrest; it is euphemistically called "detention." There are those who see a sharp distinction between arrest and detention, since a person detained is not a prisoner, nor is he placed in a cell; still, he is not free to leave the station house.

The Preliminary Examination

Upon arrest, the arrestee must be taken by the most direct route before a magistrate. The prisoner must be informed of the charge against him and of his right to counsel in every stage of the proceedings. A reasonable time must be allowed him to secure the services of a lawyer. There is then a preliminary examination, the purpose of which is to determine whether or not the arrested person should be held to await action by the grand jury or the district attorney. The examination is not so much of the prisoner as of the arresting officer and/or the complaining witnesses. Those who accuse must state the nature of their case against the defendant, who then, if he chooses, may state his side of the story. The complaints of prosecuting witnesses may be tested; perhaps their ignorance, misunderstanding, prejudice, or viciousness will be revealed and the defendant freed. Or else the magistrate believes that the evidence submitted is sufficient, reasonable, or probable, and thus orders the prisoner held for further action by either the grand jury or the district attorney. If the offense is bailable, the prisoner must be admitted to bail.[6]

Indictment

The Constitution of the State of New York provides that "No person shall be held to answer for a capital or otherwise infamous crime . . . unless on presentment or indictment of a grand jury." A capital offense is one which incurs the death penalty; an "infamous crime" is a felony; an indictment is an accusation by a grand jury.

In 1928, one Battista was arrested for burglary. While awaiting action by the grand jury, he petitioned the court for a direction that an information be filed against him, whereby he would be formally accused by the prosecutor instead of being indicted by the grand jury. His petition was granted, in accordance with an act of the legislature which became Section 222 of the Code of Criminal Procedure. Battista then pleaded guilty and was sentenced to confinement in the reformatory at Elmira.

The New York Court of Appeals held Section 222 to be in direct conflict with the constitutional provision quoted above. "The statute," said Judge O'Brien, speaking for the majority, "assumes to authorize the thing which the Constitution expressly forbids. The organic law decrees that no one shall be held to answer for an infamous crime until after a grand jury shall have considered the evidence against him. The legislative enactment says that an individual may, if he pleases, strip himself of a protection common to all within the jurisdiction of our government. This right, attempted to be conferred by statute, was not granted solely for the benefit of the criminal. Probably it was thought to be in the interest of the State. Doubtless the purpose of its attempted creation was to shorten procedure by inducing a criminal to forego a fundamental right and, by swift admission of guilt, incidentally to mitigate his penalty but essentially to hasten justice. In practice, such a course is convenient. We are not dealing with policy, expediency or convenience as viewed by the Legislature but with public fundamental rights fixed by the Constitution. . . . Section 222 of our Code seeks to and does weaken the force of our Constitution and, for that reason, it is void." [7]

The Court then considered whether, in any event, with or without a statute, such a basic constitutional right may be waived, even by a defendant. The Court answered in the negative:

Waiver is not permitted where a question of jurisdiction or fundamental rights is involved and public injury would result. A privilege, merely personal, may be waived; a public fundamental right, the exercise of which is requisite to jurisdiction to try, condemn and punish, is binding upon the individual and cannot be disregarded by him. . . . In the most solemn and absolute language the Constitution dictates the only method by which one can be held to answer for murder, burglary, arson or any other infamous crime. Without the prescribed action by a grand jury, all our other tribunals are powerless to proceed. Such action is the foundation of jurisdiction.[8]

The trial of Battista was, therefore, no trial at all for that court had been without jurisdiction to try or condemn him. And Battista for this reason could not plead double jeopardy to a subsequent indictment and trial.

The grand jury may be defined in terms of New York's Code of Criminal Procedure: "a body of persons, returned at stated periods from the citizens of the county, before a court of competent jurisdiction, and chosen by lot, and sworn to inquire of crimes committed or triable in the county." This jury is drawn by lot from lists prepared by jury commissioners; in fact, in most states grand and petit jurors are selected from the same list. The grand jury is always associated with a court and is in operation only during the term of the court. In general, in New York, a grand jury must be drawn for the following courts: the Supreme Court, the county court when specially ordered by the court or the board of supervisors, and for an extraordinary term of the Supreme Court when required. It consists of not more than twenty-three persons and not less than sixteen, and sixteen must be on hand to transact any business.

Upon being impaneled and sworn, the grand jury must be charged by the court. In doing so, the court must read to the jury or give to each juror a copy of the pertinent sections of the Code and instruct them as to the nature of their duties. You could do no better than to read Henry Fielding's charge to the grand jury for the City of Westminster in 1749. It is often forgotten that Fielding, the author of *Tom Jones, Joseph Andrews,* and *Amelia,* was also a magistrate who played a role in the reform of the English criminal law and the establishment of a police force in London. "The business of a grand jury," he said, "is only to attend to the evidence for the king; and if on that evidence there shall appear a probable cause for the accusation, they are to find the true bill, without listening to any circumstances of defense, or to any matter of law." Today, we are not concerned with the evidence for the king but with the evidence presented by the prosecuting attorney. The grand jury is not bound to hear evidence for the defendant, but it may order the production of explanatory evidence and under certain circumstances the defendant himself may appear in his own behalf. The deliberations of the grand jury are secret. At least twelve members of the jury must concur in the belief that the evidence presented to them is sufficient to lead a trial jury to find the person accused, guilty. The accusation of the grand jury is called an indictment, a bill of indictment, or "a true bill."

The truth is that the use of the grand jury is declining. With insignificant exceptions, the grand jury was abolished in England in 1933.[9] In our own country, the grand jury system has been looked upon as inflexible and overly formal. At an earlier time, the grand jury came to serve as a bulwark against royal despotism, but a condition of executive tyranny no longer exists and the courts are not tools of presidents or governors. Furthermore, the grand jury is considered as unnecessary, particularly in England, where the preliminary examination is considered sufficient. In New York, there is a preliminary examination, a necessary examination by the district attorney, to satisfy himself that he has a case to present to the grand jury, and then the grand jury examination. If a true bill is found, there is another examination before the petit jury.

The Information

In the Battista case, objection was made to the use of the "information." This is another form of accusation, only it is an accusation made by the district attorney and filed with a court of competent jurisdiction. It, too, is of ancient origin, being almost as old as the indictment; as Blackstone puts it, "as antient as the common law itself." "As the king," he said,

> was bound to prosecute, or at least to lend the sanction of his name to a prosecutor, whenever a grand jury informed him upon their oaths that there was sufficient ground for instituting a criminal suit; so, when these his immediate officers were otherwise sufficiently assured that a man had committed a gross misdemeanor, either personally against the king or his government, or against the public peace and good order, they were at liberty, without waiting for any farther intelligence, to convey that information to the court of king's bench by a suggestion on record, and to carry on the prosecution in his majesty's name. But these informations . . . are confined by the constitutional law to mere misdemeanors only. . . .[10]

Today, the use of the information is not limited to misdemeanors. The information is used in almost every case in England; in many of our states the defendant may waive indictment by grand jury; in some of the Canadian provinces, the grand jury does not exist. It is true that the grand jury is used less and less. There are those, however, who look upon its decline with dismay. Professor Holdsworth, an eminent English historian of the law, has written, "Ever since 1681, when the ignoramus[11] of a grand jury saved Lord Shaftesbury from a trial for treason, it is clear that the grand jury is capable of being a real safeguard for the liberties of the subject. These liberties need safeguards even more today than they did in 1681, because bureaucrats of Whitehall who dominate the Cabinet which in turn dominates the House of Commons have established a more effectual and a more oppressive tyranny than the Stuarts ever succeeded in establishing. We cannot in these days afford to lose one of our few remaining securities for freedom of speech and action." [12] This was written in 1933 in protest against the bill to abolish the grand jury but it was ineffectual, and largely on grounds of economy this ancient institution expired from the face of England.

It has been said that the information is as old a device as the indictment, both having originated in the twelfth century. Apparently, one mode of accusation or the other was used in connection with both greater and lesser crimes, but by the sixteenth century, in England, the indictment came to be the only mode of accusation in cases of felony. This practice developed later in the American colonies. Certainly, by the middle of the eighteenth century, the grand jury was used exclusively in felony accusations.

After a person is indicted by the grand jury or an information is brought against him by the district attorney, he is arraigned; that is, he is brought before a magistrate and the charges as set forth in the indictment or information are read to him and he is asked "How do you plead? Guilty or not guilty?" In fact, in New York there are three pleas to an indictment: guilty, not guilty, and former judgment. This last means that he has already been convicted or acquitted of the crime charged. A person may not be tried twice for the same offense.

The Insanity Plea

A defendant may plead not guilty because of insanity. This is only reasonable and has long been recognized. As Justice Tracy said in 1724: "If he [the defendant] was under the visitation of God, and could not distinguish between good and evil, and did not know what he did, though he committed the greatest offence, yet he could not be guilty of any offence against any law whatsoever; for guilt arises from the mind, and the wicked will and intention of the man. If a man be deprived of his reason, and consequently of his intention, he cannot be guilty. . . ." [13] To be deprived of his reason a man had to be "totally deprived of his understanding and memory"; he must "not know what he is doing, no more than an infant, than a brute, or a wild beast." [14]

By 1760, the good and evil test was abandoned in favor of "right and wrong," and no more was heard of the "wild beast" test. [15]

"Wild beasts," however, was not an inappropriate term for the "lunatics" of the eighteenth century. Most of them were literally "mad men," and committed to St. Mary of Bethlehem, a priory founded in 1247 and given to the corporation of London in 1547 as a royal foundation for lunatics. Bethlehem was contracted to Bedlam, a term with which we are all familiar. "In some few gaols," said John Howard in 1777, "are confined idiots and *Lunatics*. These serve for sport to idle visitants at assizes, and other times of general resort. Many of the bridewells are crowded and offensive, because the rooms which were designed for prisoners are occupied by the insane. Where these are not kept separate, they disturb and terrify other prisoners." [16]

In the eighteenth century, insanity must have been obvious to a jury, so limited and so extreme had the symptoms to be, so superficial the knowledge of mental disturbance. Of course, our knowledge of insanity and its treatment has increased tremendously, and if we are more certain about insanity we are less certain about normalcy, if there is such a thing. And to leave the matter of the sanity or insanity of a defendant to a jury is the height of absurdity. A little less absurd is the battle between psychiatrists employed by the state and by the defense. Furthermore, the legal rules for the determination of insanity from a scientific point of view are outmoded, outdated, outworn, but, unfortunately, not outcast.

For the "right and wrong" test is still with us. It is still the test of 1760 except that it has undergone certain refinements. In 1843 Daniel McNaughton—variously spelled M'Naughten, M'Naghten, McNaughten, Macnaughton, Macnaghten, and in the original Gaelic, Mhicneachdain—nursing a grievance against Sir Robert Peel, shot and killed Sir Robert's secretary, one Edward Drummond, mistaking him for the minister. Charged with murder, McNaughton's defense was to plead not guilty because of insanity. The medical testimony that the defendant was insane was strong and definite; and the jury, upon instructions from Lord Chief Justice Tindal, brought in a verdict of "not guilty by reason of insanity," and the defendant was placed in an institution. The verdict was widely discussed and apparently there was an idea that McNaughton should have been hanged. Debate in the House of Lords led to the presentation of five questions, not to the doctors, but to the fifteen High Court judges. Their replies constitute what have come to be called "the McNaughton Rules."

Among the original five questions were these:

> Question two: "What are the proper questions to be submitted to the jury where a person alleged to be afflicted with insane delusion respecting one or more particular subjects or persons, is charged with the commission of a crime (murder, for example), and insanity is set up as a defense?"
>
> Question three: "In what terms ought the question to be left to the jury as to the prisoner's state of mind, at the time when the act was committed?" [17]

These two questions were answered together. The judges' opinion was "that the jury ought to be told in all cases that every man is to be presumed to be sane, and to possess a sufficient degree of reason to be responsible for his crimes, until the contrary be proved to their satisfaction; and that to establish a defence on the ground of insanity it must be clearly proved that, at the time of committing the act, the accused was labouring under such a defect of reason, from disease of the mind, as not to know the nature and quality of the act he was doing, or, if he did know it, that he did not know he was doing what was wrong." [18]

The Rules were announced in 1843 long before "psychiatry" became a household word. Even so, the High Court judges established a non-scientific test of insanity which a jury of twelve good and true men of varied intelligence and widely differing backgrounds were to apply after hearing medical evidence from both sides.

Clarence Darrow in the Leopold-Loeb case pleaded the defendants guilty; that is, the only question before the court was the punishment, death or life imprisonment, and Darrow pleading for the latter argued the mental state of the boys at the time of the murder. District Attorney Crowe argued that the boys were sane and deserved to hang. Psychiatrists were employed by both sides and these experts apparently were of little help to Judge Caverly. "The court," he said, "is willing to recognize that the careful analysis made of the life history of the defendants and of their present mental, emotional and ethical condition has been of extreme interest and is a valuable contribution to criminology." [19] In deciding to sentence the defendants to life imprisonment, however, he said, "the court is moved chiefly by the consideration of the age of the defendants. This determination appears to be in accordance with the progress of criminal law all over the world and with the dictates of enlightened humanity." [20] This suggests that the pro and con evidence presented by the alienists for the contending parties meant next to nothing to the judge; if true, how much less would such evidence have meant to a jury? In fact, a jury, drawn from all walks of life, should not have to decide on the sanity or insanity of anybody. A jury is not qualified to do so.

At any rate, the "right-wrong" test is used in a majority of American jurisdictions. In some jurisdictions, there has been added the "irresistible impulse" test. For example, in *Smith v. United States* the Court of Appeals of the District of Columbia declared that "The accepted rule . . . is that the accused must be capable, not only of distinguishing between right and wrong, but that he was not impelled to do the act by an irresistible impulse, which means before it will justify a verdict of acquittal that his reasoning powers were so far dethroned by his diseased mental condition as to deprive him of the will power to resist the insane impulse to perpetrate the deed, though knowing it to be wrong." [21]

A real advance over the right-wrong test came in 1954 in *Durham v. United States.*[22] In 1945, Monte Durham was discharged from the Navy after a psychiatric examination revealed a "profound personality disorder" which rendered him "unfit for naval service." In 1947, he was convicted of violating the National Motor Theft Act and was placed on probation. He attempted to commit suicide and was committed to St. Elizabeth's Hospital; after two months he was discharged. In 1948, following a conviction for passing bad checks, his probation was revoked and he began service of his Motor Theft sentence. In jail his behavior was such that a lunacy inquiry was instituted; he was found to be of unsound mind. He was sent back to St. Elizabeth's where he was diagnosed as suffering from "psychosis with psychopathic personality." After fifteen months he was discharged as "recovered" and returned to jail to finish out his sentence. He was conditionally released and in short order violated one of the conditions by leaving the District. Upon learning that a warrant was out for his arrest he fled, obtaining money by passing bad checks. He was finally picked up, returned to the District, referred to a lunacy commission and found to be of unsound mind once again. Readmitted to St. Elizabeth's in February, 1951, he was diagnosed "without mental disorder, psychopathic personality." For the third time, he was discharged in May, 1951. On July 13, 1951, he was arrested for housebreaking.

At the trial in the District Court the defense was that Durham "was of unsound mind on July 13, 1951." The court rejected this defense: "I don't think it has been established that the defendant was of unsound mind as of July 13, 1951, in the sense that he didn't know the difference between right and wrong or that even if he did, he was subject to an irresistible impulse by reason of the derangement of mind. . . . There is no testimony concerning the mental state of the defendant as of July 13, 1951, and therefore the usual presumption of sanity governs." [23] Durham was convicted.

Appeal was made to the United States Court of Appeals, District of Columbia Circuit, to reverse the conviction on two grounds, the second of which we shall consider here, namely, "because existing tests of criminal responsibility are obsolete and should be superseded." The demand for a new, more reasonable and more scientific test has behind it, said Judge Bazelon, "nearly a century of agitation for reform."

In a magnificent opinion, Judge Bazelon reviews the history of the right-wrong test, presenting the views of the scientists and medical men, and the findings of various commissions. He quotes Isaac Ray, one of the founders of the American Psychiatric Association, who called "knowledge of right and wrong a 'fallacious' test of criminal responsibility." [24] He cites Judge Cardozo's strictures against the test: "Every one concedes that the present [legal] definition of insanity has little relation to the truths of mental life." [25] He cites the Report of the Royal Commission on Capital Punishment [1949-1953]: the doctors have contended that the M'Naghten test "is based on an entirely obsolete and misleading conception of the nature of insanity. . . ." [26] He quotes from *Holloway v. United States,* decided in 1945, "The modern science of psychology . . . does not conceive that there is a separate little man in the top of one's head called reason whose function it is to guide another unruly little man called instinct, emotion, or impulse in the way he should go." [27]

The court concluded that "as an exclusive criterion the right-wrong test is inadequate in that (a) it does not take sufficient account of psychic realities and scientific knowledge, and (b) it is based upon one symptom and so cannot validly be applied in all circumstances." The court also found the "irresistible impulse" test wanting "in that it gives no recognition to mental illness characterized by brooding and reflection and so relegates acts caused by such illness to the application of the inadequate right-wrong test."

The court adopted a broader test. Following the lead of the New Hampshire court in *State v. Pike*, decided in 1870, the Court of Appeals declared the rule to be "that an accused is not criminally responsible if his unlawful act was the product of mental disease or mental defect." [28]

The Court of Appeals reversed the conviction of Monte Durham and ordered a new trial in which, not the right-wrong test, but the new test, was to be applied.

This new test, however, has not met with unqualified approval. The psychiatrists approve as was to be expected; the judges, holding themselves to be bound, in the words of Cardozo, "by the shackles of a statute," generally do not. In fact, the new test up to 1961 "has been rejected in every state except New Hampshire, whence it came, and in every other federal jurisdiction in which it has been urged, save perhaps the Virgin Islands." [29]

The Selection of the Jury

To serve on a jury in New York one must be a citizen of the United States and a resident of the county; be twenty-one years of age and less than seventy; be the owner of real or personal property of the value of $250; be in the possession of one's natural faculties and not infirm or decrepit; he or she must never have been convicted of a felony or of a misdemeanor involving moral turpitude; and be of sound mind and good character, of approved integrity, sound judgment, and be able to read and write the English language understandably. Those men and women who cannot meet the requirements are disqualified.

Specifically disqualified by law are Federal, state, city, county, town, and village officials; a member of the Communist Party or of any party or organization which "advocates, advises, or teaches the duty, necessity, desirability, or propriety of overthrowing or destroying the government of the United States" or of any state "by force or violence."

A large number of persons qualified to serve as jurors may claim exemption from service if called upon to serve. The exemptions in the various states differ so widely as to defy classification. In New York, the following may claim exemption by law: clergymen; physicians, surgeons, dentists, pharmacists, embalmers, optometrists; lawyers; soldiers, sailors,

National Guardsmen, firemen, policemen; captains, pilots, engineers or other officers of vessels "making regular trips"; women; editors, editorial writers, reporters, and copyreaders. Due to state laws governing the qualifications and exemptions of jurors, "Millions of persons," Judge Knox has said, "possessing the best and most intelligent brains in all the land, are relieved, by law, of the necessity of lending aid to the courts in their search for justice." [30]

Possibly, all the exemptions specified in the preceding paragraph, except for Federal and state officials, members of the armed forces, and those who have been convicted of crime, should be abolished. Having been called, a prospective juror might reasonably plead that he was the proprietor of a one-man business "to whom jury duty would mean ruination"; or that he was the only physician or surgeon serving a rural area of 900 square miles, or the only pharmacist or embalmer. In such cases, the judge would excuse them; but why a clergyman, or a pharmacist, or an embalmer, or an optometrist, or an editor, or a reporter, should be exempt just because of his vocation is not clear. One cannot understand their being automatically excused.

The list of prospective jurors is made up from assessment rolls by commissioners of jurors. The commissioner in each county determines the competence, qualifications, eligibility, and liability of individuals for jury duty. The commissioner of jurors furnishes the appropriate officers with a list of the names of qualified jurors. The men so named are called *veniremen* and it is from this group that trial jurors are chosen.

The choosing of twelve jurors for a particular trial is called the *voir dire*. Since an attorney, in the long run, appeals to the jury for a favorable verdict, it is important that he be very careful in the selection of a jury. The law allows the attorney to protest the seating of any prospective juror in this way: The attorney may challenge the venireman *for cause,* the number of such challenges being unlimited; or he may exercise a *peremptory challenge,* where no cause need be stated.

Challenge for cause is either *general* or *particular.* If a prospective juror has been convicted of a felony or fails to meet the qualifications for jurors as set forth in the Judiciary Law, the challenge would be general. A particular challenge, on the other hand, may arise from the juror's revealing of an *implied bias,* as, for example, a blood relationship to either the defendant or the person alleged to be injured by the crime charged, or previous service on the grand jury which found the indictment, or previous service on a trial jury which tried another person for the crimes charged in the indictment, or previous service as a juror in a civil action brought against the defendant for the act charged as a crime, or, in capital cases, "the entertaining of such conscientious opinion as would preclude his finding the defendant guilty." A particular challenge is also raised if the prospective juror's state of mind in regard to the particular case indicates that he "cannot try the issue impartially and without prejudice to the substantial rights of the party challenging." In this case he will be excused for *actual bias*.

The law provides, however, that "the previous expression or formation of an opinion or impression in reference to the guilt or innocence of the defendant, or a present opinion or impression in reference thereto, is not a sufficient ground of challenge for actual bias, to any person otherwise legally qualified, if he declare on oath, that he believes that such opinion or impression will not influence his verdict, and that he can render an impartial verdict according to the evidence, and the court is satisfied, that he does not entertain such a present opinion or impression as would influence his verdict." [31] In the case of *People v. Casey*,[32] the defendant was charged with murder in the first degree, but a hung jury resulted. The trial was discussed in the newspapers and in the community and there was adverse criticism of one or more members of the jury. At the second trial, which began twenty-eight days after the commencement of the first trial, the defendant was found guilty. Appeal was made to the Court of Appeals, which reversed the judgment of the trial court and ordered a new trial.

The ground for the appeal was that at the second trial the defendant challenged several prospective jurors for actual bias, which challenges were improperly overruled by the court, contrary to the requirement of the Code of Criminal Procedure, Section 376, which has been quoted above.

One juror upon his examination testified that he had heard and read about the case; that in conversation with his neighbors he had expressed an opinion as to the guilt or innocence of the defendant and that he had said that he thought that the defendant was guilty. He was asked by the district attorney: "Notwithstanding that you have heard or read of it, or may have formed or expressed an opinion or impression, can you sit as a juror, if selected, and determine this case upon the evidence as you shall hear it from the witnesses?" And he answered, "Well, I suppose I could." [33] The court ruled that he was a good juror.

Another juror admitted that he had formed a distinctive impression as to the defendant's guilt or innocence; that he still had that impression and that it would require evidence to remove it; that, if accepted as a juror, he would go into the jury box with a prejudice in his mind. He was asked: "Would that definite, distinct impression that you have in your mind, would it shape or shadow your verdict at all?" His reply was, "Well, I would go according to the evidence, I think." There were further questions: "Apart from the evidence as it might be disclosed to you on the trial, would this previously formed impression or prejudice arising from your newspaper reading, aid at all in shaping and forming your verdict?" and he answered, "Well, I don't know that it would." He was pressed for a more definite answer: "Are you sure that it would not?" and his answer was, "No, sir; I am not sure about that." Again he was asked, "And the impression that you had, after thinking this matter all over, after reading the newspaper articles, and after the conversation that you had had with your neighbors, was a distinct impression—is with you yet—and it would go with you into the jury box, and you think might change, shade or shadow the verdict which you would give on the evidence?" The answer to this question was, "Well, it might, but it hadn't ought to." "But you say that it might; you are not sure that you could divest your mind entirely of that prejudice?" to which he replied, "No, sir." [34] The court sustained the competency of this juror.

All told, there were five prospective jurors who failed to declare that they could render an impartial verdict according to the evidence.

Speaking for a unanimous court, Judge Earl declared that "a person who has formed or expressed an opinion or impression in reference to the guilt or innocence of the defendant is still, as formerly, disqualified to sit as a juror, unless three things shall occur: (1) He must declare on oath that he believes that such opinion or impression will not influence his verdict; (2) he must also declare on oath that he believes he can render an impartial verdict according to the evidence; and (3) the court must be satisfied that he does not entertain such a present opinion or impression as would influence his verdict. Unless these three things concur the person must now, as before, be excluded from the jury box." [35]

It was argued by the prosecution, however, that the judgment of the lower court should not be disturbed since none of the persons were in fact members of the trial jury. They were excluded from the jury by the use of peremptory challenges.

Unlike challenge for cause, a peremptory challenge allows that no reason be given for excluding a person from the jury. The number of these challenges is limited to thirty, plus three allowed for each alternate juror, if the crime charged be punishable with death. If the crime is punishable by imprisonment from ten years to life, twenty peremptory challenges are allowed for the regular jury and two for each alternate juror; in all other criminal cases, five peremptory challenges are allowed for the regular jury and one for each alternate.

You may wonder why, in the case of *People v. Casey,* the appellate court reversed the judgment of the trial court when the jurors objected to by the defense did not serve on the jury anyway. In this particular case, the defendant had exhausted all the peremptory challenges allowed him by law. "He was, therefore," said Judge Earl, "by the erroneous rulings of the trial judge . . . obliged to use his peremptory challenges, and was thus deprived of the right and power to use other peremptory challenges in case he desired to." [36] The defendant, obliged to exhaust his peremptory challenges because the court failed to rule correctly when prospective jurors were challenged for cause, was harmed, his rights were abridged, and he had good cause to complain. "The defendant," said Judge Earl, "has the right to have the conscience and mind of the juror tested by a declaration under oath, not simply that he will be governed by the evidence, but by declarations which show that he believes he is in such a state of mind, so free from bias and prejudice, that he can weigh the evidence impartially, uninfluenced by any opinion or impression which he has formed. . . . Indifferency is one of the common-law characteristics of a jury, and it is inviolably secured by the constitutional guaranty of jury trial. A party put upon trial for a crime has a constitutional right by challenge, or in some other mode, to protect himself against a biased jury." [37]

Alternate Jurors

In the foregoing, I have used the term "alternate juror." In 1933, the legislature of New York passed a law which provided that, "Whenever, in the opinion of a judge of a court of criminal jurisdiction about to try with a jury a defendant against whom has been filed any indictment or information for a felony or for a misdemeanor, that it is advisable so to do, the court may cause an entry to that effect to be made in the minutes of the court, and thereupon, immediately after the jury is impaneled and sworn, the court may direct the calling of one or two additional jurors, in its discretion, to be known as 'alternate jurors.' " [38] These alternate jurors must be drawn from the same source as the regular jurors and in the same manner; they must have the same qualifications and are subject to the same examination and challenge. The alternates are seated with the regular jurors, take the same oath, and must attend the trial at all times. If the regular jurors are ordered by the court to be kept in the custody of the sheriff during the trial, the alternate jurors shall also be kept in confinement with the other jurors.

The reason for using alternate jurors is implicitly stated in the law. If, before the final submission of the case to the jury, a regular juror dies or becomes ill, or for any other reason he is unable to perform his duties, the court may order him discharged, and draw the name of one of the alternates who then takes the place of the discharged juror. When the case is given to the jury only the twelve withdraw, and the alternates are discharged.

In the case of *People v. Mitchell* [39] this law was challenged as violative of the constitutional right of a defendant to trial by jury. It was argued that the defendant had been tried by a jury of fourteen men. The Court of Appeals, in sustaining a conviction of murder in the first degree, denied this. Judge O'Brien speaking for the court declared that "Only twelve participated in the rendition of the verdict and they are the same twelve originally selected for the performance of that service. Each heard all the evidence and at no time during the course of the trial did any one of them cease to function as a juror." [40]

The use of alternate jurors, said Judge O'Brien, is "not only convenient but just both to the public and to the defendant," [41] and in no way conflicts with the constitutional right to trial by jury.

After the jury has been selected, the scene is set for a resolution of the conflict. In a criminal case the district attorney makes an opening address or statement (in a civil suit the plaintiff's attorney does this) in which he tells the jury the circumstances of the conflict, what he intends to prove, and specifies the verdict for which he is asking if the defendant has been charged with crime, or the amount of damages demanded if it is a civil suit. The opening addresses of both the plaintiff's attorney and that of the defendant (the latter may come immediately after the plaintiff's opening or he may reserve his opening until he presents his own witnesses) are usually not too long, nor too detailed. In general, the opening address must be sufficient to give the jurors an over-all view of the conflict. With such a resumé, the jurors are hopefully prepared to understand the testimony of the individual witnesses in relation to the whole as either the plaintiff's attorney or the defendant's attorney sees it. To put it another way, the attorney presents in outline a mosaic in which the jurors may more readily place the chips of evidence as they are given by the witnesses.

Direct and Cross-Examination

Following his opening address, the plaintiff's attorney calls his first witness, and examines him. This is called "direct examination." Whenever an attorney is examining his own witnesses—that is, the witnesses for his side—the examination is "direct." It is an examination of a friendly witness by a friendly attorney.

Irving Goldstein holds that "The primary object in the trial of a case should be *proving the attorney's case,* rather than disproving his opponent's case." In his view, "The most important part of the trial is the direct examination," which should be sufficiently comprehensive

(1) To prove all elements necessary to merit a favorable verdict.
(2) To present a picture of the cause of action with clarity, undertanding and interest.
(3) To present the witnesses to the greatest advantage so as to secure acceptance of their stories as true by court and jury.
(4) To present this story and picture by proper questioning according to the rules of evidence.
(5) To present all documentary evidence to prove and to corroborate the contentions of the trial lawyer.[42]

When the plaintiff's attorney completes the direct examination of his first witness—or, for that matter, of any of his witnesses—he says to the opposing counsel, "Your witness" or "Cross-examine" or "You may cross-examine." At this point the witness comes face to face with a theoretically "unfriendly" attorney.

The witnesses for the prosecution or the plaintiff, under the guidance of the district attorney or the plaintiff's attorney, tell a straightforward story; they recount fact after fact which support the story; and altogether they spin a web that might well convince a jury of its logic, intactness, and integrity. The business of opposing counsel in cross-examination is to test that story, question the facts, and, if possible, free the defendant from the web so carefully woven by the plaintiff.

Testimony which has not been subject to cross-examination is deemed to be unreliable. The witness might be prejudiced, he might have been mistaken, or he might even have perjured himself. Cross-examination might show the witness up for one or all of these defects in his testimony; cross-examination might, as well, substantiate his testimony. One or the other, cross-examination provides the conditions for "facts" to be established and the lawsuit or prosecution brought to an end.

Cross-examination is so vital and so important in ascertaining the facts of a controversy, that if a witness were to die immediately after his direct examination, the jury would be instructed to disregard his testimony altogether, solely because the facts elicited from him could not be tried, tested, proved or disproved, by cross-examination.

The right to cross-examine is sometimes thought to be the right to probe into anything and everything in a witness's life in order to discredit him; this is not true. There are limits to cross-examination. In general, "the scope of cross-examination is limited to matters inquired of on the direct examination . . ."; [43] further, "a witness may not be cross-examined as to facts collateral or immaterial to the issues unless such facts have been brought out on direct examination." [44] Whatever will contribute to explain, modify, or discredit the testimony on direct examination is allowable. Furthermore, considerable discretion resides in the court. Very often, a direct examination will elicit no more than a partial explanation from the witness. The driver of a car involved in an accident might give a picture that portrays him as an innocent victim; he might be asked, on cross-examination, whether he had been drinking before the accident occurred, although the matter of drinking had not been brought up on the direct examination. Thus, on cross-examination it is "always permissible to inquire into the details of the events testified to in chief by a witness and to develop and unfold the whole transaction about which he has only been partially interrogated." [45]

Often the attorney, in cross-examination of a witness, produces from him statements that create an impression favorable to his own client. If the impression is misleading, it may lodge in the minds of the jurors and become ineradicable unless corrected; to correct it, the opposing attorney may readdress additional questions to his own witness. This is called the *redirect*. For example, a professor of science is charged with the murder of his wife, whom he adores, but who is suffering from incurable cancer. She is in great pain, and as the pain becomes less and less subject to drugs, she begs her husband to end her life. He refuses to do this for several months; but, at last, in desperation he places some poison crystals on his wife's bed table and leaves the room. In half an hour he returns to find his wife dead. The professor at once informs the police; he is arrested and charged with murder in the first degree, for all of the elements of that degree of murder are present: premeditation, deliberation, and intent.

The district attorney's first witness was the attending physician. From him he elicited the results of his examination of the body. Among other things, the physician was asked to state the cause of death. The answer was potassium cyanide. He was asked on what he based his statement: what quantity of cyanide crystals would be required to cause certain death, and how much did he find in the stomach of the deceased?

The defense attorney, in cross-examination, attempted by his questions and the answers thereto to impress the jury with the nearness of the impending death from cancer. "Would you say that death from cancer was imminent in the near future?" "Yes." "In a matter of six months?" "Possibly." "And possibly less than that?" "Yes." "In fact, you can't precisely say how soon death from cancer might have resulted, isn't that correct?" "That is correct." When the defense attorney relinquished the witness, the prosecutor asked the witness: "Doctor, in your opinion, did death result from cancer?" And the answer was, "No."

Goldstein says that as the attorney "views the wreckage which remains after his opponent has completed his cross-examination of the most important witness in the case, it is only the trial lawyer's most painstakingly complete and thorough preparation of the facts that will make it possible for him to restore the witness in the confidence of the court and jury, especially in those instances where the opponent's telling cross-examination has apparently resulted in the witness' making so-called damaging admissions and contradictions. Suspicion has been cast upon his story by innuendo and insinuation. The beautifully interesting and connected story told by the witness on direct examination has all been disarranged. All connecting links apparently have been scattered to the four winds. Hardly anything seems to remain that would warrant the jury in giving any credence to the story told by the witness." [46] The purpose of redirect examination, says Goldstein, "is to clarify and explain all apparent contradictions, fallacies and improbabilities brought out on cross-examination." [47]

Objection and Exception

In the course of the examination of witnesses you will note, if you visit a court and watch the participants of a trial in action, that opposing counsel will arise upon occasion and object to a question put to the witness: "I object on the ground that it is a leading question"; "I object because the question suggests the answer"; "I object on the ground of hearsay"; "I object on the ground that the evidence is incompetent, irrelevant and immaterial"; "Objection on the ground that the question exceeds the scope of the evidence elicited on direct examination." These are a few examples of the *objection,* the purpose of which is to keep the proceedings, as the objecting attorney sees it, free of prejudice, error, immateriality, or any evidence in fact which is deemed by him to be illegal or improper. And the objection must be made at the time the question is asked. An attorney cannot interpose an objection the day after the question is asked; it must be done at once.

When an objection is made it is then the business of the judge to overrule or to sustain the objection. He must decide whether the question will elicit evidence which is inadmissible; if so, he will *sustain* the objection. If, on the other hand, he decides that the question and the testimony sought are legitimate and proper, he will *overrule* the objection. It is a matter of law, not of fact, which only the judge may decide. But it is not required that the judge shall take the initiative with regard to dubious evidence; this is the responsibility of the attorney.

Now, if an attorney objects to the introduction of certain evidence and the judge rules against him, he will more than likely *except* to the ruling. This is spoken of as an *exception* and it is upon these exceptions that the higher courts are asked to review the case.

The following examination illustrates the use of the objection and the exception.

Charles Shepard, a United States Army doctor, was indicted for the murder of his wife. He was tried, found guilty, and sentenced to life imprisonment.

On May 20, 1929, Mrs. Shepard was found in a state of utter collapse. A nurse, Clara Brown, was called in to attend her. Two days later, Mrs. Shepard was much improved and it was the general expectation that she would recover. On June 15th, Mrs. Shepard died of bichloride of mercury poisoning.

At the trial, Nurse Brown testified that on May 22nd, Mrs. Shepard had said that she was not going to get well, that she was going to die.

Q. At the time she told you . . . that she was going to die, did you, at that time and in that connection, have a conversation with her in reference to her condition?
A. Yes.
Q. What was it?
Mr. Kagey (defense attorney). We object to that as hearsay, not made in the presence of the defendant, incompetent, irrelevant and immaterial.
The Court. You may answer.
Mr. Kagey. We except . . . .
A. She asked me if I would do her a favor. I consented. Then she told

me to go to Major Shepard's room and in his closet, get a quart whiskey bottle off the shelf . . . .

Q. Go ahead and state what she said to you.

A. She asked me to smell the contents. I did so. She then asked me if it smelled peculiar. I told her I did not know. She asked me how much was in the bottle. I noticed there was not more than a tablespoonful . . . and told her. . . . She asked if that was enough to test for poison. I told her I did not know.

Q. Now, go ahead and state what, if anything, she said as to how she took sick, and what she did.

Mr. Kagey. We object to this as incompetent, irrelevant and immaterial, hearsay . . . .

The Court. She may answer.

Mr. Kagey. We except.

A. She stated that this was the bottle from which she drank just before collapsing on . . . May 20.

Q. What did she say as to the taste of it the night she took sick, the 20th?

Mr. Kagey. Object to this as leading.

Q. What, if anything?

Mr. Kagey. Objected to for the further reason that it is hearsay.

The Court. You may answer.

Mr. Kagey. Except.

A. It was altogether different.

Q. What did she say? Give her words.

A. It was not good.

Q. Did she say anything about how it tasted?

Mr. Kagey. Same objection.

The Court. You may answer.

Mr. Kagey. Except.

A. She said that she was being poisoned.

Q. What did she say? Give her words.

Mr. Kagey. All right; we object to this, also, as incompetent, irrelevant and immaterial, hearsay . . . .

The Court. You may answer.

A. She said "Dr. Shepard has poisoned me."[48]

This statement was admitted by the court as a "dying declaration," an exception to the rule against the admission of hearsay evidence. It might be helpful here to explain the significance of a "dying declaration" (e.g. ". . . as a 'dying declaration,' in other words a statement to be believed, in view of the speaker's realization of impending death, and consequent lack of motivation to lie.")

Dr. Shepard appealed to the Circuit Court of Appeals, which affirmed the judgment of the District Court. On appeal to the United States Supreme Court, both lower courts were reversed and a new trial ordered. Mr. Justice Cardozo in the opinion noted that "There was a timely challenge [by the defense attorney] of the ruling" by the trial judge that the statement, "Dr. Shepard has poisoned me," was admissible in evidence. Cardozo wrote:

Upon the hearing in this court, the Government finds its main prop in the position that what was said by Mrs. Shepard was admissible as a dying declaration. This is manifestly the theory upon which it was offered and received. The prop, however, is a broken reed. To make out a dying declaration the declarant must have spoken without hope of recovery and in the shadow of impending death. . . . Nothing in the condition of the patient on May 22 gives fair support to the conclusion that hope had then been lost. She may have thought she was going to die and have said so to her nurse, but this was consistent with hope, which could not have been put aside without more to quench it. Indeed, a fortnight later, she said to one of her physicians, though her condition was then grave, "You will get me well, won't you?" Fear or even belief that illness will end in death will not avail of itself to make a dying declaration. There must be "a settled hopeless expectation" . . . that death is near at hand, and what is said must have been spoken in the hush of its impending presence. . . . What was said by this patient was not spoken in that mood. . . . She spoke as one ill, giving voice to the beliefs and perhaps the conjectures of the moment. . . . She did not speak as one dying, announcing to the survivors a definitive conviction, a legacy of knowledge on which the world might act when she had gone.[49]

The doctor was granted a new trial.

Closing Address of Counsel

After the attorneys have completed the examination of the witnesses they then offer their summations or arguments to either the jury or the judge as the case may be. An attorney in summation usually begins with a compliment to the jury; he notes their patience and attention. He discusses the issue, the nature of the conflict, and, as dramatically as possible, he pictures to the jury just what happened. He has a theory as to the role his client played in the event and he reviews for the jury the evidence presented by the witnesses and which support the theory upon which he is operating. He reviews and refutes the contentions of his opponent. Finally, there is an appeal to the jury to bring in a verdict in favor of his client or, in a criminal trial, in favor of the prosecution or the defense. His main object is to win the approval of the jury for his side.

Judge's Charge to Jury

One thing now remains to be done before the issue of fact is placed in the hands of the jury and that is the judge's charge. The jury has to weigh the evidence and determine the facts; the judge instructs the jury as to the correct legal principles to apply to the facts in reaching a verdict.

The judge will instruct the jury that the burden of proof is upon the People or the State; that the defendant is to be presumed innocent until proven guilty; and that, if after consideration of all the evidence there remains a reasonable doubt as to the guilt of the defendant, he is entitled to an acquittal. A "reasonable doubt" is defined as a doubt that would cause a prudent and reasonable man to act or to pause or to hesitate to act in the determination of any of the affairs of life of the highest importance to himself. In a majority of states, in a criminal case, for the judge to omit in his charge that the defendant is presumed to be innocent until proven guilty is reversible error, which means that an appellate court is warranted in reversing the judgment of the trial court. It is error, too, when "reasonable doubt" is not properly defined.

The judge in most jurisdictions cannot comment upon the defendant's failure to take the stand in his own defense; some few states—Iowa, New Jersey, Vermont, California, Ohio, and Connecticut—do permit such comment.

In his charge, the judge must take care not "to decide the facts." He may comment upon the evidence in order to clarify the application of the law to the facts as the jury may find them, but no more. This attitude of detachment is quite unlike the practice of British courts. "By 1841," says Professor Glanville Williams, "it was recognized to be the right and duty of the judge to state what impression the evidence had produced on his mind, in order to prevent the jury being misled by worthless evidence." [50] Patrick Mahon was accused of the murder of his mistress. He pleaded "not guilty." In his summing up Mr. Justice Horace Avory had this to say:

> You can see the axe again, and judge whether, if that axe had been thrown by the woman, and struck him on the shoulder sufficiently hard to leave a bruise, and after it had struck him on the shoulder bounded off on to the door, it is possible to believe that that would break the handle. You can examine it for yourselves. Then he [Mahon] says: "Having done that she leaped across the room, clutching at my face. I did my best to keep her off. We struggled backwards and forwards. She was mad with anger, and was beginning to get the better of me." His Lordship paused. "You have seen the prisoner in the witness-box; you have seen his height and build. You know now that this woman was a woman five feet seven inches in height. Do you believe for a moment his story that she was beginning to get the better of him?" [51]

Such a statement in an American court would be deemed prejudice, undue influence upon the jury, an invasion of the province of the jury, and reversible error.

Do Juries Do What They Are Supposed to Do?

Juries do, in practice, perform the function that the law assigns to them. The jury hears the testimony of the witnesses, evaluates the evidence, determines the facts, applies to those facts the law as given by the judge, and reaches what is called a "general verdict." In a criminal case, after deliberation, the jury finds the accused "guilty" or "not guilty"; in a civil case, "We find for the plaintiff in the sum of $40,000," or "We find for the defendant." The jury does not have to explain the verdict; it merely states a conclusion.

What juries are supposed to do is a question easily answered. A more interesting and more important question is *how* in fact juries reach verdicts. Here, we enter upon a sea of speculation for, in truth, little is known of the *how* of the matter.

Jury trial was early introduced in the English colonies in America. In the early struggle with the mother country, the jury served as a bulwark against the arbitrary actions of colonial governors. Confidence in the jury was reflected in the postrevolutionary constitutions of the states and, later, in the Federal Constitution. Hamilton said that "The friends and adversaries of the plan of the convention, if they agree in nothing else, concur at least in the value they set upon the trial by jury." [52] The institution had served well as a defense against the oppression of kings, and Hamilton suggested that it would serve as well as a "barrier to the tyranny of popular magistrates in a popular government."

One could fill a five-foot shelf with deeply felt and sincere encomiums of trial by jury. One cannot question the profound role the institution has played in the lives of the American people; and yet, today, there is doubt as to its usefulness; there is more than a suggestion that trial by jury has passed its prime; that it is deficient as a mode of resolving conflicts fairly and honestly.

The late Judge Joseph N. Ulman of the Supreme Bench of Baltimore in his *A Judge Takes the Stand* held to a faith in trial by jury; and yet he was unwilling "to say that trial by jury, in its present form, is . . . the best way to try all kinds of cases." "I plead," he says, "for an open mind and a spirit of scientific investigation. If some types of disputes can be determined better by the use of substitutes for court trials rather than by court trials as we now conduct them, let us be ready and willing to take the next step, whatever it may be and wherever it may lead. The law must grow and it must change; that is true of all of life." [53]

More recently, Judge Frank has said: "It will not do . . . to make Fourth-of-July speeches about the glorious jury system, to conceal its grave defects, or merely to palliate them with superficial, cosmetic-like remedies. We need to have our public comprehend what the jury actually is like in order to arouse public interest to the point where steps will be taken to eradicate its most glaring deficiencies." [54] And considerable weight must be given the fact that the use of the jury has declined, not only in the United States but in Great Britain.

A few years ago, as part of a study of the jury, the University of Chicago Law School arranged for the secret tape-recordings of Federal jury deliberations in six civil cases in Wichita, Kansas. Microphones were concealed in the jury room with the consent of two Federal judges, the local United States Attorney, and in each case, by counsel for the parties. This study of the jury, endorsed by many distinguished legal scholars, was financed by the Ford Foundation. There was no intention of making public any of the material thus secured.

The research project was discovered, newspaper headlines followed,[55] and, on the whole, the project was condemned as un-American, violative of a sacred right, and an invasion of the jury's privacy. The Attorney-General of the United States denounced the whole proceeding, the Internal Security Subcommittee of the Committee on the Judiciary held hearings with a view to appropriate legislation "to protect the jury system of our country," and there was some talk of the impeachment of a Federal judge.

Reprinted in the Hearings of October 12, 1955, there was an editorial which, according to the Committee on the Judiciary, aptly summed up the situation: "A jury imperatively needs to carry on its deliberations in private. When it retires to consider the evidence and arguments in a case which has been argued before it, its members must be free from any outside pressure or fear of reprisal. They must be free also to discuss the case with full confidence that what they say will not go beyond the walls of the jury room. Any impairment of this privacy not only destroys the detachment with which they ought to deliberate but effectually deprives the litigants of their right to a fair trial. Uninhibited discussion becomes very difficult if there is fear of a concealed microphone." [56]

Thus it happens that by the Act of August 2, 1956, anyone who knowingly and willfully, by any means or device whatsoever, records, or attempts to record, the proceedings of any Federal grand or petit jury which is in the process of deliberating or voting "shall be fined not more than $1,000 or imprisoned not more than one year, or both." The Act goes further and imposes the same penalty upon anyone who "listens to or observes, or attempts to listen to or observe" such jury proceedings.[57]

One can hardly condemn the effort to find out something about the way juries work, since the preservation of human rights, even of life itself, depend frequently upon a jury's verdict.

We are still, therefore, dependent upon perhaps reliable, perhaps unreliable, sources, for our knowledge of how a jury reaches a verdict.

. Longenecker in his *Hints on the Trial of a Law Suit* has this to say:

"In talking to a man who had served for two weeks on juries, he stated that in one case the jury retired and the foreman made a speech something like this: 'Now boys, you know that there was lying on both sides. Which one did the most lying? The plaintiff is a poor man and the defendant is rich and can afford to pay the plaintiff something. Of course, the dog did not hurt the plaintiff much, but I think we ought to give him something, don't you?' There were several 'sures'; we thought the plaintiff might have to split with his lawyers, so we gave him a big verdict." [58]

In another case, the jurors explained the verdict as follows: "We couldn't make head or tail of the case, or follow all the messing around the lawyers did. None of us believed the witnesses on either side, anyway, so we made up our minds to disregard the evidence on both sides and decide the case on its merits." [59]

And Judge Rossman has reported that "Competent observers who have interviewed the jurors in scores of cases, declare that in many cases principal issues received no consideration from the jury." [60]

Judge Frank holds that juries, in either civil or criminal cases, have again and again arrived at a verdict by one of two or three methods: (1) in a civil case, each juror writes down the amount of money he wants to award the plaintiff; the total is added and the average taken as the verdict; (2) the jurors, by agreement, decide for one side or the other of a civil case by flipping a coin; and (3) the jurors decide by majority vote, after previous agreement to do so.[61]

This is hard to believe; and yet, where there is so much smoke there must be fire. The question, "Do juries do what they are supposed to do?" was answered in the affirmative. They do reach verdicts. But a second question, *"How* do juries reach verdicts?" was raised. The answers to this query are more or less wrapped in shadows, although judges and legal scholars have declared in no uncertain terms that juries adopt their own peculiar ways of reaching verdicts, all quite contrary to the theory of trial by jury. There is a third question to be considered: *Can* juries do what they are supposed to do? Can they hear the evidence, understand and evaluate it, comprehend the instructions of the judge, and apply those instructions to the facts and thus reach a verdict? The answer to this question is by no means clear.

The Determination of Facts

The determination of facts in a court is a problem in history. The historian, interested in who was responsible for the murder of the princes in the Tower, or the reasons for the rise and fall of the Athenian Empire, or why a mercantilist policy was injurious to the economic welfare of the American colonies, must go to the sources, which is another way of saying that he, like the lawyer, must gather his witnesses about him. The historian's witnesses are documents, official and unofficial, such as statutes, constitutions, treaties, census reports, trade reports, reports of legislative committees, contemporary letters, diaries, newspapers and periodicals, merely to mention a few. The historian is judge or jury, as the case may be. He examines these witnesses directly; he may, in a sense, cross-examine them. The letter or the diary or the newspaper account may be tested for credibility by comparison with other documents and by learning something of the political, economic, or social background of the author. He will ask of his witnesses such questions as, "How accurate an observer are you?" "Are you prejudiced?" "Do you tend to exaggerate?" "Are you to be believed?" In a word, the historian is interested in just how reliable his witnesses are.

Having secured what he deems to be the "best" evidence, the historian will then weave the "facts" together into an explanation, an interpretation; he makes out a case, and presents what may be called a summation. But a good historian will not say categorically, "Here is what happened," or "Here is the truth of the matter." He is more likely to say, "On the basis of the evidence I have found, and assuming the correctness of my interpretation, here is what I think happened."

History is a matter of probability, not of certitude.

The same is true of a court. The witnesses may be legal documents, letters, diaries, even guns, knives, and other instruments, all marked "exhibits"; but there are living witnesses as well, who testify as to what they know. The automobile accident, the robbery, or the understanding by the parties of the terms of a contract at the time of signing must be reconstructed in court. And though the event—the accident, the robbery, or the original understanding of a contract—occurred only a short time previously, the reconstruction can never exactly duplicate the original. On what is deemed the best evidence, tested by direct and cross-examination, a conclusion is reached; the judgment may be for the plaintiff, the verdict may be "guilty," but such conclusions are usually conclusions of probability, not of certainty.

The late Judge Frank in his stimulating volume, *Courts on Trial,* holds that the theory of how courts operate may be *very roughly* symbolized by the equation $R \times F = D$. The Decision, in short, is the product of the Rules times the Facts. Judge Frank declares that in a stable society the Rules can be fairly well known and understood but that "in our society . . . with the rapid changes brought about by modern life, many of the R's have become unstable." [62] For example, the modification, revision, or the overruling of some of the Supreme Court's interpretations of certain clauses of the Constitution after 1937 gave many a lawyer a feeling of uncertainty in advising his clients. "Those thinkers," continues Judge Frank, "perceiving the absence of rigidity in some rules, have assumed that the certainty or uncertainty of the D's in the $R \times F = D$ equation, stems principally from the certainty or uncertainty of the R's." [63] This assumption, Frank believes, "leads to a grave miscomprehension of court-house government," for however certain the rules may be, "the decisions remain at the mercy of the courts' fact-finding." [64]

In either a civil or a criminal case, neither judge, counsel, nor jury witnessed the event, and yet the jury must bring in a verdict either for the plaintiff or for the defendant. For the jury to reach a verdict, just what happened must be reconstructed piece by piece through testimony given by the plaintiff and the defendant, and by their witnesses, and in summation each attorney, using the evidence available to him, reconstructs a coherent picture most favorable to his client. However, a jury is usually presented with two stories, each supported by so-called "facts" presented by witnesses who are not, to say the least, infallible in their observational powers.

The witness plays so important a role in the final conclusion of a court that it is well to pause a moment and consider him. He is first of all a human being. He is within himself the victim of the adequacies and inadequacies, the strengths and weaknesses, the qualities, characteristics, and limitations of men and women generally.

On the stand, the witness is to relate his observations of an event. He must tell what he saw or heard, and even touched or smelled or tasted. He cannot, however, offer a subjective opinion unless he is an expert witness.

A witness's capacity to observe is subject to many pitfalls, one being sense perception. He may not have observed the event correctly. He may be far-sighted, near-sighted, or astigmatic. He may be color-blind. In addition, it is well known that an observer will see a larger object more clearly than a smaller one; that a more distinctive or more unusual object will be seen with more accuracy than a less distinctive or usual object; that in the observation of colors, the degree of illumination is significant; that a vertical line appears longer than a horizontal line of the same length; that an empty room appears smaller than one filled with furniture; that a vehicle moving towards one appears to be travelling at a slower rate than one moving at the same speed across one's line of vision; that sometimes we see men act as our preconceptions tell us they ought to act.

It is true, too, that the hearing capacities of people differ. Some people hear more acutely than others. Attention, interest, intensity of sound, and sickness may all affect our capacity to hear correctly.

Again, let us suppose that a witness's original observation was correct; his memory of that original observation may be faulty. Two witnesses may have observed the same event from the same point and yet the evidence they give in court may differ. It may appear that one of them is lying, but this is not necessarily true. The truth is that memory is not always reliable. Time may weaken or blur the memory of an event. Court dockets being crowded, the witness may not be able to testify to what he saw or heard for several years; and with the passage of time and the blurring of the event, imagination begins to intervene. Furthermore, our memories are not all alike. A witness may remember better what his sight told him than what his hearing told him. Also, his attentiveness at the time may determine the accuracy with which he remembers the event.

It is also possible for a witness, honestly but inadvertently, to mistake his recollection, and inaccurately report his story.

Courts are faced with a real problem in attempting to reconstruct an occurrence. The witnesses are human, they are subject to human frailty, and they sometimes know not what they say. For the "fact" as presented by a witness is not a "fact" but a recollection of a "fact," which is a very different thing. "A policeman will quite often be able to relate only what appeared in his notes, not by any means the least satisfactory kind of evidence. Seek to take him out of his framework, and to resee the events in his mind's eye, so some detail, not regarded at the moment but turning out to be important, can be recovered. In nine cases out of ten he cannot do it, though he honestly tries. His memory is of his notes, not of an observed happening." [65]

In addition to those honest witnesses who are, like most of us, subject to faulty observational powers, there are the biased witnesses and the out-and-out perjurers.

One might think that where the testimony of witnesses for both sides conflicts as to the essential points of a case, the jury would reach an impasse. Yet such conflict of testimony does not, as a matter of law, give rise to a reasonable doubt; nor does it require the court to discharge the defendant on the ground of insufficient evidence. The jury should attempt to reconcile such conflicting evidence as much as possible, since it is presumed that the witnesses are honest. If the testimony cannot be reconciled, the jury must then decide who is to be believed and who is not. And here, it is said, the jurors must depend upon their own common sense and powers of observation, their own sensitivity and experience in life. Does the witness answer questions put to him in a straightforward, honest way? Is he evasive? What kind of character is he? What is his reputation? Does he appear to be biased? Does he appear to be a person of integrity or not? The demeanor of the witness, Wigmore has said, is always in evidence. "The task of the juror," says Osborn, "is to interpret this language without words, as well as he can, and distinguish the true from the false. . . . An important phase of the study of this wordless language is no doubt a scrutiny of everything about a speaker that may indicate sincerity or insincerity. The steps down seem to be unnaturalness, uneasiness, nervousness, hesitation, affectation, concealment and deceit, and the steps up seem to be outspokenness, naturalness, frankness, openness, and properly qualified statements." [66] Assuming an intelligent, perceptive, and attentive jury, oral testimony should contribute to the detection of falsehood and uncertainty, and for this reason appellate courts are reluctant to go behind the verdict of the jury which has witnessed the witnesses. But, "it is an exaggeration," says Glanville Williams, "to suppose that a lie can be detected merely by observing the way in which the witness utters it, for some liars are bold and some honest witnesses are hesitating and nervous." [67] Another observer has said, "The worst woman I ever knew . . . had a face which for purity and innocence I can only compare with Raphael's 'Madonna,' and some of the best men and women who have crossed my path would have been convicted instanter under any laws founded on Cesare Lombroso's theories." [68]

Thus, a court is not dealing with "facts" but "assumed facts," and the equation of Judge Frank's, rough as it is, becomes $R \times AF = D$.

As if juries did not have trouble enough with the evidence, there is still the further difficulty of the jury's understanding of the law as stated by the judge in his charge. Like everyone else, judges have their limitations, and some, in the charge, reveal an incapacity to express themselves clearly. Too often, it is said, instructions are given hurriedly and in a mumbling manner. Furthermore, when judges give what in effect is a law lecture worthy of advanced law students and involving abstruse concepts of the most esoteric nature, it is little wonder that some juries simply give up, ignore both the evidence and the law, and "decide the case on the merits." The jury's task is not an easy one.

The irony of the plight of the jury is that those who complain most bitterly about the shortcomings of the jury system are the very ones who have sought and secured legislative exemption from jury duty. The subversion of a great judicial institution has come, to a degree at least, from the indifference of the so-called "best" people who either have no time or do not wish to be bothered.

A Note on Civil Procedure

A civil suit begins with a *summons* directed by the plaintiff's attorney in the name of the court in which the issue is to be tried, to the defendant. This merely announces the impending suit and orders the defendant to appear and to answer the plaintiff's claim within a certain period of time or else lose the suit by default, which means that the court would hand down a judgment without hearing the defendant's side of the story. The summons is usually accompanied by the *complaint*. Here the cause of action is set forth: the defendant owes the plaintiff $5,000, or he maintains a nuisance on his property to the injury and discomfort of the plaintiff, or the defendant has failed to honor the terms of a contract. The defendant is entitled to ask for a *bill of particulars* describing the complaint in considerable detail.

Within twenty days, if the case is to come before the New York Supreme

Court, the defendant must make his answer unless he secures an extension of time from the court. Let us say that he denies the allegations contained in the complaint: he does not owe the plaintiff $5,000, or he does not maintain a nuisance, or he has not dishonored the terms of a contract. The issue is thus joined and the attorneys for each side go to work gathering evidence. By the use of the *subpoena,* witnesses can be compelled to appear; by the use of the *subpoena duces tecum* a person is compelled, not only to appear, but to bring certain books, papers, or records, with him.

In a civil suit, a jury may be called, but this right may be waived by the parties. If a jury is to be selected, each prospective juror is examined by the parties and those revealing bias or prejudice may be challenged for cause and dismissed by the court. Each side has six peremptory challenges.

Following the selection of the jury, the plaintiff's attorney makes his opening remarks, in which he outlines the complaint and states what he intends to prove. The first witness is called to the stand, where he takes the oath to tell the truth and nothing but the truth. As in a criminal case, the witnesses are subject to direct and cross-examination. When all the plaintiff's witnesses have been examined, the plaintiff "rests." At this point, the defendant's attorney is likely to move that the complaint be dismissed as a matter of law on the ground that the plaintiff had not "proved" his case. The judge must decide whether or not to dismiss. If he does so decide, the suit is over, unless the plaintiff appeals to a higher court against the judge's ruling; if not, the defendant must produce his own witnesses to demolish, if he can, the plaintiff's contentions. These witnesses, like the plaintiff's, are questioned by both sides.

In a civil case, unlike a criminal case, the defendant ordinarily takes the stand and gives evidence; but, as in a criminal case, the defendant, or any witness for that matter, cannot be required to give testimony which might incriminate him.

Finally, the defense rests. Each attorney goes to the jury appealing for a verdict. The judge charges the jury; and after deliberation, the jury finds for the plaintiff or the defendant.

The methods of proof in a civil case are not unlike those in a criminal case. There is one great difference. In a criminal proceeding, proof of guilt must be "beyond a reasonable doubt." In a civil case, proof rests upon a *preponderance of evidence.* This means "that the party having the burden of proving certain facts must make it appear more probable than not that those facts existed." [69]

The Importance of Procedure

In the early part of this book emphasis was put upon the fact that men reveal, and always have revealed, a tendency to disagreement and conflict. Society came to disapprove and to condemn the irresponsible resolution of individual differences through private vengeance and the blood feud, and men began to submit their disputes to third parties. Under the aegis of a priestly class, the procedures of proof involved the intervention of God. In time, ordeal and battle were discarded and more rational methods of proof were substituted for them. This development roughly paralleled the emergence of courts and lawyers. Procedural law acquired a greater significance than substantive law and as the centuries wore on, courts developed an extremely complex system of procedural rules which culminated in early nineteenth-century England in the conditions described so forcefully by Dickens in *Bleak House.*

Dissatisfaction with procedural mazes brought reforms in both England and the United States. For example, equity and law were consolidated and the old common law system of pleading was reduced to complaint, answer, and reply. And yet in 1906 Roscoe Pound could cite procedure as one of "the most efficient causes of dissatisfaction with the present administration of justice in America." [70] He went on to say that "our system of courts is archaic and our procedure behind the times. Uncertainty, delay and expense, and above all the injustice of deciding cases upon points of practice [procedure], which are the mere etiquette of justice, direct results of the organization of our courts and the backwardness of our procedure, have created a deep-seated desire to keep out of court, right or wrong, on the part of every sensible business man in the community." [71] Substitute "almost everybody" for "every sensible business man," and we approach the truth.

What is the purpose of procedure?

It would seem that behind procedure there lie two chief purposes: (1) to expedite the attainment, as far as human intelligence, perceptiveness, and honesty allow, of a reasonably accurate reconstruction of the issue in conflict; and (2) fairness to the parties in dispute.

Although a greater simplification of procedure is still to be realized, the means of a fair, honest trial are at hand. Whether a trial is fair, however, depends upon the quality of the men on the bench and the attorneys.

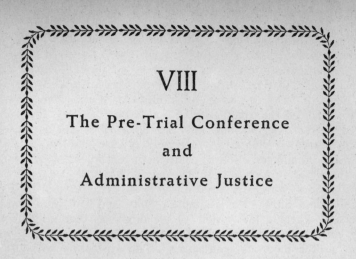

VIII

The Pre-Trial Conference
and
Administrative Justice

This chapter deals with two matters, each marking a departure from the traditional way of doing things, one of which is the product of congestion in the courts, the other the product of a complex industrial civilization. The first is called the *pre-trial conference,* the second, *administrative adjudication.* The first is a twentieth-century development and represents an interesting change, in both the United States and Great Britain, in the methods of resolving a civil dispute; the second, though not unknown earlier, commenced a vigorous career in the second half of the 19th century.

The Pre-Trial Conference

A good, busy lawyer will try to keep his client out of court. He will confer with opposing counsel in hopes of reaching a settlement acceptable to the parties who are thus saved time, energy, and money, not to speak of the anxiety attendant upon delays due to docket congestion. If no agreement satisfactory to the parties can be reached, then there is nothing to do but prepare for trial.

Judges have followed the example of the good lawyer simply because the courts are bursting at the seams with an enormous case load. In the *Annual Report of the Director of the Administrative Office of the United States Courts* for 1961, it is said that "On June 30, 1961, the district courts were burdened with 64,128 pending civil actions. Of these, 34,712, constituting 54 per cent of the pending civil caseload, had been on the docket for less than one year; 22,351, or 35 per cent, had been pending from 1 to 3 years; and 7,065, or 11 per cent, had been pending more than three years." [1] In New York State, "On June 30, 1955, there were pending and undisposed of almost 47,000 cases in the Supreme Court. . . . Delays between the date when a case is placed on the trial calendar and the date when it is reached for trial ran to 45 months in one county and ranged from 9 to 40 months in eleven other counties. . . ." [2]

A partial answer to the problem of court congestion has been found in the judicial *pre-trial conference.*

The general purpose of the pre-trial conference, moderated by a judge, is to reduce the caseload in the courts by (1) getting the parties to arrive at a settlement before trial, and (2) if settlement is impossible, to shorten the length of the trial by stipulations of the parties as to the precise issues, facts, the number and qualifications of expert witnesses, the nature of the injury, medical and hospital expenses and other matters, which consume much time in the course of a formal trial.

According to Harry D. Nims, the first systematic use of the pre-trial conference occurred in Detroit in 1929. In that year, "Chief Judge Ira W. Jayne and his associate judges of the Circuit Court . . . began to hold such conferences, as a routine matter, in cases awaiting trial in their court. In these conferences, the judge did not act as a judge usually acts in the trial of a lawsuit, but as a friend of the lawyers and the litigants, his purpose being to help them find ways to simplify the coming trial . . . and so reduce the time and expense involved in disposing of it." [3] This was done on the court's own initiative.

The experiment was successful. "Calendars," says Nims, "were reduced, trials simplified, many cases ended in the pre-trial conferences." [4] Judges and lawyers came to Detroit from other states to witness the experiment and were duly impressed. The use of the pre-trial conference spread until it became almost standard practice in most of the states.

Judge James C. Donnelly of Boston's Superior Court has said that "In 1935 the congestion on the jury list in the Superior Court was such that the time lapse between the entry of a case in court and the trial date was in the neighborhood of five years." Though he did not attribute an improved situation in his court to pre-trial alone, the practice did lessen the case load so that in 1950, "elapsed time now between entry and trial has been cut . . . to just under two years and six months." [5]

In 1938, the pre-trial conference was incorporated as Rule Sixteen of the Federal Rules of Civil Procedure, and this was approved by Congress. Rule Sixteen provides that

In any action, the court may in its discretion direct the attorneys for the parties to appear before it for a conference to consider:

(1) The simplification of issues;
(2) The necessity or desirability of amendments to the pleadings;
(3) The possibility of obtaining admissions of fact and of documents which will avoid unnecessary proof;
(4) The limitation of the number of expert witnesses;

(5) The advisability of a preliminary reference of issues to a master for findings to be used as evidence when the trial is to be by jury;

(6) Such other matters as may aid in the disposition of the action.

The court shall make an *order* which recites the action taken at the conference, the amendments allowed to the pleadings, and the agreements made by the parties as to any of the matters considered, and which limits the issues for trial to those not disposed of by admissions or agreements of counsel; and *such order when entered controls the subsequent course of the action,* unless modified at the trial to prevent manifest injustice. The court in its discretion may establish by rule a pre-trial calendar on which actions may be placed for consideration as above provided and may either confine the calendar to jury actions or to non-jury actions or extend it to all actions.[6]

In the 1957 *Report* of the Director of the Administrative Office of the United States Courts it is said that

More than half of the district courts are now using this procedure regularly in all civil cases coming on for trial. Figures collected by the Administrative Office show an increase of 50 per cent in the number of pre-trial conferences in the last 2 years. An excellent example of what can be done with pre-trial is furnished by the Eastern District of Louisiana where the 2 judges terminated 1,281 civil cases in 1957, or an average of 640.5 each. . . . Every civil case is pre-tried in that district before it reaches a trial calendar and the judges attribute their ability to dispose of this volume of litigation to their use of pre-trial.[7]

To instruct lawyers of the District of Columbia bar in the methods of the pre-trial conference, a demonstration was staged in Washington in 1950.[8]

This mock pre-trial conference was moderated by Alexander Holtzoff, a judge of the United States District Court for the District of Columbia. Mr. Joseph Bulman represented the plaintiffs, Morris and Nancy Brown, while Mr. George Horning represented the defendant, the Municipal Transit Company.

This was a negligence case, an action for personal injuries and property damage. Morris Brown, driving his own car and accompanied by his wife, was proceeding westerly on Nebraska Avenue when he was struck by the defendant's bus proceeding in a northerly direction along Connecticut Avenue. The plaintiffs claimed that the automobile was crossing the intersection on a green light and that the bus was moving against a red light. Both Mr. and Mrs. Brown suffered severe injuries. They were asking for damages amounting to $20,000.

The defendant, on the other hand, denied the allegations of the plaintiffs and claimed that it was Morris Brown, his judgment somewhat diminished by drink, who ran his car through a red light; the collision was due solely to Brown's negligence. The defendant counter-claimed in the sum of $295.25 for damage to the bus.

As to matters stipulated by the parties, there were the following: that Morris Brown was owner and operator of the automobile and that Plaintiff No. 2 was his wife; and that the intersection was controlled by traffic lights and that they were in operation at the time of the collision. It was agreed, too, by the parties that, subject to relevancy and competency, the following stipulations would be admitted in evidence at the trial *without formal proof:* routine hospital records, X-ray photographs of the injuries sustained by the plaintiffs, a photograph of the locale of the collision, a photograph of the damaged automobile for the purpose of showing the point of impact, an official weather report for the afternoon of the accident, medical and hospital bills, a bill for the repair of the plaintiff's car, a bill for the repair of the bus, and a plan of the intersection. As Judge Holtzoff said, "we have eliminated a great deal of trial time by these stipulations."

The Court: Have you gentlemen explored the possibility of an adjustment of this matter?

Mr. Bulman: Your Honor, I have made demand upon the company since I have filed suit, but I am frank to admit that there has been no offer forthcoming.

Would Your Honor be interested in the amounts I claim for the respective plaintiffs?

The Court: I would be very glad to have you state what you are asking in compromise.

Mr. Bulman: Your Honor can see from the claims here that both plaintiffs suffered severe permanent injuries.

On behalf of the plaintiff Nancy Brown—that is, the wife—I ask $7,500. On behalf of the husband, I ask $9,500. I think those amounts are fair and reasonable in view of the fact that we have over $2,000 worth of special expenses and that medical care may continue in the future by reason of these permanent injuries. I think that is a very fair offer.

The Court: What do you say, Mr. Horning?

Mr. Horning: I am somewhat surprised at a settlement demand of $17,000 which is now made, when during the negotiations for settlement prior to the suit, and even at the time of the taking of the deposition, my file indicates that Mr. Bulman was willing to settle those claims for $5,000. So, at this time, when he comes up with a $17,000 offer, it seems that it puts us further apart than we ever were. I might state to Your Honor that, as Your Honor knows, we have a board that appraises the value of these cases. The board carefully considered this case. We felt that there was not any liability at all; that our bus was being operated in a proper manner; that it had entered the intersection on a green light; and that it had the right-of-way. The automobile struck the bus at the right front door. We have two passengers who were seated in the front of the bus, where they had a grandstand view of it, both of whom have given statements, and whose names and addresses I furnished to Mr. Bulman.

I assume he has interviewed them. They substantiate the claim of the bus driver.

We have, on the other hand, Mr. Brown driving his automobile, certainly feeling gay from this cocktail party, at a high rate of speed, anxious to get to Woodward & Lothrop's, a mile away, before 6 o'clock, when it closed, and entering this wide intersection on a red light.

We feel in view of that situation that the case is one which should be tried. Of course, if Mr. Bulman were to come down to something more reasonable, I might resubmit it. In fact, at this time I might state to Your Honor that I would recommend that we forgo our counterclaim of about $300 and perhaps pay, just as nuisance value, what it would cost us to try the case, in the neighborhood of $500, making a total out-of-pocket of around $800 as the result of the accident, rather than to try the case.

The Court: Well, the settlement value of a case like this, of course, depends on the extent to which there are disinterested witnesses to substantiate the claims of the parties. You say you have two passengers to support the contention that it was the plaintiff's car which ran through the red light.

Mr. Horning: Yes, Your Honor.

The Court: Have you any disinterested witnesses?

Mr. Bulman: Yes. First, I would invite the attention of the Court to the fact that the board which Mr. Horning speaks of is not a jury. They have proven wrong in the past. This is something Your Honor knows of. Secondly, I am rather amazed in this case that they have only two witnesses, because it was early in the afternoon, and the bus was fully loaded, and they show up with two witnesses.

I interviewed both of those witnesses and found they were seated somewhere about in the middle of the bus, and the bus was rather crowded, so I think their positions of observation were not any too good.

On the other hand, luckily for my clients, on that corner there is a gas station, and there was a gas station attendant there. He was not doing anything at the moment. He had a grandstand seat of this entire thing, and he tells us—and we have a statement from him—to the effect that our car entered on the green light, and he is positive. I think, Your Honor, that that spells out a distinct question of fact to go to the jury. Because of that, Your Honor, I do not think that our demands are so far fetched. They may be a little high, but I have never known the Municipal Transit Company to give me any more money than I have demanded. If Mr. Horning is willing to take it up with the company, I will be very happy to talk to my clients.

The Court: This is a case with disinterested witnesses on both sides. There is a conflict on a crucial issue. No one can tell what the outcome may be. There is this about it, Mr. Horning. This is the kind of case where, if you get a verdict against you, it can be a very heavy verdict because of the nature of the injuries. As you know, juries in this jurisdiction have been giving very heavy verdicts if they decide for the plaintiffs and if there are serious permanent injuries.

But, of course, Mr. Bulman, it seems to me you run a very serious risk of having the jury decide for the defendant. It is one of those uncertain cases. It might go either way, depending on the impression made by the disinterested witnesses. It seems to me, under the circumstances, that it might behoove you to abate your demand somewhat.

Mr. Bulman: Your Honor, I do not feel we are taking any risk with a $500 offer.

The Court: No; I am sure Mr. Horning would be willing to pay considerably higher than that.

Mr. Horning: Well, it is $800, Your Honor, waiving the counterclaim.

Mr. Bulman: I am fully appreciative of the risks my clients entail in this case, Your Honor, but I am governed by the fact that they have in the neighborhood of $2,000 worth of out-of-pocket expenses.

Of course, Mr. Horning is not concerned with this, but the plaintiffs do have to pay me a fee, and the result is that what we get in settlement is not net to themselves.

However, if Mr. Horning is serious in trying to get this case out of the way, I think I would be willing to recommend $7,500 for both cases.

The Court: What do you say to that, Mr. Horning? I think that is more within the bounds of reason than the original demand.

Mr. Horning: As Your Honor knows, I have worked before you for a long time. You have helped us to settle many cases in pretrial. I would like to ask Your Honor what your candid view about the case is and what we should do.

The Court: Well, before I do that, I would like to know whether you are willing to go substantially higher than $800.

Mr. Horning: Yes, Your Honor; if Your Honor feels that it is a case we should settle, and should settle for more than that, I am willing.

The Court: It seems to me that this is a case where a fairly substantial settlement would be warranted, because you run a very serious risk of having a very heavy verdict against you if the plaintiff prevails, because of the nature of damages.

On the other hand, Mr. Bulman, I think that if the case is to be settled, the plaintiffs must be reasonable also. I recall there was a case tried before me not so long ago in which the plaintiffs rejected a substantial offer, and then the jury brought in a verdict for the defendant. I think your clients should bear that possibility in mind.

Mr. Bulman: That was not my case, Your Honor.

The Court: Would you be willing to pay $5,000, Mr. Horning?

Mr. Horning: Does Your Honor feel that that is fair and reasonable, in view of the circumstances?

The Court: I think it is. Of course, I am not trying to force my views on you, gentlemen. I do not have to repeat that you gentlemen are entitled to have a jury determine the issues. But in view of the fact that you invited my comments, it seems to me that $5,000 would be a reasonable amount to pay, because it would be insurance against a very heavy verdict. Would your client be willing to accept $5,000?

Mr. Bulman: Your Honor, I do not think they would go that low; but if Your Honor could manipulate his thoughts to the price of $6,000, we might be very much interested in that.

The Court: What do you say about that?

Mr. Horning: Of course, as Your Honor knows, I have great respect for

Your Honor's judgment in these cases. You have wide experience in them. I will be happy to go back to my client and to the board and report what has transpired here today; and further, I will state to Your Honor that I will recommend settlement in the figure Your Honor has set. I trust we will be able to effect a settlement and avoid a lengthy trial.

The Court: Well, apparently we are only a thousand dollars apart at this moment.

What do you say about that?

Mr. Bulman: Your Honor, I will tell my clients Your Honor's view. They have great respect for the Court's view, more than for counsel's. If Your Honor thinks $5,000 is a reasonable sum, I am sure they will go along.

The Court: I think that is a reasonable sum, considering the possibilities of this case and its uncertainties.

Well, gentlemen, in the meantime, will you please sign the pretrial memorandum?

The case will go on the trial assignment and will be reached in about three weeks. But I hope you will come back and report within the next few days that you have settled this case for the amount we have tentatively agreed upon.

Administrative Adjudication

Were a foreigner to ask an American just where disputes between government and citizen and between citizen and citizen were settled, the response would be "in the courts." If the questioner pressed the American to be specific about these courts he would probably mention the Federal District Courts, the Courts of Appeals, and the United States Supreme Court; on the state level, he would refer to city courts, small claims courts, county courts, and such appellate courts as Maryland's Court of Appeals, Minnesota's Supreme Court, Maine's Supreme Judicial Court, and Delaware's Court of Errors and Appeals. Our American's answer is correct but it is, by no means, a complete answer.

Within the last hundred years in the United States, on both state and national levels, there has developed a system of administrative courts or tribunals concerned with the public welfare and endowed with immense power of decision over private interests, whether of person or property. It is not too much to say that today administrative agencies decide more cases affecting private interests than all the regular courts combined.

Laissez-faire

The role of government in 1800 was generally limited to three functions: the protection of person, the protection of property, and the protection of the country as a whole from external dangers. By 1900, the picture had changed. Government was still the protector of person, property and country, but its role, which had been passive in behalf of the public welfare, now became active. By 1950, as a result of two world wars, a depression, and an expanding population, the intervention of government in the affairs of men was so great that any resemblance to the government of 1800 was purely coincidental.

The United States in 1900 was no longer predominantly agricultural. Great cities, trade unions, high finance and the modern corporation, all begotten for good or ill by a virile industrialism, dominated the scene. There was a rugged, restless, and unrestrained drive for money and power which only a few could realize. Great fortunes were made, the wealthy became wealthier and the poor became poorer. The United States Commission on Industrial Relations in its *Report* for 1915 declared that 2 per cent of the people in the United States owned 60 per cent of the national wealth while 65 per cent of the people owned but 5 per cent of that wealth. There were few millionaires in 1860; by 1892, the number had jumped to 3,561.[9]

At the same time, the great majority of men and women, either as workers or consumers, were grievously exploited by unscrupulous employers and manufacturers. Men worked hard for subsistence wages; women labored for long hours in factories or sweat shops, some no better than fire traps, or in unsanitary, unclean, and poorly ventilated bakeshops and candy establishments. Children did not escape the cruel and inhuman treatment given them by a class at least as irresponsible as some of the plantation owners of the ante-bellum South. As the rich built their palaces, more and more people lived in slums.

The use of chemicals to prevent the spoilage of meats and fruits, to restore stale and rancid butter to its original appearance, and to deodorize rotten eggs, meant that often enough the housewife did not know what she was buying. The most despicable and insidious form of exploitation was the patent medicine makers' unhesitant adding of habit-forming drugs to soothing syrups for babies.

Men suffered accidents in the course of their employment and had no effective remedy against the employer who, as has been pointed out, could divest himself of any responsibility behind the common law defenses of contributory negligence, assumption of risk, and the fellow-servant rule.

If the employer wished to justify such conditions he could invoke a laissez-faire philosophy and speak of the benefits, to all the people, of unfettered competition as a guarantee of ample goods at fair prices; he could expound the notion of a free individual in a free society; and preach the doctrine of freedom of contract as between unorganized workers and huge corporations. Such myths were part of the intellectual equipment of most of the justices of the United States Supreme Court throughout the last quarter of the nineteenth century and the first quarter of the twentieth.

It was exploitation pure and simple that engendered resentment and led finally to an interest on the part of both the states and the Federal government in the welfare of the people.

The Public Welfare

It is unnecessary to do more than mention certain manifestations of this interest. Congress, in 1887, passed the Interstate Commerce Act, which, aimed at the railroads, forbade discrimination against shippers, arbitrary freight rates, and rebates. In 1890, there came the Sherman Anti-trust Act which struck at price-fixing and monopoly and forbade combinations in restraint of trade. The Pure Food and Drug Act was enacted in 1906; its purpose was to prevent "the manufacture, sale, or transportation of adulterated or misbranded or poisonous or deleterious foods, drugs, medicines, and liquors, and for regulating traffic therein . . ." The second Employers Liability Act (1908) has already been discussed. The Federal Trade Commission Act of 1914 was intended to prevent unfair methods of competition, while the Clayton Act of the same year prohibited price discrimination, business consolidations and combinations. The Adamson Act of 1916 gave the eight hour day to employees of the railroads.

The states, too, were busy with social legislation. Many states passed child labor laws, laws governing minimum wages and maximum hours of labor for women, safety codes and factory acts. To provide a greater distribution of wealth, some of the states passed income and inheritance tax laws. And many of the states, through the enactment of Workmen's Compensation Laws, abolished those employer's common law defenses that worked hardship upon the workman who was the victim of industrial accident or occupational disease.

The Delegation of Legislative Powers

The complexities of twentieth-century industrialism in the United States brought not only such statutes as have been mentioned above but new and more expeditious methods of dealing with current problems. One method is that of the delegation of power by Congress to a commission or board or to an officer of an executive department to adopt what are called rules or supplementary legislation having the force of law. According to the late James Hart,

It is now generally admitted that delegated rule-making is a practical necessity not only in time of emergency but also in the normal operation of twentieth-century government. In the simple days of the agricultural era, statutes could be relatively concrete, specific, and detailed. With the coming of the industrial age, however, not only are the conditions to be regulated highly complex and rapidly changing, but unprecedented problems have emerged. . . . The net result has been a gradual change in the regulatory role of Congress, which has been compelled, in many cases, to provide only the general principles of regulation, and to devolve upon administrative authorities the task of applying those general principles. Frequently it has authorized such authorities to *concretize* such principles, before applying them to particular cases, by the issuance of rules and regulations of more specific content. The conclusion that, under modern conditions, this is a necessary and normal technique of regulation is increasingly verified by experience in the several states.[10]

When, for example, the Interstate Commerce Commission fixes future rates for the transportation of passengers and freight on interstate railways, it is supplementing an act of Congress; it is making law. When the Secretary of Agriculture makes regulations covering the importation and interstate transportation of plants and animals in accord with a policy set forth in an act of Congress, he is making law. The Secretary of the Treasury makes law when he issues rules for the enforcement of the internal revenue statutes.

Subordinate legislation is a reflection of the fact that Congress, unaided, cannot effectively deal with the myriad problems of present-day industrial America.

The Quasi-Judicial Power

We come now to a second power delegated to organs of administration, a power particularly pertinent to the subject of this book, and that is the power to resolve disputes arising between private parties or between government and the private citizen. This is called the quasi-judicial function.

Congress has seen fit to endow certain administrative agencies with judicial power for two reasons: first, because of the extreme complexity of modern-day social and economic life; and second, because of the inadequacy of the regular courts in meeting that complexity. The advantages of the quasi-judicial function are the expert knowledge of the administrator-judge, and the speed, flexibility, and relative informality of the proceedings.

The judicial power exercised by an administrator or commission is not similar to the proceedings in a regular court of law, but there are judicial characteristics: notice and hearing, for example, are the counterparts of a law court's summons and complaint and trial. If the rules are not the same as the law's, if there is flexibility and "informality," there is still the resolution of conflict, whoever the parties may be.

It was said a moment ago that when the Interstate Commerce Commission fixes future railroad rates it is making law. When, however, the same agency resolves a dispute between a carrier and a shipper over a given rate, it is acting in a judicial capacity. The Federal Trade Commission is exercising a judicial function when it seeks to discover, on complaint, whether a given business is or is not guilty of unfair trade practices and to punish the violator if the complaint is proven true. Ordinarily the grant of a license is an administrative matter, but when application is made to the Federal Communications Commission for a license to establish a new radio station, the quasi-judicial function emerges in reaching a decision either to grant the permit or not.

Workmen's Compensation Board

At the start of the present century, most American workmen had to rely upon the common law doctrine of employer's liability to secure redress for accidents and diseases incurred in the course of labor. We have already discussed this doctrine as well as the several common law defences available to the employer: the fellow-servant rule, assumption of risk, and contributory negligence. These doctrines, in an age of great factories and giant corporations, left the injured workman almost helpless in court, so difficult was it to prove the employer's negligence.

Yielding to the demands of labor for reform, Congress and some of the state legislatures either modified or abolished these defenses. This, however, was not enough. The injured workman still had to battle the employer in the courts, a long and costly process he could ill afford.

The answer to the problem was Workmen's Compensation. Following the example of Germany (1884) and England (1897), several of the states, beginning with Maryland in 1902, adopted Workmen's Compensation Acts. At first, these acts ran into trouble in the courts: (1) they interfered with freedom of contract as between employer and employee; and (2) they imposed an unfair burden upon the employer since it was he who paid the bill whether he had been negligent or not. In a series of decisions beginning in 1915, however, the Supreme Court recognized the validity of Workmen's Compensation.

Let us examine briefly the operation of New York's Workmen's Compensation Act.

The Workmen's Compensation Board is part of New York's Department of Labor. The Board consists of thirteen members appointed by the governor for seven-year periods.[11] Referees are appointed by the Board to hear and determine claims for compensation and the decisions of the referees are deemed to be decisions of the Board unless that body overrules or modifies those decisions.[12]

In the application of the Compensation Act, its terms are to be liberally construed.

The employer must, by law, carry insurance—either in a fund administered by the state or with a private company—to insure prompt and full payment of any award. The employee pays nothing; the entire cost is borne by the employer.[13]

The hearing before a referee of the Workmen's Compensation Board in New York is a quasi-judicial proceeding. By law, the claim is presumed to be a valid one.[14] Either party, that is, the claimant on one side and the employer or carrier (insurance company) on the other, may present evidence and be represented by counsel. The referee may examine the claimant and his witnesses and cross-examine the witnesses of the employer.

The usual common law or statutory rules of evidence are declared by law to be inapplicable to these hearings, nor is the Board or referee bound by technical or formal rules of procedure.[15] For example, declarations of a deceased employee are receivable in evidence and, if corroborated by circumstances or other evidence, are sufficient to establish the accident or injury.[16] The Board or the referee has power to issue subpoenas to compel the attendance of witnesses and the production of records, books or papers.[17] Witnesses, of course, testify under oath.

The employer or carrier will protest an award when it is believed that the injury or death or occupational disease did not arise out of and in the course of the employment. From the decision of the referee, appeal may be had to the Board; and from the Board to the Appellate Division of the Supreme Court, Third Department, and thence to the Court of Appeals. It is not necessary to file exceptions to the rulings of the Board in order to bring a case before the Appellate Division.[18]

A consideration of a few contested cases will suggest the liberality with which the Board adjudicates the claims of injured workmen. They will also indicate the role of the appellate courts in keeping the Board within the terms of its enabling act.

Pasquel v. Coverly

Marie Pasquel on the death of her husband sought and secured an award from the Workmen's Compensation Board. The award was opposed by the employer but was affirmed by the Appellate Division of the Supreme Court.

The decedent, employed by one Coverly, an agent for Mutual of Omaha in White Plains, New York, was required occasionally to visit other Mutual agencies in the state to explain bookkeeping procedures. In March, 1954, Pasquel was sent to the Kingston office, seventy-seven miles distant from his home. With a friend, he arrived at one o'clock and completed his work by five. He and his companion then drove to a point just north of Newburgh where they had dinner with a relative of the decedent. After dinner, the three men drove to Newburgh where

Pasquel visited two automobile salesrooms for the purpose of buying a car. They then stopped in a tavern where they had several drinks and returned to the relation's home where they played cards until three in the morning. On the return to White Plains, Pasquel crashed into a tree and thus met his death.

The Court of Appeals[19] reversed the Appellate Division and annulled the award, holding that the accident and death did not arise out of the employment. "The circumstance," said Judge Van Voorhis, "that he combined business with some pleasure would not defeat the claim, unless the accident resulted from risks produced by the personal activities. We think that it did. Here it was the employer's business which sent the traveler forth upon the journey, but it was not the employer's business which brought exposure to the perils in consequence whereof he died. In order to be compensable, death or disability must not only have arisen in the course of the employment, it must also have arisen 'out of' the employment." [20]

Palermo v. Gallucci

Anthony Palermo was driving his employer's truck when it was struck by a mail truck. Palermo was thrown out and lay unconscious on the pavement. He was taken to a hospital where his injuries were diagnosed as contusion of one elbow and abrasion of the scalp. X rays indicated no intracranial injury. Palermo consulted his own physician, Dr. Arnold Nathan, whose diagnosis was not unlike that of the hospital physicians. Palermo went back to work. Less than three weeks later Palermo died of coronary occlusion and coronary thrombosis. An autopsy was performed by a pathologist at the direction of the coroner, Dr. Laviano.

Palermo's widow claimed compensation from the Workmen's Compensation Board and an award was made to her on the ground that the coronary attack was "causally related" to the injury the deceased had sustained in the auto collision during the course of his employment." From this decision, appeal was made to the Appellate Division by the employer, who argued that the death was not the result of the accident. The award was affirmed. The case then went to the Court of Appeals,[21] which had before it one question: was there substantial evidence to support the finding of the Board?

At the hearing before the Board, Dr. Laviano testified for the employer, Dr. Nathan for the widow. The former averred that without doubt the heart and other contents of the chest were shaken by the accident, but, on the basis of information given him by the pathologist, he felt that "this thrombus was not due to the accident but was something that developed later." Dr. Nathan testified that the force of the blow when Palermo was thrown from the truck may well have produced the heart injury. As he declared, a sudden compression in the chest, the pressing of the heart up against the chest wall, possible injury to the coronary vessels which lie close to the heart's surface, might well result in a reaction "where we have the production of or clotting of blood within the vessel wall at the site of the injury. And we have the resultant coronary occlusion." [22]

The Court of Appeals affirmed the decision of the Appellate Division. Judge Conway's opinion was that

> In sum, there are in this case two conflicting expert opinions each one based upon the same facts. The selection of either is an exercise of fact-finding power which is entirely within the province of the Board and outside the limited jurisdiction of this court. It is not our function to render a decision upon the basis of which expert opinion we deem is more weighty or persuasive. The testimony of each expert was sufficiently direct and specific to create an issue of fact and to warrant a finding either for or against causal relation. That issue has been resolved by the appropriate body—the Board—in favor of the claimant widow, and the record leaves us no course but to affirm.[23]

Herman v. Greenpoint Barrel Co.

At a company Christmas party in 1956, the employer furnished quantities of intoxicating liquor and food. Two young men engaged in a drinking competition, consuming liquor "by the cupful." By three o'clock in the afternoon both young men were found to be unconscious and were taken to their homes. By six o'clock one of the young men was dead.

The Workmen's Compensation Board granted an award, the Board finding that the decedent "died as a result of the large quantities of liquor consumed and that death was due to generalized visceral congestion, pial edema, cerebral edema, and acute ethyl alcohol poisoning; that the furnishing by the employer of alcohol at the party for the purpose of improving employer-employee relations and assisting in building morale among employees constituted a risk of the employment, and that the death of decedent arose out of and in the course of his employment." [24] The employer contested the award.

The decision of the Board was reversed by the Appellate Division: "While the occurrence took place upon the premises of the employer, who furnished the liquor and food, it is no basis for a finding in favor of the claimant. The intoxication was the result of excessive personal use of alcohol which departed from any rational relationship to the work." [25] The Court of Appeals affirmed the dismissal of the claim.

Johnson v. Loew's

Claimant, a seventeen-year-old boy, was employed as a messenger. When not running errands, the claimant and other messengers sat on a bench in the reception room of the employer's office. One afternoon during a slack period, the messengers began to shoot paper clips through a window by means of rubber bands. The claimant placed a clip in a band but instead of flying away from him it flew back and injured his left eye. The Workmen's Compensation Board awarded compensation. This was affirmed by the Appellate Division and later by the Court of Appeals.[26]

The claimant's immediate supervisor was aware of the clip-shooting and did not condone it; but the boys had not been expressly forbidden to engage in the practice. The employer argued that the claimant did not sustain the accident "out of and in the course of his employment." The Board contended that "under the circumstances, claimant's act of shooting the paper clip . . . did not remove him from the scope of his employment." [27]

A British Case

Like Congress and the state legislatures, Parliament has conferred judicial powers upon ministers, departmental officers, and administrative bodies, for the reason that these agencies can deal more expeditiously with the many special, complex, and pressing problems of modern life, particularly in a welfare state. These agencies could act with greater speed than the courts and bring to bear upon disputes an expert knowledge the judges did not possess. The welfare state does not admit the luxury of long, legal tie-ups in the courts. Furthermore, Parliament is supreme and no Act of Parliament may be declared unconstitutional by any court.[28]

There is no intention here to discuss administration in Great Britain, but a case decided in 1956 in the House of Lords will indicate the extent to which (in one sphere of state activity, at least) the Parliament has shorn the courts of power.

In 1948, a house and eight and one-half acres of land were taken from Mrs. Kathleen Smith on order of the East Elloe Rural District Council for the purpose of erecting a number of low-cost, low-rent, housing units called Council houses. This was done in accordance with law. There had been a public local inquiry or hearing, the Minister of Health had confirmed the order, and in due course the compulsory purchase price for the house and land had been fixed at £3000. Mrs. Smith's house was demolished and the Council houses erected.

Six years later, Mrs. Smith went to court seeking damages from the Council for trespass to her land and an injunction to prevent further trespass; she sought, also, a declaration that the order of 1948 had been "wrongfully" made and confirmed in "bad faith" by the Council, the clerk of the Council, and the Minister of Health.

Now, of the right of the Council to acquire the land, there is no question. The procedure of acquisition required by Parliament was scrupulously followed. And in order to give finality and security from challenge to compulsory acquisitions of land, Parliament passed in 1946 the Acquisition of Land (Authorization Procedure) Act.[29] Paragraph 15 provided (in part) that "If any person aggrieved by a compulsory purchase order desires to question the validity thereof . . . on the ground that the authorization of a compulsory purchase thereby granted is not empowered to be granted under this Act . . . he may, within six weeks" from the date of the confirmation of the order, make application to the High Court. Under certain circumstances, not of interest here, the court may suspend or quash the operation of the purchase order. But, subject to Paragraph 15, Paragraph 16 provides that "a compulsory purchase order . . . shall not, either before or after it has been confirmed . . . be questioned in any legal proceedings whatsoever."

One would expect that the imputation of fraud or bad faith would reopen the whole question of the purchase despite the six weeks' limitation; but no, the court of first instance set aside the writ of summons before a statement of claims could be introduced. Throughout this case, the courts, including the House of Lords, had no idea as to the nature of the "bad faith."

The argument before the Lords centered around paragraph 16, to the effect that however general its language it "must be construed so as not to oust the jurisdiction of the court where the good faith of the local authority or the Ministry was impugned and put in issue." [30] Where the words "compulsory purchase order" occurred in the Act, it was argued, "they are to be read as if the words 'made in good faith' were added to them." The House of Lords could not accept this interpretation. The words of the paragraph were clear enough and did not admit of any qualification. "It cannot be predicated of any order," said Viscount Simonds, "that it has been made in bad faith until it has been tested in legal proceedings, and it is just that test which paragraph 16 bars." [31]

Lord Morton, in a concurring opinion, supposes a compulsory purchase order which compels a man to sell the house which has been his home and the home of his family for decades. After the order is made, he learns that the local district council wished to satisfy a grudge against him, or for reasons more sinister wished to dislodge him. This man is forever precluded from going to any court to have the order set aside. But, as Lord Morton declared, it is "within the powers of Parliament to achieve this result, and, in my opinion, it has been achieved by paragraphs 15 and 16." [32]

The word "court" evokes in our minds the austere and righteous judge, black-robed upon the bench, the opposing counsel, the defendant whose freedom or property is at stake, the questioning and cross-questioning of the witnesses, the objections made and the exceptions taken, the impassioned summations, the cold and logical charge to the jury, and finally, the verdict. Such an image is the essence of the "judicial" and there are those who believe firmly that any proceeding that does not accord with this image is not judicial and is, therefore, suspect.

This is unfortunate. The courts play an essential role in our society and system of government and we could not do without them. This is like saying that the sun will rise tomorrow morning or that a human being cannot exist without oxygen. Yet the truth is that our courts are the product of a simpler, more leisurely civilization and they are ill-adapted to deal with *all* the countless conflicts of a rapidly moving, swiftly changing, machine age. It has been estimated that "in the course of an average work day about 62 workers will have been killed, 350 will have suffered some permanent impairment, and 7,600 more will have suffered injuries which will keep them from work for an average of about 18 days." *Res ipsa loquitur:* the thing speaks for itself.

If, in administrative adjudication, the complicated procedures of the courts are lacking, this does not mean that *all* judicial aspects are absent. There must be notice; a man must know the case he has to meet. There must be a hearing; he ought not to be condemned unheard. And, of course, these newer courts must, in their decisions, take care to remain within the framework of the legislative enactment which is the basis of their power.

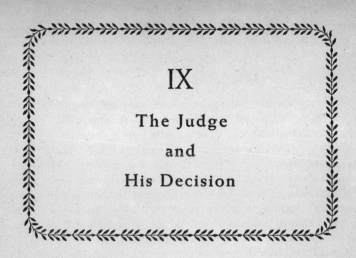

IX

The Judge
and
His Decision

Louis Repouille, an alien residing in New York, deliberately put to death his thirteen-year-old son on October 12, 1939. Repouille was the sole support of a family which included five children, one of whom was an idiot, blind, mute, and deformed, incapable of taking care of himself in any way. Repouille chloroformed this child because the care of the four normal children was jeopardized by the burden imposed upon him by the fifth.

Repouille was indicted for manslaughter in the first degree, tried, and found guilty of manslaughter in the second degree, the jury recommending the "utmost clemency." He received a suspended sentence and was immediately placed on probation. He was discharged from probation in December, 1945.

Repouille filed a petition for citizenship on September 22, 1944. Although the Nationality Act of 1940 [1] provided that an alien seeking to become a citizen must have been a person of "good moral character" for five years preceding the actual date of filing, the District Court granted the petition. From this order, the District Attorney in behalf of the Immigration and Naturalization Service appealed to the Circuit Court of Appeals for a reversal on the ground that during the five year period Repouille had suffered a moral lapse. The appellate court, speaking through Judge Learned Hand, reversed the District Court and dismissed the petition. [2]

The Act in question did not define the phrase "good moral character." However pitiful the circumstances, did Repouille reveal an absence of "good moral character" in taking his child's life? Judge Hand felt that

It is reasonably clear that the jury which tried Repouille did not feel any moral repulsion at his crime. Although it was inescapably murder in the first degree, not only did they bring in a verdict that was flatly in the face of the facts and utterly absurd—for manslaughter in the second degree

153

presupposes that the killing has not been deliberate—but they coupled even that with a recommendation which showed that in substance they wished to exculpate the offender. Moreover, it is also plain, from the sentence which he imposed, that the judge could not have seriously disagreed with their recommendation.[3]

Judge Hand was aware that many people of unimpeachable virtue "think it morally justifiable to put an end to a life so inexorably destined to be a burden to others, and . . . condemned to a brutish existence, lower indeed than all but the lowest forms of sentient life." [4] He was aware, too, that many people—probably most people—do not equate law and ethics: "there have always been conscientious persons who feel no scruple in acting in defiance of a law which is repugnant to their personal convictions, and who even regard as martyrs those who suffer by doing so." [5]

Did "good moral character" mean the generally accepted moral conventions of the time? Yes, Judge Hand could answer, but what are the generally accepted moral conventions of the time? He believed that this would be a difficult test to apply in the absence of "some national inquisition, like a Gallup poll." Should the verdict of the jury be seized upon "as a reliable measure of current morals?" Judge Hand would hesitate to accept the verdict as decisive, since a similar offender in Massachusetts was imprisoned for life.

"Left at large as we are," said Judge Hand, "without means of verifying our conclusion, and without authority to substitute our individual beliefs, the outcome must needs be tentative." [6] However that may be, Judge Hand felt reasonably secure in holding that the moral conventions of the time did not admit of the right of the individual to play the role of God and to decide when another's life should end.

There was a dissent in this case. Judge Jerome Frank believed that the tentativeness and uncertainty and lack of knowledge of his brethren was inexcusable. "Good moral character" was to be measured by "the generally accepted moral conventions at the time" and that these conventions were to be found quite simply in "the attitude of our ethical leaders." [7] He would have remanded the case to the District Court with instructions to secure reliable information on the subject on the basis of which the district court judge might "reconsider his decision and arrive at a conclusion." If another appeal followed, "we can avoid sheer guessing, which alone is now available to us, and can reach something like an informed judgment." [8]

The Unanswerable Question

How do judges decide cases? Skating on thin ice is as nothing compared to an attempt to answer this question. The dangers are manifold; but, even if contemplation of the subject is dotted with "ifs" and

"ands" and "buts," even if thought upon the problem is rife with speculation, even if "fools rush in where angels fear to tread," the question is
still intriguing, absorbing, and unanswerable.

In the case just discussed, the three judges were acquainted with the
facts, they had read the briefs, they had heard the oral arguments, and
they knew the law. And yet, two voted to reverse the District Court, and
one voted to remand. Why?

Constitutional and Statutory Clauses

If a statute is so clear, so free of doubt as to its meaning, there
is nothing for the judge to do (assuming its constitutionality) but to
apply it. But many statutes contain ambiguous words and phrases which
are not defined and which admit of several meanings. Certainly, the
extremes of bad and good moral character might be easily determined.
The dipsomaniac, the forger, the molester of children, the arsonist, and
the purveyor of drugs to adolescents, would be, in anyone's mind, no
proper candidate for citizenship on the basis of good moral character.
It is the in-between cases that may cause trouble. Except for one lapse,
Repouille was a person of good moral character and the majority recognized this; but it would seem that in the dissent, Judge Frank suggests
that a survey of the attitudes of the nation's ethical leaders might reveal
that Repouille's act was not immoral at all.

Like "good moral character," the great clauses of the Constitution are
not defined and since 1789 have yielded a rich harvest of judicial exegeses.
Due process of law, equal protection, freedom of the press, commerce
among the states, and the contract clause, are examples of concepts
which have been subject to judicial scrutiny and creativity, interpreted
and reinterpreted as they have been under the stress of changing conditions and times.

Cardozo and the Judicial Process

"When constitution and statute are silent," said Cardozo, "the
judge must look to the common law for the rule that fits the case." [9]
Here, too, only rarely is there a precise rule that fits the case; and often
enough, there are conflicting rules, either of which, by analogy, might apply satisfactorily to the facts.

Cardozo says that there are four methods available to judges in deciding cases: the methods of philosophy (the rule of analogy), evolution,
custom, and sociology. Only with the first and last shall we be concerned, because these two are particularly pertinent to our discussion.
The first is the way of precedent and *stare decisis*. "It is an established

rule," said Blackstone, "to abide by former precedents, where the same points come again in litigation; as well to keep the scale of justice even and steady, and not liable to waver with every new judge's opinion." [10] Men are entitled to expect in their relations with other men, and with government, that the rules of society as applied by the courts shall be free of whimsicality, irresponsibility, and arbitrariness, to the end that a degree of certainty and stability shall be attained. *Stare decisis* has its good points, but as we have pointed out in Chapter VI, this method carried to the limits of its logic would mean stultification.

The second method, called by Cardozo the method of sociology, includes "justice, morals and social welfare, the *mores* of the day." [11]

A certain Francis B. Palmer made a will in 1880, leaving small legacies to his two daughters, Mrs. Riggs and Mrs. Preston, and the bulk of his estate to his grandson, Elmer Palmer. Elmer knew that upon his grandfather's death he would inherit a considerable property.

In 1882, Francis Palmer married a second time. He also manifested an intention of revoking those provisions of his will in Elmer's favor. To prevent this, Elmer murdered his grandfather.

The will was made out in proper form, it had been probated, and "it must have effect according to the letter of the law." From behind prison walls, Elmer claimed his property.

Mrs. Riggs and Mrs. Preston sought to have the will, so far as it devised and bequeathed property to Elmer, cancelled and annulled. The General Term of the Supreme Court upheld Elmer's claim to the property.

Before the New York Court of Appeals, the only question for decision was, can Elmer have the property? The court in a five-two decision said that he could not. [12]

"It is quite true," said Judge Earl, "that statutes regulating the making, proof and effect of wills, and the devolution of property, if literally construed, and if their force and effect can in no way and under no circumstances be controlled or modified," [13] then Palmer's estate is secure in the hands of the murderer. The binding force of a will, so it was argued, cannot be broken even where the legatee murders the testator to prevent him from making any proposed changes in his will.

It was argued, too, that by depriving the murderer of his inherited property, the Court would be enhancing "the pains, penalties and forfeitures provided by law for the punishment of crime." [14]

On the basis of either one of these principles or "paths," or both of them, the Court of Appeals could have affirmed the General Term.

But, there was another principle available to the judges. True, the purpose of the statutes was to enable the maker of a will to dispose of his estate to the objects of his bounty after death and to be assured that the donees should have the property given them. There is this, though: "all laws as well as all contracts may be controlled in their operation and effect by general, fundamental maxims of the common law. No one," said Earl, "shall be permitted to profit by his own fraud, or to take advantage of his own wrong, or to found any claim upon his own iniquity, or to acquire property by his own crime." [15] This was the principle or path followed by the Court. The will was broken.

The question which is of real interest, as it was to Cardozo, is "why and how the choice was made between one logic and another." Why was the one principle selected in preference to the others? "One path was followed, another closed, because of the conviction in the judicial mind that the one selected led to justice." [16]

Cardozo, commenting on this case, said

> Analogies and precedents and the principles behind them were brought together as rivals for precedence; in the end, the principle that was thought to be most fundamental, to represent the larger and deeper social interests, put its competitors to flight. I am not greatly concerned about the particular formula through which justice was attained. . . . What concerns me now is . . . the underlying motive, the indwelling, creative energy, which brings such devices into play. The murderer lost the legacy for which the murder was committed because the social interest served by refusing to permit the criminal to profit by his crime is greater than that served by the preservation and enforcement of legal rights of ownership.[17]

Why did the judges in *Hynes v. New York Central Railroad* [18] choose the concept of the traveller on the highway in preference to the concept of the trespasser? Why did the judges in *Woods v. Lancet*[19] choose to overrule the principle that one could not recover damages for injuries sustained before birth and, in doing so, create a new principle? Why did the judges in *MacPherson v. The Buick Company* choose to broaden the rule as to the liability of the manufacturer to the ultimate user or consumer with whom he is not bound by contract? [20] Why did the judges in *People v. Rosenheimer*[21] choose to uphold a state law which required a person involved in an automobile accident to remain on the scene or to report the mishap, in preference to the rule that a person should not be compelled to incriminate himself? In more recent years, why did the United States Supreme Court in the segregation case of *Brown v. Board of Education*[22] reject the path of the separate but equal doctrine for a more honest interpretation of the equal protection clause of the Fourteenth Amendment?

Frank's Views of the Judicial Process

"The judge in reaching a decision," said Judge Frank, "is making a judgment. And if we would understand what goes into the creating of that judgment, we must observe how ordinary men dealing with ordinary affairs arrive at their judgments." [23] When we do this, Frank notes, we find that the ordinary man decides first, and then seeks reasons in support of that decision.

Frank holds that the lawyer presenting a case in court must "begin with a conclusion which will insure his client's winning the lawsuit." [24]

He goes on to say that "in theory, the judge begins with some rule or principle of law as his premise, applies this premise to the facts, and thus arrives at his decision." [25] This theory, so Frank believes, does not accord with the facts. "Since the judge is a human being and since no human being in his normal thinking processes arrives at decisions (except in dealing with a limited number of simple situations) by the route of any such syllogistic reasoning, it is fair to assume that the judge, merely by putting on the judicial ermine, will not acquire so artificial a method of reasoning. Judicial judgments, like other judgments, doubtless, in most cases, are worked out backward from conclusions tentatively formulated." [26]

We may omit close consideration of the lawyer in court. As Frank says, the conclusion he begins with is not his conclusion; it is his client's, and it is the business of the lawyer to convince the court of the validity of that conclusion.

Frank's assertion, however, that both the ordinary man and the judge begin with "conclusions tentatively formulated" fails to give the whole picture. What causes them to arrive at these conclusions in the first place?

Let us assume an ordinary man dealing with one of the ordinary affairs of life: the purchase of a car. According to Frank's theory, having reached the "more or less vaguely formed" conclusion to buy a car, the man then seeks reasons in support of his decision: the old car needs new tires and a costly overhauling, it uses an excessive amount of gasoline and oil, and there are frequent breakdowns and some difficulty in getting parts. Another reason might be that with all the repairs necessary on the old car, it might be cheaper to buy a new one.

There are, however, other ways of thinking and reaching conclusions. Instead of the factors mentioned being reasons in support of a *previously and independently reached* conclusion, it would seem more reasonable to assume that from the condition of the old car, there emerged the conclusion to purchase a new car.

To say, as Frank says, that a judge reaches his decisions on the basis of previously reached, independent conclusions, and that his opinions are mere rationalizations, is too simple a picture. It overlooks too much.

True, the judge is a human being. Like the rest of us, he was born and grew up, the subject of influences, good, bad, and indifferent. As an adult he reflects an experience of life, its hopes and fears, its joys and sorrows, its successes and failures, its secondary victories and primary defeats or vice versa.

Our man on the bench, however, is something more. He *is* a judge. He is also a lawyer. For years he has talked, eaten and slept law. In law school, he came upon case after case in contracts, torts, procedure, agency, wills, constitutional and administrative law; he drank deeply of their contents, mulled over them, argued for and against them, absorbing doctrine, precedent and rule. As a practicing attorney, the lawyer's way of thinking —getting the facts, finding the appropriate cause of action, distinguishing one case from another--deepens within him, and more deeply colors his approach to lawyer's problems. When he comes to be a judge and must resolve the conflicting conclusions of the parties to a dispute, he brings to bear upon the conflict, not the thinking of the ordinary man, but the thinking of a mind trained and practiced in the law. He is, as Karl Llewellyn has said, "law-conditioned." [27]

If judicial judgments are "worked out backward from conclusions tentatively formulated," they are, first of all, conclusions that come within the context of the lawyer's training and experience. Secondly, as in the instance of the ordinary man and his motor car, the conclusions of a Cardozo arise because of a knowledge of men and their condition, an awareness of social change, and a sensitivity to the needs of society. They arise, too, from a sense of justice and fair-dealing. On the other hand, there are judges whose knowledge, awareness, and sensitivity are narrow and parochial, and whose concept of their role in society lacks courage, insight and initiative, and whose labors tend to uphold the status quo. But, whether wise or not, judges necessarily act within the limits of the law.

How can one say that, you ask? Is it not obvious that judges are making law all the time? Yes, that is true; but there is this to remember, that in making law, the judges keep well within the web of the law. What does this mean? It means that judges, and particularly judges of the highest courts have, as Cardozo said, a choice of paths to follow in deciding a case. The word "particularly" is used in reference to the highest courts because their choices cannot be questioned or overruled by a higher court. Although lower court judges have a choice, too, none of them like to be overruled and they therefore tend to hew to a line already drawn by the highest court. Thus, in *Woods v. Lancet,* Judge Shientag concurred with the majority of the Appellate Division, not because he approved of the decision, but because of a ruling of the Court of Appeals thirty years earlier. A study of the majority and dissenting opinions of any case will reveal good law; but it will be noted that the majority followed one legal path, the minority, another. Above all, these differing opinions reflect choice; and nothing, said Thomas Reed Powell, will save the judges "from the pain of choosing at every step."

The law gives the impression of rigidity, and the impression is correct. Rigidity must exist if men are to know a degree of certainty and stability. But there is more than this. There is resilience and flexibility, as the cases attest, without which the impact of law would be as the touch of a dead hand.

Mr. Justice Holmes said that "the life of the law has not been logic;

it has been experience," [28] and there is truth in this. The vitality of the law has been the experience of mankind and the response of living judges to that experience. But, as Cardozo commented, "Holmes did not tell us that logic is to be ignored when experience is silent." [29]

Learned Hand and "Good Moral Character"

There are those who believe that the judicial function should consist solely and simply in the literal application of law or principle, no more, no less. There are others whose view of the judge's duty allows extreme latitude to the extent that whatever the law or precedent, the judge should follow the dictates of his own conscience. Judge Learned Hand believed neither view correct. The former, he calls the "dictionary" school; "no matter what the result is, he [the judge] must read the words in their usual meaning and stop where they stop." [30] The latter, he regards as inevitable when one is "interpreting any written words. When a judge tries to find out what the government would have intended which it did not say, he puts into its mouth things which he thinks it ought to have said, and that is very close to substituting what he himself thinks right." "Let him beware . . . ," says Judge Hand, "or he will usurp the office of government." [31]

What does a judge do when the statute or precedent is not clear, when words and phrases are not defined and thus leave the judge "at large"?

To return to the phrase "good moral character," the question arose again in *Schmidt v. United States.*[32] The District Court had denied one Schmidt his petition for naturalization on the ground that he had failed to establish that he was a person of good moral character for the five years preceding the filing of the petition. Before an examiner, Schmidt had admitted that "Now and then I engaged in an act of sexual intercourse with women. These women have been single and unmarried women. As to the frequency of these acts I can only state that they occurred now and then. My last such act took place about half a year ago with an unmarried woman." [33] The Court of Appeals reversed the District Court and the petition was granted.

In his decision, Judge Hand was again troubled, as well he might be, by the meaning of good moral character. Its basis was certainly the moral feeling now prevalent in the country, but how is that moral feeling to be determined? "Even though we could take a poll," he said, "it would not be enough merely to count heads, without any appraisal of the voters. A majority of the votes of those in prisons and brothels, for instance, ought scarcely to outweigh the votes of accredited churchgoers. Nor can we see any reason to suppose that the opinion of clergymen would be a more reliable estimate that our own." [34]

Judge Hand reviewed a few of the cases. A single act of adultery was alone enough to prevent an alien's naturalization; but an alien who, unable to secure a divorce, had been living for years in a faithful but adulterous union was admitted. The court said: we did not "believe that the present sentiment of the community views as morally reprehensible such faithful and long continued relationships under the circumstances here disclosed." [35] An alien was admitted to citizenship despite the fact that he had violated the law of Connecticut in marrying his niece, by whom he had four children. The court thought that the community's moral sense would not be outraged by such a union. Finally, Hand cited *Repouille v. United States.*

One more case of "good moral character" may be considered. Johnson, the petitioner, came to this country in 1913. He married in 1923 and had one son. He had left his wife, and though he was ordered to pay for her support, he rarely did so. He found it difficult to hold a job. In 1944, a probation officer of the Domestic Relations Court stated that Johnson and his wife had been known to that court since 1931. Johnson admitted that he had lived "in illicit relations" with a woman named Urich between 1937 and 1942, that is, within the probationary five year period. The District Court granted Johnson's petition.

The Court of Appeals reversed the order and denied the petition.[36]

It will be remembered that Judge Frank, dissenting in *Repouille v. United States,* had expressed the opinion that the moral conventions of the time might be elicited from the nation's ethical leaders. In *Johnson v. United States,* Judge Hand answered this argument more fully, and incidentally pointed up the difficulties of the judging process.

We must own that the statute imposes upon courts a task impossible of assured execution; people differ as much about moral conduct as they do about beauty. There is not the slightest doubt that to many thousands of our citizens nothing will excuse any sexual irregularity; for some indeed this extends even to the subsequent marriage of an innocent divorced spouse. On the other hand there are many thousands who look with a complaisant eye upon putting an easy end to one union and taking on another. Our duty in such cases, as we understand it, is to divine what the "common conscience" prevalent at the time demands; and it is impossible in practice to ascertain what in a given instance it does demand. We should have no warrant for assuming that it meant the judgment of some ethical élite, even if any criterion were available to select them. Nor is it possible to make use of general principles, for almost every moral situation is unique; and no one could be sure how far the distinguishing features of each case would be morally relevant to one person and not to another. Theoretically, perhaps we might take as the test whether those who would approve the specific conduct would outnumber those who would disapprove; but it would be fantastically absurd to try to apply it. So it seems to us that we are confined to the best guess we can make of how such a poll would result.[37]

One who contemplates the judging process from the outside, looking in through the shaded windows of the mind, finds visible only a very sketchy outline of this process. And it is questionable whether seeing this outline gives us claim to any "knowledge" of the actual process. For, as Mr. Justice Holmes has said, judicial decisions depend "on a judgment or intuition more subtle than any articulate major premise." [38] Thus, what has been said here is conjecture. But one truth emerges clearly: to repeat what we said in the beginning, it is the men who count. Men, through the agony of resolving human conflict, make a judicial system what it is. Their quality and character, intelligence and dignity, make the law a living, vital entity combining the wisdom of the past with the realities of the present, to the end that men shall know justice.

Notes

Cases (Federal, state, and British) are cited by title, date of decision, volume number, abbreviated title of the report, and page number. Earlier cases are cited under the name of the reporter or reporters who prepared them for publication. British statutes are cited by regnal year, name of sovereign, small c. (for chapter), and chapter number. For an excellent account of citations, the reader should consult Miles O. Price, *A Practical Manual of Standard Legal Citations* (New York: Oceana Publications, 1950).

Chapter I

[1] Lochner v. New York (1905) 198 U.S. 45.

[2] Highway Law, § 290, subdivision 3.

[3] People v. Rosenheimer (1913) 209 N.Y. 115, 124.

[4] *Science and the Modern World* (New York: The Macmillan Company, 1954), p. 289.

[5] *Leviathan*, Part I, ch. xiii. Unhappily, or maybe it is just realistic, Hobbes' view of the nature of man seems to find a responsive chord in the minds of present-day students. This is why I have mentioned Hobbes rather than Hooker or Locke or Rousseau.

[6] *Ibid.*

[7] Students who are interested in further exploring this idea may well read Joseph Conrad's *Heart of Darkness* and William Golding's *Lord of the Flies.*

[8] *Federalist Papers,* No. 51. This is not quite true. If angels drove automobiles, a rule might require that they keep to the right side of the road. This rule, I think, would be based, not on conflict, but on convenience. Such a rule, however, reduces an area of potential conflict.

[9] See the first few paragraphs of John C. Calhoun: *A Disquisition on Government.*

[10] H. L. A. Hart, *The Concept of Law* (Oxford: Clarendon Press, 1961), p. 1. However, neither chemistry nor medicine is the convenient pigeon-hole it once was. Chemistry, physics, biology, mathematics, and other sciences have become so interrelated that the lines between them have become indistinct. If it were worth the trouble, scientists could easily develop a literature in answer to the question, What is physics, or biology, and so on. Some mathematicians are interested in the question, Is mathematics a "science" or a "language"?

[11] *Addresses of Charles Evans Hughes, 1906-1916* (2nd ed.; New York and London: G. P. Putnam's Sons, 1916), p. 185.

[12] Oliver Wendell Holmes, *Collected Legal Papers* (New York: Harcourt, Brace & World, Inc., 1920), p. 173.

[13] *The Bramble Bush, on Law and its Study* (New York: Oceana Publications, 1951), p. 12.

[14] This statement says nothing about the part played by administrative agencies in resolving disputes, a question which is discussed later on.

[15] Southern Pacific Company v. Jensen (1917) 244 U.S. 205, 222.

[16] James Harrington, "Oceana," in *Ideal Commonwealths* (rev. ed.; London & New York: The Colonial Press, 1901), p. 183. Judge Jerome Frank has said that this phrase means a government of laws administered by the "right" kind of men. Although we can all agree with this statement, it means little. Naturally, most of us want the "right" men in government; we want "good" legislators, "good" civil servants, "good" ambassadors, "good" governors, a "good" president, and "good" judges. What is meant by "right," by "good"? The ideal, applicable to lawyers and judges alike, was broadly expressed by the late Karl Llewellyn:

> In accepting the honor and responsibility of life in the profession of the law, I engage, as best I can, to work always with care and with a whole heart and with good faith; to weigh my conflicting loyalties and guide my work with an eye to the good, less of myself than of justice and of the people; and to be at all times, even at personal sacrifice, a champion of fairness and due process, in court or out, for all, whether the powerful or the envied or my neighbors or the helpless or the hated or the oppressed.

Taken from *Announcements,* The Law School, The University of Chicago, 1962-1963.

[17] (1905) 103 App. Div. (N.Y.), 246.

[18] Loudon v. Scott (1920) 58 Mont. 645.

[19] *The Speeches of Sir Samuel Romilly in the House of Commons* (London: James Ridgway and Sons, 1820), Vol. I, 124.

[20] Francis Bacon, *Essays,* No. 1.

[21] Quoted in Sir Alfred Denning, *The Road to Justice* (London: Stevens & Sons, Limited, 1955), p. 1.

[22] 10 Howell's *State Trials,* p. 267.

[23] 7 & 8 Will. III, c. 3.

[24] 12 Geo. III, c. 20.

[25] See A. L. Goodhart, "Acquitting the Guilty," in *The Law Quarterly Review,* Vol. 70 (Oct. 1954), pp. 514-526.

[26] *Ibid.,* pp. 521-525.

[27] *Ibid.,* pp. 518-519.

[28] John Forster, *The Life of Charles Dickens* (Philadelphia: J. B. Lippincott Co., 1873), Vol. II, 99.

[29] *Ibid.*

[30] 15 & 16 Vict., c.c. 80, 86.

[31] *Bleak House,* ch. 1. In the Preface to this novel, Dickens makes clear that *Jarndyce* v. *Jarndyce* is not entirely the product of his imagination. He wrote: "At the present moment (1853) there is a suit before the Court which was commenced nearly twenty years ago . . . and which is (I am assured) no nearer to its termination now than when it was begun. There is another well-known suit in Chancery, not yet decided, which was commenced before the close of the last century. . . . If I wanted other authorities for Jarndyce and Jarndyce, I could rain them on these pages. . . ." *Bleak House* (London: Chapman and Hall, 1897), Vol. I, p. xiv.

[32] Temporary Commission on the Courts to the Governor and the Legislature of the State of New York, *Report, 1956* (Albany: Williams Press, Inc., 1956), p. 13.

[33] (New Haven: Yale University Press, 1932).

[34] *Ibid.,* p. 39.

[35] Moore v. Dempsey (1923) 261 U.S. 86, 89-90.

[36] *Ibid.,* 91.

[37] (1930) 254 N.Y. 192.

[38] *Ibid.,* 194-195.

[39] *Ibid.*, 196.
[40] *Ibid.*, 198-199.
[41] *Ibid.*, 195.
[42] *Ibid.* Italics supplied.
[43] *Ibid.*, 199-200.
[44] *Report on Lawlessness in Law Enforcement* (Washington: Government Printing Office, 1931), p. 347.

Chapter II

[1] Sir William Blackstone, *Commentaries on the Laws of England* (Oxford: Clarendon Press, 1778), Vol. III, 343.

[2] Guy Carleton Lee, *Leading Documents of English History* (London: George Bell and Sons, 1900), pp. 88-89. One might argue that the outcome of the test was preordained by the form of the ordeal since anyone tied up and thrown into a stream would sink, and anyone carrying a hot iron for a number of paces would be severely burned. The interesting question is what determined the use of fire rather than water? Citing Glanville as an authority, Blackstone declares that the former was "confined to persons of higher rank, the latter to the common people." *Commentaries, op. cit.*, Vol. IV, 342.

[3] *Ibid.*, pp. 87-88.

[4] A thrymsa was a third of a shilling. "Near thirteen hundred pounds of present money," wrote David Hume in 1761. See his *History of England* (Oxford: Talboys and Wheeler, 1826), Vol. I, 195.

[5] The Salisbury Oath. See Lee, *Leading Documents in English History, op. cit.*, p. 120.

[6] *The Anglo-Saxon Chronicle*, ed. by Dorothy Whitelock (London: Eyre and Spottiswoode, 1961), pp. 198-199.

[7] An old English land measure.

[8] F. E. Harmer, *Anglo-Saxon Writs* (Manchester: Manchester University Press, 1952), pp. 395-396.

[9] I have omitted in the text any reference to the assize *Utrum* which related to the question whether land possessed by the church was held by the usual feudal tenure or as frankalmoign, and the assize *Darrein Presentment,* the purpose of which was to identify the person who last had the right of presentation of an ecclesiastical benefice. Both questions were to be settled in the king's court.

[10] B. Wilkinson, *Constitutional History of Medieval England* (London: Longmans, Green and Co., 1958), Vol. III, 179-180.

[11] William Stubbs, *The Constitutional History of England* (Oxford: Clarendon Press, 1891), Vol. I, 648.

[12] Magna Carta, ch. 18. *Darrein Presentment* or last presentation: a real action which lay against anyone who interfered with the plaintiff's right to present a benefice, or ecclesiastical living, to his own appointee. But seet Footnote 9, Chapter II.

[13] 13 Ed. I, c. 30.

[14] *Royal Writs in England from the Conquest to Glanvill* (London: Bernard Quaritch, 1959), pp. 402-403.

[15] Arthur T. Vanderbilt, *Cases and Other Materials on Modern Procedure and Judicial Administration* (New York: Washington Square Publishing Corp., 1952), pp. 1327-1328.

[16] Blackstone, *Commentaries, op. cit.*, Vol. I, 67.

[17] *Ibid.*, p. 68.

[18] *Ibid.*

[19] *Ibid.*, p. 69.

[20] *Ibid.*, pp. 76-78.

[21] Thomas Robinson, *The Common Law of Kent: or, the Customs of Gavelkind. With an Appendix concerning Borough-English* (London: F. Cogan, 1741).

[22] Blackstone, *Commentaries, op. cit.*, Vol. II, 83.

[23] *Ibid.*

[24] *Ibid.*, Vol. I, 79.

[25] C. H. S. Fifoot, *English Law and its Background* (London: G. Bell and Sons, Ltd., 1932), p. 91.

[26] (1843) 12 M. & W. 324, 353. Taken from Thomas Edward Scrutton, "Roman Law Influence in Chancery, Church Courts, Admiralty, and Law Merchant," in *Select Essays in Anglo-American Legal History* (Boston: Little, Brown & Company, 1907), Vol. I, p. 213.

[27] Scrutton, *ibid.*, pp. 214-215.

[28] Blackstone, *Commentaries, op. cit.*, Vol. III, 108.

[29] *Ibid.*, Vol. I, 79.

[30] *Ibid.*, p. 80.

[31] Carleton Kemp Allen, *Law in the Making* (Oxford: Clarendon Press, 1951), pp. 118-119.

[32] *Ibid.*, p. 119.

[33] *Ibid.*

[34] *Ibid.*, pp. 119-120.

[35] *Ibid.*, p. 122.

[36] *Ibid.*

Chapter III

[1] B. Wilkinson, *Constitutional History of Medieval England, 1216-1399* (London: Longmans, Green and Co., 1958), Vol. III, 145-146.

[2] William Paley Baildon (Ed.), *Select Cases in Chancery, A. D. 1364 to 1471* (London: Bernard Quaritch, 1896), p. 110.

[3] *Ibid.*

[4] Lumley v. Gye (1853), 2 Ellis and Blackburn, 216.

[5] Lumley v. Wagner (1852), 1 De Gex, Macnaghten & Gordon, 604.

[6] (1893) 1 Chancery 126.

[7] W. T. Barbour, "The History of Contract in Early English Equity," in *Oxford Studies in Social and Legal History* (Oxford: Clarendon Press, 1914), Vol. IV, p. 121.

[8] *Ibid.*

[9] *Ibid.*

[10] *Ibid.*

[11] Augustus Jessopp, *The Coming of the Friars* (London: T. Fisher Unwin, 1908), p. 37.

[12] See *supra* p. 33.

[13] 27 Hen. VIII, c. 10.

[14] George W. Keeton, *Shakespeare and His Legal Problems* (London: A. & C. Black, Ltd., 1930), pp. 13-14.

[15] Paul S. Clarkson and Clyde T. Warren, *The Law of Property in Shakespeare and the Elizabethan Drama* (Baltimore: The Johns Hopkins Press, 1942), p. 151.

[16] See in general, E. L. Woodward, *The Age of Reform, 1815-1870* (Oxford: Clarendon Press, 1939); George Macaulay Trevelyan, *Lord Grey of the Reform Bill* (New York: David McKay Co., Inc., 1920); and Justin McCarthy, *The Epoch of Reform, 1830-1850* (London: Longmans, Green and Co., 1920).

[17] 9 & 10 Vict. c. 95.

[18] 20 & 21 Vict. c. 77, §39.
[19] 20 & 21 Vict. c. 85.
[20] 7 & 8 Geo. IV, c. 28. "Benefit of clergy" protected the priest or clerk from the rigors of the criminal law. A priest accused of felony and brought before a regular court would plead his clergy and thereupon be turned over to the ecclesiastical courts for trial. This was later extended to all persons who could read a certain Psalm, in Latin, commonly called the "neck verse."
[21] For the story of the movement to reduce the number of capital offences, see Leon Radzinowicz, *A History of English Criminal Law and its Administration from 1750,* Vol. I, *The Movement for Reform* (London: Stevens & Sons, 1948).
[22] 6 & 7 Will. IV, c. 114.
[23] Common Law Procedure Act, 15 & 16 Vict. c. 76. See also statutes referred to in following note.
[24] 36 & 37 Vict. c. 66; 38 & 39 Vict. c. 77. Amendments to these statutes were passed in 1877, 40 & 41 Vict. c. 9; 1879, 42 & 43 Vict. c. 78; and 1881, 44 & 45 c. 68. The best account of the old forms of action is Frederic William Maitland's, "The Forms of Action at Common Law," reprinted in Arthur T. Vanderbilt, *Cases and Other Materials on Modern Procedure and Judicial Administration* (New York: Washington Square Publishing Corp., 1952), pp. 1266-1330.

Chapter IV

[1] See Sir Frederick Pollock and Frederic William Maitland, *The History of the English Law Before the Time of Edward I* (London: Cambridge University Press, 1898), pp. 140-144.
[2] See *supra* p. 26.
[3] Guy Carleton Lee, *Leading Documents of English History* (London: George Bell and Sons, 1900), p. 138.
[4] *Ibid.*
[5] *A Short History of English Law* (Boston: Little, Brown, and Company, 1913), pp. 51-52.
[6] William Blackstone, *Commentaries on the Laws of England* (Oxford: Clarendon Press, 1778), Vol. III, 374.
[7] 1 Cobbett & Howell, *State Trials,* 869.
[8] *Ibid.,* 899.
[9] *Ibid.*
[10] *Ibid.*
[11] *Ibid.,* 900.
[12] *Ibid.*
[13] *Ibid.*
[14] *Ibid.*
[15] *Ibid.,* 901.
[16] *Ibid.*
[17] 6 Cobbett & Howell, *State Trials,* 951.
[18] *Ibid.,* 999.
[19] *Ibid.,* 1008.
[20] William Blackstone, *Commentaries on the Laws of England, op. cit.,* Vol. IV, 349.
[21] *The Book of English Law* (Boston and New York: Houghton Mifflin Company, 1929), p. 167.
[22] William Blackstone, *Commentaries on the Laws of England, op. cit.,* Vol. IV, 18.
[23] *Ibid.,* pp. 18-19.

[24] *The Speeches of Samuel Romilly in the House of Commons* (London: James Ridgeway and Sons, 1820), Vol. I, 131, footnote.

[25] *Ibid.,* pp. 131-132, footnote.

[26] William Blackstone, *Commentaries on the Laws of England, op. cit.,* Vol. III, 379.

[27] *Certiorari:* a writ or order issuing from a higher court directing a lower court to send to it for review the record of a case pending or terminated therein. The purpose of the review is the correction of (1) procedural errors, or (2) the interpretation of the law as it relates to the given case. *Mandamus:* a writ or order issued by a court to an inferior court, a person, or officer of a corporation, directing the recipient to perform a nondiscretionary, ministerial act pertaining to office or duty. *Prohibition:* a writ or order issued by a higher court to the judge and parties of a suit in a lower court directing them to abandon the cause in that particular court on the ground that that court has no jurisdiction over the case.

[28] *The Machinery of Justice in England* (2nd ed.; London: Cambridge University Press, 1953), pp. 36-37.

[29] Sir Charles Grant Robertson, *Select Statutes, Cases, and Documents* (9th ed.; London: Methuen & Co., Ltd., 1949), p. 97.

[30] 3 Cobbett & Howells, *State Trials,* 1.

[31] *Ibid.,* 3.

[32] *Ibid.,* 59.

[33] *Ibid.,* 53.

[34] Guy Carleton Lee, *Leading Documents of English History, op. cit.,* pp. 349-350.

[35] 6 Cobbett & Howells, *State Trials,* 1194.

[36] *Ibid.,* 1196.

[37] *Ibid.,* 1198.

[38] Sir Charles Grant Robertson, *Select Statutes, Cases, and Documents, op. cit.,* p. 98.

[39] *Ibid.,* pp. 95-96.

[40] *Ibid.,* p. 96.

[41] *Ibid.,* p. 98.

[42] William Blackstone, *Commentaries on the Laws of England, op. cit.,* Vol. I, 136. Italics supplied.

[43] *Ibid.,* Vol. III, 438.

[44] (1898) 169 U.S. 649.

Chapter V

[1] Van Ness v. Pacard (1829) 2 Pet. 137, 144.

[2] Quoted from William MacDonald, *Select Charters and other Documents Illustrative of American History, 1606-1775* (New York: The Macmillan Company, 1914), p. 77.

[3] Paul Samuel Reinsch, "The English Common Law in the Early American Colonies," in *Select Essays in Anglo-American Legal History* (Boston: Little, Brown, & Company, 1907), Vol. I, p. 382.

[4] *Ibid.,* p. 388.

[5] *Ibid.,* p. 369.

[6] Of course, there were lawyers in the colonies, and four delegates to the Constitutional Convention of 1787, who had been trained in England in one of the four Inns of Court: Lincoln's Inn, the Middle Temple, the Inner Temple, and Gray's Inn. These are private, unincorporated associations exclusively empowered to confer the degree or rank of barrister, in other words, of calling to the bar.

[7] Page Smith, *John Adams* (Garden City, N.Y.: Doubleday & Company, Inc., 1962), Vol. I, 34.

[8] *Ibid.*, p. 42.

[9] For an account of the Litchfield school, see Alfred Zantzinger Reed, *Training for the Public Profession of the Law* (New York: The Carnegie Foundation for the Advancement of Teaching, 1921), pp. 128-133; and Margaret L. Coit, *John C. Calhoun, American Portrait* (Boston: Houghton Mifflin Company, 1950), pp. 36-43.

[10] Blackstone was born in 1723 and died in 1780. He studied at Pembroke College, Oxford. He was called to the bar in 1746. With little success as a barrister, he returned to Oxford where in 1753 he began his famous "Lectures" on the laws of England. These form the basis of the *Commentaries*. On the strength of the lectures, Blackstone was elected the first Vinerian professor of law at Oxford. He had some experience in Parliament, a brief stay on the Court of King's Bench, and finally was appointed to the Common Pleas.

[11] Alfred Zantzinger Reed, *Training for the Public Profession of the Law, op. cit.*, p. 111.

[12] *Ibid.*

[13] *Commentaries on the Laws of England* (8th ed.; Oxford: Clarendon Press, 1778), Vol. I, 125.

[14] *Ibid.*, p. 129.

[15] *Ibid.*, Vol. IV, 335.

[16] *Ibid.*, p. 291.

[17] *Ibid.*, p. 297.

[18] Edited by Max Farrand (New Haven: Yale University Press, 1937).

[19] Daniel J. Boorstin, *The Mysterious Science of the Law* (Boston: Beacon Press, 1958), pp. 3-4.

[20] William L. Prosser, *Handbook of the Law of Torts* (St. Paul: West Publishing Co., 1941), p. 1.

[21] *Ibid.*

[22] *Ibid.*, p. 3.

[23] Wilkinson v. Downton [1897] 2 Queen's Bench 57.

[24] Hay v. Cohoes Corp. (1849) 2 N.Y. 159, 160.

[25] *Ibid.*

[26] *Ibid.*, 161

[27] *Ibid.*

[28] *Ibid.*

[29] (1866) Law Reports, 1 Exchequer case, 265; Law Reports, 3 House of Lords, 330.

[30] *Ibid.*

[31] *Ibid.*

[32] Rickards v. Lothian [1913] Appeal Cases 263.

[33] Blyth v. Birmingham Waterworks Co. (1856) 11 Exchequer 781.

[34] A. P. Herbert, *Uncommon Law* (London: Methuen & Co., Ltd., 1935), pp. 3-4.

[35] (Bloomington: Indiana University Press, 1955), pp. 215-221.

[36] *Ibid.*, p. 216.

[37] Byrne v. N.Y.C. & H.R.R. (1881) 83 N.Y. 620, 621.

[38] Wagner v. International Ry. Co. (1921) 232 N.Y. 176, 179.

[39] *Ibid.*, 179-180.

[40] *Ibid.*

[41] Palsgraf v. Long Island Ry. Co. (1928) 248 N.Y. 339.

[42] Palsgraf v. Long Island Ry. Co. (1927) 222 App. Div. (N.Y.) 166, 167.

[43] (1773) 2 W. Blackstone, 892.

[44] (1847) 4 Denio (N.Y.) 464.

[45] (1882) 19 Johns. (N.Y.) 381.

[46] Palsgraf v. Long Island Ry. Co. (1927) 222 App. Div. (N.Y.) 168-169.

[47] Palsgraf v. Long Island Ry. Co. (1928) 248 N.Y. 341.
[48] *Ibid.*, 343.
[49] *Ibid.*
[50] *Ibid.*
[51] *Ibid.*
[52] *Ibid.*, 350.
[53] A definition widely used by the courts.
[54] William L. Prosser, "Palsgraf Revisited," in 52 *Michigan Law Review* (November, 1953), p. 6.
[55] *Ibid.*, p. 20.
[56] Palsgraf v. Long Island Ry. Co. (1928) 248 N.Y. 342.
[57] *Ibid.*, 342-343.
[58] William L. Prosser, "Palsgraf Revisited," *op. cit.*, p. 22.
[59] See *supra*. p. 75.

Chapter VI

[1] Hulett v. Swift (1865) 33 N.Y. 571, 572.
[2] *Ibid.*, 574.
[3] (1584) 8 Coke's *Reports* 32.
[4] Hulett v. Swift, *op. cit.*, 572-573.
[5] Wilson v. Bumstead (1881) 12 Nebr. 1. Quoted in Roscoe Pound and Theodore F. T. Plucknett, *Readings on the History and System of the Common Law* (3rd ed.; Rochester: The Lawyers Co-operative Publishing Co., 1927), p. 272.
[6] Robert A. Sprecher, "The Development of the Doctrine of *Stare Decisis* and the Extent to which it should be Applied," in 31 *American Bar Association Journal* (Oct., 1945), p. 501.
[7] Benjamin N. Cardozo, *The Paradoxes of Legal Science* (New York: Columbia University Press, 1928), p. 8.
[8] Fred Rodell, *Woe Unto You, Lawyers!* (New York: Pageant Press, 1957), pp. 116-118.
[9] Tallon v. Interborough Rapid Transit Co. (1922) 232 N.Y. 410, 412.
[10] *Ibid.*
[11] *Ibid.*
[12] *Ibid.*, 415.
[13] Matter of Littler v. Fuller Co. (1918) 223 N.Y. 369, 371.
[14] Tallon v. Interborough Rapid Transit Co., *op. cit.*, 413-414.
[15] *Ibid.*, 414.
[16] Hynes v. New York Central Railroad (1919) 188 App. Div. 178.
[17] *Ibid.*, 182.
[18] (1921) 231 N.Y. 229.
[19] *Ibid.*, 235.
[20] *Ibid.*, 234.
[21] *Ibid.*
[22] *Ibid.*, 236.
[23] Benjamin N. Cardozo, *The Growth of the Law* (New Haven: Yale University Press, 1927), pp. 100-101.
[24] Woods v. Lancet (1951) 278 App. Div. 913.
[25] 232 N.Y. 220.
[26] *Ibid.*, 221.
[27] Woods v. Lancet, *op. cit.*, 914.
[28] (1900) 184 Ill. 359, 370.
[29] *Ibid.*, 371. Woods v. Lancet, *op. cit.*, 914-915.

[30] (1951) 303 N.Y. 349.

[31] (1884) 138 Mass. 14.

[32] Woods v. Lancet, 303 N.Y. 349, 354.

[33] *Ibid.*, 356.

[34] "The Path of the Law," in *Collected Legal Papers* (New York: Harcourt, Brace & World, Inc., 1920), p. 181.

[35] Morris Cohen, *Reason and Nature* (New York: Harcourt, Brace & World, Inc., 1931), p. 125.

[36] Henri Poincaré, *The Foundations of Science* (New York: The Science Press, 1913), p. 155.

[37] *The Anatomy of Science* (New Haven: Yale University Press, 1926), p. 7.

[38] *Ibid.*, p. 9.

[39] *The Paradoxes of Legal Science, op. cit.*, p. 6.

[40] MacPherson v. Buick Motor Co. (1916) 217 N.Y. 382, 397.

[41] *Ibid.*, 396.

[42] *Ibid.*

[43] MacPherson v. Buick Motor Co. (1914) 160 App. Div. 55, 58.

[44] *Ibid.*, 58-59.

[45] *Ibid.*, 60.

[46] MacPherson v. Buick Motor Co. (1916) 217 N.Y. 383.

[47] *Ibid.*, 384.

[48] 6 N.Y. 397.

[49] MacPherson v. Buick Motor Co. (1916) 217 N.Y. 385.

[50] 89 N.Y. 470.

[51] MacPherson v. Buick Co. (1916) 217 N.Y. 386.

[52] 195 N.Y. 478.

[53] *Ibid.*, 480.

[54] MacPherson v. Buick Co. (1916) 217 N.Y. 387.

[55] *Ibid.*, 389.

[56] *Ibid.*

[57] (1932) 259 N.Y. 292.

[58] *Ibid.*, 294.

[59] *Ibid.*, 295.

[60] M'Alister (or Donoghue) v. Stevenson [1932] Appeal Cases 562.

[61] Edward H. Levi, *An Introduction to Legal Reasoning* (Chicago: The University of Chicago Press, 1949), pp. 73-74. In the foregoing section, the writer is greatly indebted to Professor Levi's stimulating and enlightening study.

[62] Priestley v. Fowler (1837) 3 Meeson & Welsby 1. Quoted from P. H. Winfield, *Cases on the Law of Tort* (London: Sweet & Maxwell, Ltd., 4th ed., 1948), pp. 56-58.

[63] *Ibid.*, p. 57.

[64] *Ibid.*, pp. 57-58.

[65] (1842) 4 Metcalf (45 Mass.) 49. Quoted from Carl Raushenbush and Emanuel Stein, *Labor Cases and Materials* (New York: F. S. Crofts & Co., 1941), p. 541.

[66] *Ibid.*, p. 542.

[67] William L. Prosser, *Handbook of the Law of Torts* (St. Paul: West Publishing Co., 1941), p. 377.

[68] Gibson v. Erie Ry. Co. (1875) 63 N.Y. 449, 452.

[69] (1879) 100 U.S. 213.

[70] Gibson v. Erie Ry. Co., *op. cit.*, 454.

[71] Hough v. Ry. Co. (1879) 100 U.S. 213, 224-225.

[72] 35 Stat., p. 65.

[73] *Ibid.*, p. 66.

[74] *Ibid.*

[75] Munn v. Illinois (1876) 94 U.S. 113, 134.

[76] Seaboard Air Line v. Horton (1914) 233 U.S. 492.

[77] *Ibid.,* 495, 496.

[78] *Ibid.,* 497.

[79] *Ibid.,* 503.

[80] 318 U.S. 54, 62 (footnote 14).

[81] 53 Stat., p. 1404.

[82] Tiller v. Atlantic Coast Line (1943) 318 U.S. 54, 55-56.

[83] *Ibid.,* 56.

[84] *Ibid.,* 57.

[85] *Ibid.,* 58.

[86] *Ibid.*

[87] *Ibid.,* 72, 73.

Chapter VII

[1] Traffic infractions are specifically excluded from the category of crime.

[2] 141 N.Y. 185.

[3] *Ibid.,* 190.

[4] *Ibid.*

[5] *Ibid.*

[6] See New York Code of Criminal Procedure, § 552, for offenses not bailable.

[7] People ex rel. Battista v. Christian (1928) 249 N.Y. 314.

[8] *Ibid.,* 317-318.

[9] 23 & 24 Geo. V, c. 36. Administration of Justice (Miscellaneous Provisions) Act, 1933.

[10] William Blackstone, *Commentaries on the Laws of England* (Oxford: Clarendon Press, 1778), Vol. IV, pp. 309-310.

[11] *We are ignorant.* At one time, this word was inscribed on a bill of indictment by the grand jury when it was rejected for insufficent evidence.

[12] Quoted in Lester Bernhardt Orfield, *Criminal Procedure from Arrest to Appeal* (New York: New York University Press, 1947), p. 141.

[13] Rex v. Arnold (1724) 16 Cobbett & Howell, *State Trials,* 695, 764.

[14] *Ibid.,* 765.

[15] Rex v. Ferrers (1760) 19 Cobbett & Howell, *State Trials,* 886.

[16] John Howard, *The State of the Prisons in England and Wales* (3rd ed.; London, 1784), p. 8.

[17] See Royal Commission on Capital Punishment, 1949-1953, *Report* (London: Her Majesty's Stationery Office, 1953), p. 391.

[18] *Ibid.*

[19] Quoted in Irving Stone, *Clarence Darrow, For the Defense* (Garden City: Doubleday & Co., 1941), p. 418.

[20] *Ibid.,* pp. 418-419.

[21] (1929) 36 F. (2d) 549.

[22] 214 F. (2d) 862.

[23] *Ibid.,* 865-866.

[24] *Ibid.,* 870.

[25] *Ibid.* See Benjamin N. Cardozo, "What Medicine Can do for Law," in *Law and Literature* (New York: Harcourt, Brace & World, Inc., 1931), p. 106.

[26] *Ibid.,* 871.

[27] *Ibid.* This case is to be found at 148 F. (2d) 665.

[28] *Ibid.,* 874-875.

[29] Charles W. Halleck, "The Insanity Defense in the District of Columbia—A Legal Lorelei," as reprinted in U.S. Congress, Senate, Subcommittee of the Com-

mittee on the Judiciary, *Hearings, Constitutional Rights of the Mentally Ill*, 87th Cong., 1st Sess., 1961, p. 373.

[30] John C. Knox, "Jury Selection," in 22 *New York University Law Quarterly Review* (July, 1947), p. 437.

[31] New York Code of Criminal Procedure, § 376 (2).

[32] (1884) 96 N.Y. 115.

[33] *Ibid.*, p. 119.

[34] *Ibid.*, p. 120.

[35] *Ibid.*, pp. 118-119.

[36] *Ibid.*, p. 123.

[37] *Ibid.*, p. 125.

[38] New York *Code of Criminal Procedure*, § 358-a.

[39] (1934) 266 N.Y. 15.

[40] *Ibid.*, p. 18.

[41] *Ibid.*, p. 19.

[42] *Trial Technique* (Chicago: Callaghan and Company, 1935), p. 247.

[43] Gabriel V. Mottla, *New York Evidence, Proof of Cases* (Rochester: The Lawyers Cooperative Publishing Company, 1954), p. 216.

[44] *Ibid.*, p. 217.

[45] Irving Goldstein, *Trial Technique, op. cit.*, p. 489.

[46] *Ibid.*, p. 593.

[47] *Ibid.*, p. 594.

[48] Taken from the dissenting opinion of Judge Phillips, Shepard v. United States (1933) 62 F. (2d) 683, 686-687.

[49] (1933) 290 U.S. 96, 99-100.

[50] *The Proof of Guilt* (London: Stevens & Sons Limited, 1955), p. 238.

[51] Stanley Jackson, *Mr. Justice Avory* (London: Victor Gollancz Ltd., 1935), p. 310.

[52] *The Federalist Papers*, No. 83.

[53] *A Judge Takes the Stand* (New York: Alfred A. Knopf, 1933), p. 115.

[54] Jerome Frank, *Courts on Trial* (Princeton: Princeton University Press, 1949), p. 110.

[55] See *New York Times,* October 6th, 7th, 8th, 13th, and 14th, 1955.

[56] U.S. Congress, Senate, Internal Security Subcommittee of the Committee on the Judiciary, *Hearings, Recording of Jury Deliberations*, 84th Cong., 2d Sess., 1955, p. 2.

[57] U.S.C.A., Title 18, § 1508.

[58] Quoted from Jerome Frank, *Courts on Trial, op. cit.*, p. 114. See Rolla R. Longenecker, *Some Hints on the Trial of a Lawsuit* (Rochester: The Lawyers Cooperative Publishing Company, 1927).

[59] *Ibid.*

[60] *Ibid.*

[61] *Ibid.*, pp. 114-115.

[62] *Ibid.*, pp. 14-15.

[63] *Ibid.*, p. 15.

[64] *Ibid.*

[65] Albert Lieck, *Bow Street World* (London: R. Hale Ltd., 1938), pp. 238, 243. See also F. C. Bartlett, *Remembering* (London: Cambridge University Press, 1932).

[66] Albert S. Osborn, *The Mind of the Juror as Judge of the Facts* (Albany: Boyd Printing Co., 1937), p. 86.

[67] *The Proof of Guilt, op. cit.*, p. 80.

[68] F. W. Ashley, *My Sixty Years in the Law* (London: John Lane, The Bodley Head, 1936), p. 163.

[69] Gabriel V. Mottla, *New York Evidence, Proof of Cases, op. cit.*, p. 20.

[70] "The Causes of Popular Dissatisfaction with the Administration of Justice," in

Ray D. Henson, ed., *Landmarks of Law* (New York: Harper & Row, Publishers, 1960), p. 189.

[71] *Ibid*. See also Fred Rodell, *Woe Unto You, Lawyers!* (New York: Pageant Press, Inc., 1957), Ch. IX.

Chapter VIII

[1] Reprinted with *Reports of the Proceedings of the Judicial Conference of the United States, 1961* (Washington: Government Printing Office, 1962), p. 135.

[2] *1956 Report of the Temporary Commission on the Courts to the Governor and the Legislature of the State of New York* (Albany: Williams Press, Inc., 1956), p. 13.

[3] *Pre-Trial* (New York: Baker, Voorhis & Co., Inc., 1950), p. 3.

[4] *Ibid*.

[5] 11 Federal Rules Decisions, 3.

[6] Fed. Rules Civ. Proc., rule 16, 28 U.S.C.A. Italics supplied.

[7] (Washington: Government Printing Office, 1958), p. 97.

[8] (1952) 11 Federal Rules Decisions, 15, 25-28.

[9] G. P. Watkins, *The Growth of Large Fortunes* (Publications of the American Economic Association, 3rd Series, 1907), Vol. VIII, No. 4, 146.

[10] *An Introduction to Administrative Law with Selected Cases* (New York: F. S. Crofts & Co., 1940), p. 154.

[11] Workmen's Compensation Law, § 140.

[12] *Ibid.*, § 150.

[13] *Ibid.*, § 25.

[14] *Ibid.*, § 16.

[15] *Ibid.*, § 36.

[16] *Ibid.*, § 37.

[17] *Ibid.*, § 38.

[18] *Ibid.*, § 55.

[19] In the Matter of the Claim of Marie Pasquel v. Coverly (1958) 4 N.Y. 2d. 28.

[20] *Ibid.*, 30-31.

[21] In the Matter of the Claim of Rose Palermo v. Gallucci & Sons (1959) 5 N.Y. 2d. 529.

[22] *Ibid.*, 535.

[23] *Ibid.*, 532-533.

[24] In the Matter of the Claim of Sally Herman v. Greenpoint Barrel & Drum Reconditioning Co., (1960) 8 N.Y. 2d. 880.

[25] *Ibid*.

[26] In the Matter of the Claim of James Johnson v. Loew's Inc. (1960) 8 N.Y. 2d. 757.

[27] *Ibid.*, 758.

[28] However, a court may find subordinate legislation to be *ultra vires*.

[29] 9 & 10 Geo. VI, c. 49.

[30] Smith v. East Elloe Rural District Council [1956] 2 Weekly Law Reports, 888.

[31] *Ibid.*, 894.

[32] *Ibid.*, 900.

Chapter IX

[1] Nationality Act of 1940, 8 U.S.C.A. § 707 (a) (3).

[2] Repouille v. United States (1947) 165 F. 2d. 152.

[3] *Ibid.*, 153.

[4] *Ibid.*
[5] *Ibid.*
[6] *Ibid.*
[7] *Ibid.*, 154.
[8] *Ibid.*, 155.
[9] Benjamin N. Cardozo, *The Nature of the Judicial Process* (New Haven: Yale University Press, 1928), pp. 18-19.
[10] William Blackstone, *Commentaries on the Laws of England* (Oxford: Clarendon Press, 1778), Vol. I, 69.
[11] Benjamin N. Cardozo, *The Nature of the Judicial Process, op. cit.*, p. 31.
[12] Riggs v. Palmer (1889) 115 N.Y. 506.
[13] *Ibid.*, 509.
[14] *Ibid.*, 508.
[15] *Ibid.*, 511.
[16] Benjamin N. Cardozo, *The Nature of the Judicial Process, op. cit.*, p. 41.
[17] *Ibid.*, pp. 41-43.
[18] See *supra* p. 86-89.
[19] See *supra* p. 89-91.
[20] See *supra* p. 92-96.
[21] See *supra* p. 4-5.
[22] (1954) 347 U.S. 483.
[23] Jerome Frank, *Law and the Modern Mind* (New York: Coward-McCann, Inc., 1930), p. 100.
[24] *Ibid.*
[25] *Ibid.*, p. 101.
[26] *Ibid.*
[27] Karl N. Llewellyn, *The Common Law Tradition* (Boston: Little, Brown & Co., 1960), pp. 19-20.
[28] Oliver Wendell Holmes, Jr., *The Common Law* (Boston: Little, Brown & Co., 1938), p. 1.
[29] Benjamin N. Cardozo, *The Nature of the Judicial Process, op. cit.*, p. 33.
[30] Learned Hand, *The Spirit of Liberty* (New York: Alfred A. Knopf, Inc., 1952), p. 107.
[31] *Ibid.*, p. 108.
[32] (1949) 177 F. 2d. 450.
[33] *Ibid.*
[34] *Ibid.*, 451.
[35] *Ibid.*
[36] (1951) 186 F. 2d. 588.
[37] *Ibid.*, 589-590.
[38] Quoted from Charles P. Curtis, *Law as Large as Life* (New York: Simon and Schuster, Inc., 1959), p. 15.

Glossary

For terms not included in the following list, consult the Index. Beware of these definitions. Whole books have been written about some of the items. Brief definitions are useful up to a point, but, as one legal maxim has it, "Error abides in generalities."

Acquittal. The decision of the petit jury that the defendant is not guilty.

Action. A proceeding in court to determine the legal rights of the parties.

Allegation. The statement given by a party to an action, that sets forth what he expects to prove.

Answer. In a civil suit, the document served upon the plaintiff by the defendant, in answer to the complaint.

Appellant. The party who appeals to a higher court because he is dissatisfied with the decision of the lower one.

Assault. The violent attempt or threat to hurt another.

Assize. In England, until the end of the 13th century, statutes were called Assizes—the Assize of Clarendon, for example. Today, the term applies to the trial of issues, either civil or criminal, by judges of the High Court on circuit.

Bail. Security (money or bail bond) by which a prisoner, charged with crime, can be released. Bail may be given by the prisoner himself or his sureties, and insures that he will appear for trial when so ordered. Not all crimes are bailable.

Battery. The unlawful use of violence upon another. Battery always includes assault.

Benefit of Clergy. Originally, the exemption of clergymen from the ordinary criminal process. Such clergymen who ran afoul of the law were tried in the ecclesiastical courts. Later, it was a means of escaping the death penalty and extended to all persons who were connected with the Church; and still later, to anyone who could read. The reading test consisted of the fifty-first Psalm, commonly called the "neck" verse.

Bona fide. In good faith.

Change of venue. The removal of a case for trial from one district or county to another district or county. This is done in criminal cases, particularly in order to avoid a trial before a judge and/or jury prejudiced against the defendant.

Chattel. Personal property other than freehold land: a cow, an automobile, furniture, and so forth.

Common carrier. A transportation system, available to all, which undertakes to move persons or property for a stated charge.

Complainant. One who brings suit against another.

Complaint. A statement of the cause of action against the person named therein.

Contempt of court. The failure or refusal to obey a court order.

Contract. Usually a written agreement, enforceable in a court of law, made by two or more persons.

Court of first instance. A court in which a controversy is heard and determined for the first time.

Court of last resort. A court from which there is no appeal.

Court of record. A court whose proceedings are recorded "for a perpetual memorial and testimony," thereby giving a record to which later judges may refer. This court has power to punish for contempt.

Damages. A sum of money awarded by a court as compensation to a person who has suffered loss or injury to his person, property, or rights through the unlawful act, or failure to act, or negligence of another.

Decision. The determination of a court of competent jurisdiction in settlement of a controversy. The decision of an appellate court is simply the affirmance or reversal of the court below. The "opinion" of the court is not part of its decision.

Decree. The judgment of a court of equity; as, for example, a divorce decree.

Defendant. A person against whom a suit or prosecution is brought.

Demurrer. The defendant's answer to a charge against him which admits the plaintiff's allegation but denies any legal responsibility. "I admit," said the defendant, "that I ran away from the scene of the accident contrary to a New York statute, but that statute is unconstitutional."

Dissenting opinion. The opinion of an appellate judge, in which he gives his reasons for disagreeing with the majority decision.

Freehold. Full ownership of land.

Immaterial. Evidence which neither proves nor disproves the issue of a trial.

Impeach. To question the truthfulness of a witness's testimony.

Incompetent. Testimony which cannot be admitted in evidence, such as hearsay evidence.

Intestate. One who dies without leaving a will.

Irrelevant. Testimony is irrelevant when it has no bearing on the issue of trial.

Issue. The point to be tried and which develops from the pleadings of the plaintiff and the defendant; a point which is affirmed by one party and denied by the other.

Judgment. The official decision of a court of competent jurisdiction in a controversy submitted to it, respecting the rights and claims of the two parties; the adjudication of guilt and the fixing of punishment.

Jurisdiction. The authority under which a court hears and decides a controversy. The jurisdiction of the Federal courts is found, basically, in Article III of the Constitution of the United States.

Leading case. A case that is deemed to be authoritative and thus followed in subsequent cases of like import.

Leading question. A question, asked the witness, that suggests the answer and is therefore inadmissible.

Liability. Legal obligation "to do, pay, or make good something"; legal responsibility in general.

License. Formal permission granted by an appropriate governmental authority to carry on some business or profession or activity, as, for example, permission to manufacture intoxicating liquors, to practice medicine, or to operate an automobile.

Litigants. The parties to a suit.

Malfeasance. The doing of an unlawful act; the word often describes official misconduct.

Manslaughter. The unlawful killing of a human being, characterized by the absence of premeditation, deliberation, or intent.

Maxim. A tersely stated principle of law as, for example, "No man should be judge in his own cause"; "A delegated power cannot be further delegated."

Misfeasance. The negligent doing of a lawful act.

Mortgage. A contract whereby real estate is pledged as security for a loan of money. If the security consists of personal property, the agreement is called a chattel mortgage.

Motion. An application during the course of a trial made by one of the litigants, requesting a rule or order granting some form of relief. The defendant moves for an arrest of judgment, or for a new trial, or to quash the indictment.

Murder, first degree. The killing of another with premeditation, deliberation, and intent. The killing of another during the commission of a felony, even though there was no premeditation, deliberation, or intent, is murder in the first degree and is called "a felony murder."

Nolle prosequi. Formal entry upon the record by the prosecutor that he "will no further prosecute" the case. Frequently abbreviated to "nol-pros."

Obiter dictum. The utterance of a judge that is incidental or collateral to the opinion he is giving and has no direct bearing upon the case before him.

Opinion. The reasons given for the decision reached by an appellate court.

Ordinance. A rule established by a local authority for the regulation of some activity within the community.

Plaintiff. The party who brings suit against another.

Pleadings. The claims and defenses of the litigants.

Police power. The power of a state of the Union to regulate the activities of its citizens in behalf of public health, public safety, public morals, and public convenience.

Presentment. An accusation of crime by a grand jury from their own knowledge and observation, without any bill of indictment being laid before them.

Prima facie. On the face of it; at first sight.

Prima facie *evidence.* Evidence deemed by law to be sufficient to establish a fact, if that fact cannot be disproved.

Probate. The proof that a written instrument is the last will and testament of a deceased person.

Proximate cause. That which, in a natural sequence and without any effective intervening cause, results in an event or injury.

Puisne. In the English court system, an associate justice.

Quash. To void or annul. When the evidence is such that a valid judgment cannot be reached, an indictment will be quashed.

Recognizance. An obligation entered into before a court to appear at the assizes or criminal court, to keep the peace, or to pay a debt.

Recovery. A judgment of a court of law awarding damages.

Reports. Published volumes which contain accounts of cases argued and decided in the courts.

Res judicata. In noncriminal cases, the counterpart of double jeopardy. The expression means that an issue has already been decided by a court. The issue being *res judicata,* it cannot be tried a second time.

Respondent. The party contending against an appeal from a lower court to a higher court.

Riparian. Relating to the bank of a river. A riparian owner is the possessor of land on the bank of a river.

Sentence. In a criminal case, the punishment imposed by the judge.

Stipulation. An agreement reached by opposing attorneys in the course of litigation and relating to certain facts, the qualifications of expert witnesses, and medical bills, among other things.

Suit. In either law or equity, an action of any kind.

Testator. One who makes a valid will. He is said to have died testate.

Testimony. The giving of evidence by a witness under oath.

Trespass. Unlawful entry and damage to another man's property; unlawful interference with the person and property of another.

Ultra vires. In English law, particularly: beyond the law. An administrative body which went beyond the powers, duties, and limits of its enabling act (that is, an Act of Parliament) would be acting *ultra vires* and with no force and effect. This is the British version of judicial review.

Venue. The district or county in which the crime or injury is alleged to have occurred.

Verdict. The decision or conclusion of the petit jury in a criminal proceeding.

Waiver. The relinquishment of a right.

Warrant. A writ issued by a court, authorizing the seizure of a certain person or a certain property.

Will. A legal declaration, usually in writing, of a person's wishes as to the disposition of his property after his death.

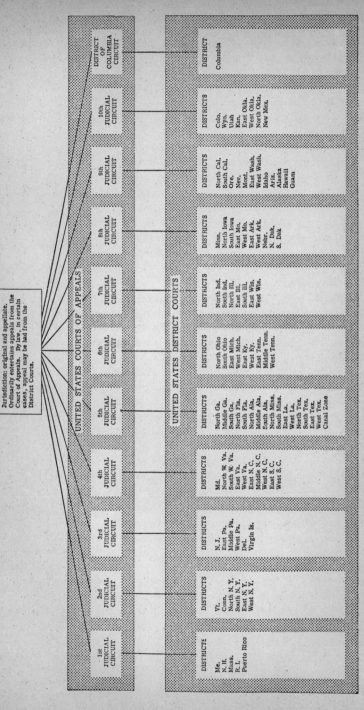

Chart of the United States Courts (abbreviated)

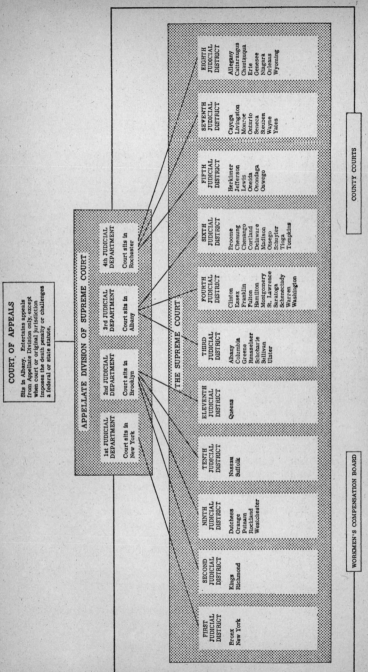

COURT OF APPEALS

Sits in Albany. Entertains appeals from Appellate Division only, except when court or original jurisdiction imposes the death penalty or challenges a federal or state statute.

APPELLATE DIVISION OF SUPREME COURT

1st JUDICIAL DEPARTMENT	2nd JUDICIAL DEPARTMENT	3rd JUDICIAL DEPARTMENT	4th JUDICIAL DEPARTMENT
Court sits in New York	Court sits in Brooklyn	Court sits in Albany	Court sits in Rochester

THE SUPREME COURT

FIRST JUDICIAL DISTRICT
Bronx
New York

SECOND JUDICIAL DISTRICT
Kings
Richmond

NINTH JUDICIAL DISTRICT
Dutchess
Orange
Putnam
Rockland
Westchester

TENTH JUDICIAL DISTRICT
Nassau
Suffolk

ELEVENTH JUDICIAL DISTRICT
Queens

THIRD JUDICIAL DISTRICT
Albany
Columbia
Greene
Rensselaer
Schoharie
Sullivan
Ulster

FOURTH JUDICIAL DISTRICT
Clinton
Essex
Franklin
Fulton
Hamilton
Montgomery
St. Lawrence
Saratoga
Schenectady
Warren
Washington

SIXTH JUDICIAL DISTRICT
Broome
Chemung
Chenango
Cortland
Delaware
Madison
Otsego
Schuyler
Tioga
Tompkins

FIFTH JUDICIAL DISTRICT
Herkimer
Jefferson
Lewis
Oneida
Onondaga
Oswego

SEVENTH JUDICIAL DISTRICT
Cayuga
Livingston
Monroe
Ontario
Seneca
Steuben
Wayne
Yates

EIGHTH JUDICIAL DISTRICT
Allegany
Cattaraugus
Chautauqua
Erie
Genesee
Niagara
Orleans
Wyoming

WORKMEN'S COMPENSATION BOARD

COUNTY COURTS

Chart of the Courts of New York State (abbreviated)

Index

Actions, 30-31
Acton v. Blundell, 35
Adams, John, trains for the law, 63-64
Address, opening, 120; closing, 125
Administrative adjudication, 142ff.
Aethelred, early writ of, 25
Aids, feudal, 22
Alfred, laws of, and the *wergild,* 20
Allaire v. St. Luke's Hospital, 90
Allen, C. K., 37-38
Alternate jurors, 119; *People v. Mitchell,* 119-120
Analogy, reasoning by, 92ff.; Edward H. Levi on, 97; *MacPherson v. Buick Motor Co.,* 92ff.; *Smith v. Peerless Glass Co.,* 96
Arrest, 105ff.; *People v. Wilson,* 106-107
Assumption of risk, 98, 99-100; *Gibson v. Erie Ry. Co.,* 99-100; *Seaboard Air Line v. Horton,* 101-102; *Tiller v. Atlantic Coast Line,* 102-104
Athelstan, laws of, and the ordeal, 19

Bazelon, David L., test of insanity, 114-115; *Durham v. United States,* 113ff.
Blackstone, Sir William, description of the ordeal, 19; on the common law, 31ff.; on common law and custom, 37; criticized by C. K. Allen, 37-38; on trial by jury, 53, 56; on *habeas corpus,* 60; *Commentaries,* 64ff.; and the United States Constitution, 65-67; Boorstin on, 67; on the information, 110
Bleak House, 12
Boorstin, Daniel J., on Blackstone, 67
Borough-English, 23
Bōt, 20
Bracton, 35
Brown v. Board of Education, 157
Byrne v. N.Y.C. & H.R.R., 72

Cahn, Edmond, 72
Calye's Case, 81

Cardozo, Benjamin N., and *People v. Zackowitz,* 15-17; and *Wagner v. Int. Ry. Co.,* 73-74; and *Palsgraf v. Long Island Ry. Co.,* 74-77; and *stare decisis,* 83; and *Hynes v. N.Y.C.R.R.,* 86-89; and *MacPherson v. Buick Motor Co.,* 92-96; on legal definition of insanity, 114; and *Shepard v. United States,* 123-125; on deciding cases, 155-156, 157
Certainty, and the law, 5, 91-92; Holmes on, 92; Cardozo on, 92; and the practice of medicine, 9
Challenge, for cause, 116ff.
Chancery, 12, 29-30, 40ff.
Change, social, and the law, 2-5, 142ff.
Charge, judge's, to jury, 125-126
Chivalry, tenant in, 22
Clarendon, Assize of, 52
Codes, French, 34-35
Common law, 31ff.; in America, 62ff.; and statutes, 100ff.
Common Pleas, Court of, 27ff.
Contributory negligence, 100
Corpus Juris Canonici, 36
Corpus Juris Civilis, 34-36
Courts, Anglo-Saxon and Norman, 18ff.
Criminal Appeal, Court of, 11
Crime, defined, 105
Cross-examination, 120-121
Cross v. Andrews, 81
Curia Regis, 23-24, 26, 29
Custom, and the common law, 31ff.; C. K. Allen on, 37-39

Damages, and common law, 41
Darrow, Clarence, 113
Decision of judge, 153ff.
Declaration of Independence, 65
Delegation of power, 144-145
Demurrer, 4
De pace habenda, writ of, 26
Detention, 107
Devlin v. Smith, 95
Dickens, Charles, 12

Dietrich v. *Northampton,* 91
Direct examination, 121-122
Domesday Book, 27
Drobner v. *Peters,* 89, 91
Durham v. *United States,* 113ff.

Employers' Liability Act, 1908, 100ff.;
   amended, 1939, 102
Equity, 40ff.; and common law, 46ff.
Examination of witnesses, 120-122
Exception, 122ff.
Exchequer, Court of, 23, 27, 31

Facts, determination of, by judge or jury,
   129ff.
Farwell v. *Boston & Worcester Ry. Co.,*
   98-99
Fellow-servant rule, 98-99
Felony, 105
Feudalism, 21ff.
Fief, 22
Fielding, Henry, charge to grand jury,
   109
Franciscan friars, and origin of the trust,
   44-45
Frank, Jerome, on the jury system, 127-
   128, 129; on reaching verdicts and
   decisions, 130-131, 133, 157ff.; dissent
   in *Repouille* v. *United States,* 154
Frankalmoign, tenant in, 22

Gavelkind, 33, 45
General customs and common law, 31-
   33; how determined, 32
Gibson v. *Erie Ry. Co.,* 99-100
Glanvill, 35
Gloucester, Statute of, 1278, 27
Goldstein, Irving, on direct examination,
   120; on the redirect, 122
Goodhart, A. L., 11
Grand Assize, 26, 51
Grand jury, defined, 109; decline of, 109-
   110
Grand Serjeanty, 22
Guille v. *Swan,* 75

Habeas corpus, and *Moore* v. *Dempsey,*
   13-15; early defects of, 57; *Darnel's
   Case,* 57-58; *Jenkes' Case,* 59-60; in the
   United States Constitution, 60; Black-
   stone on, 60; and *United States* v.
   Wong Kim Ark, 60-61
Habeas Corpus Act, 57
Hand, Learned, 153-154, 160-161; and

Repouille v. *United States,* 153-154;
   on "good moral character" and *Schmidt*
   v. *United States,* 160-161
Hay v. *Cohoes Co.,* 69-70
Herbert, A. P., on the "reasonable man,"
   71
Hobbes, Thomas, 6
Holmes, Oliver Wendell, Jr., definition
   of law, 7; and *Moore* v. *Dempsey,* 13-
   15; 96-97, 159-160, 162
Hough v. *Ry. Co.,* 100
Hughes, Charles Evans, definition of law,
   7
Hulett v. *Swift,* 81-82
Hynes v. *New York Central Co.,* 86-89,
   157

Indictment, 108-109
Information, the, 110-111
Injunction, 41-43
Inquest, 51
Insanity plea, 111ff.
Ivanhoe, trial by battle, 20

Jackson, R. M., 56
Jeffreys, George, Lord Chief Justice, 10
Jenks, Edward, 52, 53
Johnson v. *United States,* 161
Judicature Acts, 1873-1875, 49
Jury, Grand, 50
Jury, Petit, origins of, 50-51; and *Throck-
   morton's Case,* 53-54; and *Bushell's
   Case,* 54-55; Blackstone on, 56; selec-
   tion of, 115ff.; exemptions, 115-116;
   function of, 127ff.
Justice, 10-17
Justices in eyre, 28

Keeton, G. W., 47
King's Bench, Court of, 27, 31
King's Peace, 24

Laissez-faire doctrine, 142-143
Law, basis of, 5; definitions of, 7-8; and
   social change, 2-5, 142ff.
Lawyers, in the American colonies, 62;
   training of, during and after the
   colonial period, 63; the influence of
   Blackstone's *Commentaries,* 64ff.
Leopold-Loeb Case, 113
Leviathan, The, 6
Littler v. *Fuller Co., Matter of,* 85-86
Llewellyn, Karl, definition of law, 7
Lochner v. *New York,* 3-4

Lumley v. *Gye,* 42-43
Lumley v. *Wagner,* 43-44

Mahon Case, 126
MacKenzie v. *Carman,* 9
MacPherson v. *Buick Motor Co.,* 92ff., 157
McNaughton Rules, 112-113
Madison, James, 6
Magna Carta, 27
Medicine and law, compared, 9-10
Merchant of Venice, The, 46-48
Misdemeanor, 105
Moley, Raymond, 13
Moore v. *Dempsey,* 13-15, 17
Mort d'ancestor, Assize of, 26, 28

Negligence, and the reasonable man, 71ff.; and *Wagner* v. *Int. Ry. Co.,* 73-74; and *Palsgraf* v. *Long Island Ry. Co.,* 74-78; *Scott* v. *Shepard,* 75; *Vandenburgh* v. *Truax,* 75; *Guille* v. *Swan,* 75; contributory, 100
Nims, Harry D., on pre-trial conference, 137
Nisi prius, 28
Novel Disseisin, Assize of, 26, 28
Novus actus interveniens, 78

Oath, 19
Oath-helpers, 19
Objection, the, 122ff.
Ordeal, by fire, 19; by water, 19; decline of, 52
Original writ, 29-30; example, 30

Particular customs, and common law, 33
Peine forte et dure, 11, 52-53
People ex rel. Battista v. *Christian,* 108-109
People v. *Casey,* 117-119
People v. *Mitchell,* 119-120
People v. *Rosenheimer,* 4-5, 57
People v. *Wilson,* 106-107
People v. *Zackowitz,* 15-17
Peremptory Challenge, 116ff.
Petition of Right, and *habeas corpus,* 58-59
Petty serjeanty, 22
Pone, writ of, 26-27
Praecipe, the writ, 25-26
Precedent, 81ff.
Pre-trial, 136ff.
Preliminary examination, 107-108

Priestley v. *Fowler,* 98
Procedure, 105ff.; civil, 133-134; importance of, 134-135
Proximate cause, 77-78

Quasi-judicial power, 145-146

Relief, 22
Repouille v. *United States,* 153-154, 161
Riggs v. *Palmer,* 156-157
Right, writ of, 25
Rodell, Fred, 83-84
Roman Law, 34-36
Ryan v. *Mutual Tontine Association,* 44
Rylands v. *Fletcher,* 70-71

Schmidt v. *United States,* 106-161
Scrutton, T. E., 35-36
Scutage, 22
Seaboard Air Line v. *Horton,* 101-102
Self-incrimination, exception to rule of, 4-5
Shepard v. *United States,* 123-125
Sheriff, 18, 23
Smith v. *East Elloe Rural District Council,* 150-152
Smith v. *Peerless Glass Co.,* 96
Smith v. *United States,* and the "irresistible impulse" test, 113
Socage, 22
Specific performance, 43-44
Stare decisis, 80ff.
State v. *Pike,* 115
Statler v. *Ray Manufacturing Co.,* 95
Statutes and the common law, 100ff.
Strict liability, 69-71; and *Hay* v. *Cohoes Co.,* 69-70; *Rylands* v. *Fletcher,* 70-71
Subpoena, 41

Tallon v. *Interborough Rapid Transit Co.,* 84-86
Tenants-in-capite, 21
Tenure, 21ff.
Thomas v. *Winchester,* 94-95, 96
Tiller v. *Atlantic Coast Line,* 102-104
Tolt, writ of, 26
Tort, definition of, 68; intentional, 69; strict liability, 69-71; negligence, 71ff.
Torture, use of, 11
Trial by battle, 20
Trial by jury, 50ff.; Henry II and, 51
Trusts, origins, 44-45

Ulman, Joseph N., on trial by jury, 127
Uses (see Trusts)
Uses, Statute of, 45

Van Caenegem, R. C., 29-30
Vacarius, and Roman Law, 35

Wardship, 22
Warrant of arrest, 105-107
Wergild, 20
Westminster, Statute of, 1285, 40
Whitehead, Alfred North, 5

Wilkinson v. *Downton,* 69
William I, and the English system of land-holding, 21
Witenagemot, 23
Woods v. *Lancet,* 89-90, 157, 159
Workmen's Compensation, 146ff.; *Pasquel* v. *Coverly,* 147-148; *Palermo* v. *Gallucci,* 148-149; *Herman* v. *Greenpoint Barrel Co.,* 149; Johnson v. Loew's, 150
Writs, executive, 24ff.; original, 25, 29, 31; and actions, 30-31

The American Assembly Series

AUTOMATION AND TECHNOLOGICAL CHANGE,
  edited by John T. Dunlop—S-AA-7
THE CONGRESS AND AMERICA'S FUTURE,
  edited by David B. Truman—S-AA-13
THE COURTS, THE PUBLIC, AND THE LAW EXPLOSION,
  edited by Harry W. Jones—S-AA-15
THE FEDERAL GOVERNMENT SERVICE (Second Edition),
  edited by Wallace S. Sayre—S-AA-14
GOALS FOR AMERICANS: The Report of the President's
  Commission on National Goals—S-AA-3
OUTER SPACE: Prospects for Man and Society,
  edited by Lincoln P. Bloomfield—S-AA-5
THE POPULATION DILEMMA,
  edited by Philip M. Hauser—S-AA-10
THE SECRETARY OF STATE,
  edited by Don K. Price—S-AA-2
THE UNITED STATES AND CANADA,
  edited by John Sloan Dickey—S-AA-12
THE UNITED STATES AND THE FAR EAST (Second Edition),
  edited by Willard L. Thorp—S-AA-6
THE UNITED STATES AND JAPAN,
  edited by Herbert Passin—S-AA-16
THE UNITED STATES AND LATIN AMERICA (Second Edition),
  edited by Herbert L. Matthews—S-AA-9
THE UNITED STATES AND THE MIDDLE EAST,
  edited by Georgiana G. Stevens—S-AA-11